TRENDS
ISSUES
IN ELEMENTARY LANGUAGE ARTS

TRENDS AND ISSUES IN ENGLISH LANGUAGE ARTS
1999 EDITION

NATIONAL COUNCIL OF TEACHERS OF ENGLISH
1111 W. KENYON ROAD, URBANA, ILLINOIS 61801-1096

Staff Editor: Kurt Austin
Interior Design: Tom Kovacs for TGK Design; Carlton Bruett
Cover Design: Carlton Bruett

NCTE Stock Number: 55022-3050

TRENDS AND ISSUES IN ENGLISH LANGUAGE ARTS

Keeping track of the myriad issues in education can be a daunting task for those educators already stretched to get thirty hours into a twenty-four hour day. In an effort to inform and support English educators, the National Council of Teachers of English annually offers this volume featuring current trends and issues deemed vital to the professional conversation by our membership at large. Whether specialists or generalists, teachers know that no single "trend" or "issue" could touch the interest and concerns of all members of NCTE; with these books—one for each section of the Council: Elementary, Secondary, College—we aim to chronicle developments in the teaching and learning of English language arts.

The wealth of NCTE publications from which to draw the materials for *Trends and Issues* proves a double-edged sword. Publishing thirteen journals (bimonthly and quarterly) and twenty to twenty-five books annually provides ample content, yet what to include and what not? Of course, timeliness and pertinence to the issues of the day help shape the book, and, more important, we aim to meet our primary goal: Is this valuable to our members? This edition of *Trends and Issues*, we believe, offers readers a seat at the table, a chance to join the discussion. At the college level the trends and issues cited for this year are "Diverse Students, Diverse Teachers," "Ethics in Teaching, Research, and Publishing," and "Service Learning and Social Change." At the K–12 levels members cited "Multimedia in the Classroom," "Second Language Learners," and "How Politics Have Shaped Our Thinking and Our Classrooms" as those topics of current relevance to them as English language arts professionals.

We hope that you'll find this collection a valuable resource to be returned to often, one that facilitates professional development and reminds us that we all have a stake in the language arts profession.

NCTE invites you to send us those trends and issues in the English language arts that you feel are the most relevant to your teaching. Send your comments to our Web site at www.ncte.org (click on "Trends and Issues") or e-mail directly to John Kelley at jkelley@ncte.org.

Faith Schullstrom
Executive Director

CONTENTS

I. MULTIMEDIA IN THE CLASSROOM

1. The Classroom   3
   Marilyn Jody and Marianne Saccardi

2. Let's Go to the Movies: Rethinking the Role
   of Film in the Elementary Classroom   10
   Michele Whipple

3. The Challenge of Change: Exploring Literacy and Learning
   in Electronic Environments   24
   Charles Kinzer and Donald J. Leu, Jr.

4. Integrating Technology in the Classroom   45
   Linda McMillen, Sherrell Shanahan, Kathleen Dowd,
   Joyce MacPhee, and Jennifer Hester

II. SECOND LANGUAGE LEARNERS

5. "I Know English So Many, Mrs. Abbott":
   Reciprocal Discoveries in a Linguistically Diverse Classroom   69
   Suzette Abbott and Claudia Grose

6. A Chinese Boy's Joyful Initiation into American Literacy   88
   Jane S. Townsend and Danling Fu

7. Finding the "Right Measure" of Explanation for
   Young Latina/o Writers   105
   Liliana Barro Zecker, Christine C. Pappas, and Sarah Cohen

8. Doing His Own Thing: A Mexican-American Kindergartner
   Becomes Literate at Home and School   124
   Margaret M. Mulhern

III. How Politics Have Shaped Our Thinking and Our Classrooms

9. In Which Governor Bush's Business Council Holds a Pre-summit
Meeting in Texas   143
Denny Taylor

10. A Note on Terms: Conceptualizing Phonics and Whole Language   172
Constance Weaver

11. Believing in What's Possible, Taking Action to Make a Difference   177
Ellen H. Brinkley *with* Connie Weaver, Pen Campbell,
Marianne Houston, Jean Williams, Virginia Little,
Mary Monaghan, Lauren Freedman, Bob and Jo Bird

12. The California Reading Situation: Rhetoric and Reality   191
Jeff McQuillan

1 MULTIMEDIA IN THE CLASSROOM

The definitions of reading and literacy are changing rapidly as technology becomes more and more a part of our everyday culture. As teachers and teacher educators, we must learn to recognize these changes and learn to take advantage of the challenges they offer our classrooms and our curricula. The following articles provide insight and instruction on how to incorporate technology into the elementary classroom without placing undue demands on teachers' and students' already demanding lives. Instead of adding multimedia activities to the classroom, for example, the authors of these articles suggest ways to augment what students are already learning through the use of computer programs, film, the Internet, videotape, and so on.

Uniting all of these articles is the belief that reading is only meaningful if the reader comprehends the text. Moreover, the more chances a reader has to make choices about what he or she reads, to respond in meaningful ways to a text, and to draw connections between life experiences and the text, the more comprehensible the text will become. Jody and Saccardi, for example, show how electronic mail allows students to share their own written responses to literature and have literature discussions with students anywhere in the world who are interested in the same books or topics. Furthermore, the authors illustrate the central role the teacher plays in facilitating learning and communication among the students.

Each article offers different approaches to using technology in the classroom, not only to increase students' levels of comprehension, but to engage them in the reading process and to broaden their sense of literacy and of themselves as learners. For example, in "Let's Go to the Movies: Rethinking the Role of Film in the Elementary Classroom," Michele Whipple encourages us to allow readers to create meaningful intertextual connections by expanding our definition of text to include film as well as other media such as computer programs, television, photographs, and videotape. "Validation of alternate texts," she writes, ". . . through their emphasis in the classroom, may allow those students who are in some way at-risk in their literacy development to participate in the classroom discourse, to become part of the classroom community, to be validated as learners and people."

While each of the four articles focuses on integrating technology into the classroom and the curriculum rather than tacking it on as "something else" for educators to teach their students, the final two articles offer in-depth analysis and review of many computer programs, instructional software, interactive literature on CD-ROM, and World Wide Web sites, designed to become an integral part of the classroom.

1 The Classroom

Marilyn Jody and Marianne Saccardi

Dear Gary Paulsen,

I like reading your books because they always end right. What I mean by that is some books are good until the end. Then they make the end so unrealistic that it ruins it. Yours aren't like that or at least not the ones I've read. I've read these books of yours: *Hatchet, Woodsong, Dogsong, Dancing Carl, The Crossing,* and *The Winter Room.*

—Lynn, a fifth grader

Whether we teach in a self-contained elementary classroom or are responsible for a single subject in middle school through university, as teachers we are all too well aware of the limits of time and the limitlessness of the task. At national conferences we have heard leading educator Donald Graves lament that teachers have such demands placed upon them that many give in to employing a "cha-cha-cha" curriculum on the dance floor of the classroom, flitting from subject to subject in short quick steps in an effort to "get it all in." And with talk of even more national and state requirements finding their way into the curriculum, it seems clear that we cannot fit much more into the limited amount of time we have with students. If there is anything teachers do *not* need, it is another "add-on" program, however beneficial it may appear. Our first goal, then, in this book, is to show how to

Reprinted from Chapter 2 of *Using Computers to Teach Literature* by Marilyn Jody and Marianne Saccardi.

integrate an electronic-mail project into what we are *already* doing in the classroom, using the computer as a tool to accomplish our goals far better than we could without it. Thus the schedule we discuss below should not be seen as allowing a confiscation of several weeks from that which we must accomplish in the classroom, but as encouraging enrichment of what we are already doing *in* the classroom during those valuable weeks, by adding to our own perspectives those of the students, teachers, and—sometimes—authors who are now an actual part of our classroom reading and research community via computer network.

In a recent editorial in the *New York Times,* author Saul Bellow stated, "The literacy of which we are so proud often amounts to very little. You may take the word of a practicing novelist for it that not all novel readers are good readers" (A25). Reading results in learning, in exploring new ideas, in innovative applications only if our students understand what they are reading. With greater demands than before being placed upon them, with "higher standards" as common buzzwords throughout the educational community, we realize that we must bring our students beyond merely reading words on the page to critical understanding of what those words mean. In the past, we have given them various standardized tests to measure their comprehension skills. We have spent many classroom hours asking comprehension questions atter they have read stories or chapters. What we propose here is not spending additional time on reading skills, or, conversely, ignoring skills altogether for more "meaningful" instruction. Instead, we suggest that classroom time be reallocated, from time spent on drills or testing to time spent on dialogue about books. It is a simple but powerful shift in emphasis. The K–12 students we have worked with in the BookRead Project read more books, with greater understanding, than ever before. Because they became invested in the computer network exchange, they were eager to make sense of what they were reading in order to communicate their ideas to their distant reading partners. And, as an added bonus, they tried harder to use conventional spelling and grammar so that their writing would be understood—and, in fact, did so competitively, so that their school would not be embarrassed!

Arranging a Schedule

A first step in setting up an online project is to schedule a time in the school year when you and your students can most easily set aside several weeks (six weeks is a realistic time frame) for a computer dialogue with another class.

We have found that one project in the fall and another in the spring is a comfortable goal. With your school calendar at hand, try to eliminate times when you know your class will be pulled in other directions—for a school play, testing weeks, holidays, big sporting events, etc.

Choosing an Author or a Topic of Study

Once your time frame is established, your next task will be to find an author whose books you feel will "hook" your students and get them asking for more. Or, rather than focus on a single author, you could target a topic that you and your students have decided to investigate during the year and gather a variety of books on that topic for study and discussion over a computer network. As Byrum and Pierce emphasize in *Bringing Children to Literacy: Classrooms at Work,* this does not mean devising a neat unit of study to be used to teach other areas of the curriculum, but rather devising one that is genuinely entered into by both students and teacher, one which uses the other areas of the curriculum to investigate the subject at hand. In these authentic learning experiences, the class becomes a community of learners who are working for a common goal, who are courageous enough to take risks and to delve into material which stretches their capabilities. For these students, the curriculum is not something imposed on them, but rather a course of study they and their teacher work out together as they plan what they want to discover about a topic as well as what kinds of research and activities they want to pursue. The classroom becomes a busy, happy place where children are active participants in their own learning. When that learning is informed by literature, and when that literature is shared and discussed with another class engaged in the same study, the insights and learning are multiplied many times over.

For example, a class might express an interest in whales. Many books, both fiction and nonfiction, picture books as well as novels, are available to use, both to provide information for your investigation of these fascinating creatures and to fuel online conversations with a partner class. In his novel *The Hostage,* Theodore Taylor poses the question of whether a killer whale should be captured and sold to an amusement park or allowed to remain free. A Japanese mother tells her child the story of a woman who rescues her daughter from the underwater home of the whales in *Okino and the Whales* by Arnica Esterl. The excitement of going on a whale watch is recounted by Frances Ward Weller in *I Wonder If I'll See a Whale.* A lonely old man waits for the yearly migration of orcas and imparts his love of whales to his granddaughter in Sheryl McFarlane's *Waiting for the Whales.* Young children can practice their counting while being enthralled by Ed Young's beautiful illustrations in Tony Johnston's *Whale Song.* Some of the best nonfiction writers for children have written books on whales: *All About Whales,* by Dorothy Hinshaw Patent; *Great Whales, the Gentle Giants,* by Patricia Lauber; and *Whales,* by Gail Gibbons are just a few. Myra Cohn Livingston has selected poems about whales by leading poets for her collection *If You Ever Meet a Whale.* Older children may enjoy Shulamith Levey Oppenheim's *The Selchie's Seed,* about a young girl, descended from the Selchie folk, who becomes fascinated by a mysterious white whale. You can read some of these books aloud, or any others you might select, depending on the ages, abilities, and interests of your students. Students can also read and study others, individually or in groups. What children glean from these books—the questions they wonder about or the ideas they form as they read them, as well as the activities and investigations (perhaps their own "whale watch") in which they become involved during their study—is the "stuff" of their computer conversations.

Even when we feel that we don't have much room to make choices in what we teach because of curriculum constraints, we can still fill our lessons and discussions with literature and share what we are learning with other students online. Consider what you are required to teach during the year in all the disciplines. Is there a period in history that must be covered in class which would be enriched by historical fiction and authors who write excellent books on the subject for young people? Is an especially gripping science topic scheduled for study? There are a host of fine nonfiction writers for children whose writings would grace and enrich the science curriculum. High school English teachers who wish to undertake a computer project might consider the books their students are already required to read as part of the English program. Of course, these teachers cannot drop this core of mandatory books, but there are ways to work them into a computer project. The obvious solution would be to find a partner class which is reading the same books and engage in a dialogue with those students. Another possibility would be to find an author of young adult books who writes engagingly about the themes contained in the required books and to study that author's books to enlarge students' understanding of them. Or, teachers might want to consult their colleagues in the history or science departments to set up a team-teaching approach. The more you can integrate a computer project into what you or your colleagues are already doing, the less burdened you and your students will feel, the more support you will receive from other teachers in the building, and the greater the impact such an experience will have on all concerned.

Try to give your students as much input as possible in choosing an author. After all, they will be spending several weeks of their time, both at home and in school, reading and discussing that author's work. The more they feel a part of the decision-making process, the more enthusiastic they will be about the project. What authors are their favorites? Which ones would they like to know more about? Which genres do they enjoy or which ones do you wish to teach in a given term? With the incredible increase in books of poetry for children, anthologies as well as collections on special subjects, you might want to consider a poetry project for one term and a fiction study for another. Folklore is another genre rich in books for children of all ages.

Your Partner Class

It is important that you find a teacher whose class wishes to read the same books and who has a time frame that is compatible with your own. We will say more about how to find such partners, but for now, let's discuss some things you should keep in mind as you think about arranging a match. Again, it is important that your students join you in the decision-making process. Do your students want to write to a class as a whole, do they want to work in small groups, or do they want to be assigned an individual "pen pal" for the duration of the dialogue? Do boys want to talk to boys, girls to girls? Will teachers respond to students? To each other? Will teachers make their conversations with each other about the books available to the students? Will you want to invite an author to join the conversation? A computer discussion can take place very well without an author on board, but having one certainly does add interest. Do you have funds to pay an author to "visit" online? Can the cost be shared with a partner school or schools? Certainly, you would have to pay an author much less to engage in a computer conversation from the convenience of his or her home than you would to have that author travel to your school. Is there a local, regional, or national network link available to you that might supply authors?

Be sure to set up mutually agreed upon guidelines for the project with your partner teacher and class *beforehand,* so that all concerned know exactly what is required of them when they agree to participate. We have found that when a project falters, it is often because expectations were not clearly spelled out in the beginning. How long will the project run? When will it begin and end? How often will you exchange messages? How much teacher involvement will there be? How much conversation, if any, about topics other than the books in the project will be allowed? We have found, especially with high school students, that they are likely to talk at length online about their social and personal lives, often in response to reading-inspired topics. Students in BookRead Projects were fascinated with the idea that the kids they were talking to came from a different part of the country and had different ideas and customs. They wanted to air those ideas before they got down to the business of discussing books. And often these personal discussions became the link to their understanding of the books. For example, one young person who had confessed to his distant pen pal that he had family problems, wasn't trying in school, and had experimented with drugs changed his mind about how "boring" it was to read after he identified with the similarly troubled hero of Sue Ellen Bridgers's novel *Permanent Connections.* His comment was that the main character must have been "based on a real person."

It is important for both the teachers and the students to know in advance whether such exchanges are acceptable. Many classes we worked with made videotapes introducing themselves to their partner class before the online project actually began. These tapes were great fun to make, generated early enthusiasm for the project, and helped to build group cohesiveness. Some students even viewed their partner class's tape with the idea of choosing a particular student with whom to exchange ideas, while others preferred the excitement of anonymity.

Classroom Organization

If large chunks of your school day are already given over to reading and discussing literature, then you will not have many adjustments to make in your schedule or your teaching. You will continue to spend that time reading and writing, the only difference being that, in addition to sharing their ideas with one another, your students will also be talking to distant reading partners on the computer. If you do not have large blocks of time built in for reading and writing, some schedule rearranging must be done. Since students' lives outside the classroom are so busy, it is important to give them time in class to read and discuss books. While we expect them to read at home as well, the amount of class time we devote to reading and writing speaks to our students more powerfully than anything else can about our own priorities.

The Computer

In order for your students to begin their online computer discussion, it helps enormously to have access to a computer in your classroom. If you do not have one, perhaps a computer can be moved in for the duration of the project. Although it would be ideal (how often can we expect that?), this computer need not even have a modem or be connected to a dedicated telephone line. Students can simply use a word-processing program to make their comments and save them on disk at any time during the day that is convenient for them. Then, either at the end of each day, or a few times a week, depending upon how often you and your partner teacher have agreed to exchange messages, you can go to a computer that is connected to the network and "upload" (copy and send) the text of your students' messages, along with your own. At the same time, you can "download" (copy from the network and save) messages from the other class to a disk and either print out copies for your students or have them read the responses on the computer screen back in the classroom. You can even do these uploading and downloading operations in the evening at home if you have a computer that enables you to do so.

Teachers who must rely on computers in another space, such as a computer lab or a library, have a bit more arranging to do, so the sooner you discuss your plans with others in the building, the more cooperation you can expect. Of course, the person in charge of the lab has to know about your project and be willing to work with you. If your class has scheduled computer time during the week, students can type their messages at that time. All the messages can be saved, transferred to one disk, and quickly uploaded to your partner school. If this sounds complicated, rest assured that it isn't. Have the media specialist teach you the few simple procedures involved rather than you having to rely on others whose time may not always be at your disposal. If you don't have enough computer lab time, you may be able to arrange to use another teacher's time in exchange for some of your computer lab time, once your project is completed.

2 Let's Go to the Movies: Rethinking the Role of Film in the Elementary Classroom

Michele Whipple

Films have traditionally played a less prominent role in the elementary language arts curriculum than other instructional materials. While they have frequently been used as a supplemental resource, follow-up activity, form of reward, filler, and as background noise, films have rarely been approached as serious material for literacy instruction. Fortunately, recent developments in what qualifies as "text," in conjunction with research on response-based language arts instruction, have facilitated our developing understandings of the value of this medium. Preliminary application of these findings have shown film to be an accessible and engaging material which can bind children together and bring validation to their varied home and school literacy experiences. Hence, I would like to suggest here that films are a valuable instructional material for the elementary teacher and that they deserve a closer look.

Expanding Literature Learning Through Film

I first became interested in the use of film with elementary students while working on a longitudinal research project investigating the changing literacy experiences of a group of students as they moved through grades 5–7 (Walmsley, Rosenthal, & Whipple, 1997). As part of this study, I engaged in biweekly conversations with several children about books they had been reading both in and out of their classrooms.

Reprinted from *Language Arts*, November 1998.

Following a book conversation with Jason, a fifth-grade student, he began to tell me about a movie his class had watched earlier in the week. The movie, entitled *April Morning* (Goldwyn & Halmi, 1987), was based on a novel of the same name by Howard Fast (1961). Ironically, I had recently read the original text for a graduate class. Excited about our recent experiences, Jason and I began to talk about this title, making comments and asking questions of one another. Here is a segment of our exchange:

JASON: In social studies, we're learning about the
              Revolutionary War and we watched a movie
              called *April Morning.*

MICHELE: You did? I read *April Morning* for my class (at the
              university). It's by Howard Fast, right? I didn't
              even know there was a movie.

JASON: It's a great movie.

MICHELE: I loved the book . . . I felt especially bad in the
              beginning.

JASON: When his dad died?

MICHELE: Yeah, but also for the soldiers.

JASON: They just stood there and got shot. . . .

There were several characteristics of the extended version of this conversation that struck me as significant and that altered the manner in which I both engaged in and viewed literature conversations from that point on. First, in talking with Jason about our related experiences surrounding the title, *April Morning,* I was struck by his involvement in the exchange. He was genuinely excited about the film and the fact that I could possibly fill in some of the *gaps* he felt existed in his understanding of the story (Iser, 1989). In addition, as I read over the transcript of this conversation and compared the nature of Jason's responses to those he had made in previous *official* conversations concerning tradebooks, it was evident that he had ventured into areas of the text and response which he had not addressed in prior exchanges (i.e., analysis of the plot and the actions of the characters). I then realized that had this opportunity not arisen, I may have never seen this side of Jason's "response personality." Thus, I would have had only a partial picture of Jason as a reader and responder.

Secondly, I began to recognize that just as books and other forms of written communication are considered *texts,* so are alternate forms of story such as films, oral dialogue and narratives, and audio and computer communications (Bakhtin as cited in Holquist, 1990; Cox, 1994; Myers, 1996; Rosenthal, 1997). I wondered on how many occasions, prior to this one with *April Morning*, Jason and the other children participating in the study had attempted to bring their film experiences to our conversations and I had urged them back to talking about written text.

It was for these reasons that I decided to investigate the instructional and response opportunities that arise when we broaden our definitions of what counts as *text* to include film. In order to supplement these findings and to assess the future of instructional film use in the elementary classroom, I also felt it necessary to explore these possibilities in light of recent trends in language arts. This lead me to examine the relationship of Louise Rosenblatt's transactional theory (1938/1976, 1978) to film viewing and to review the related literature.

Lack of Focus on the Elementary Level

As a result of my experience with Jason, I became increasingly interested in film use with elementary students. In the months which followed, I began scouring the library for resources only to find that, in general, the information available on film use in the classroom is considerably limited. In addition, the majority of what is accessible to teachers focuses on students of middle school (Witkin, 1994), high school (Senger & Archer, 1989; Shull, 1989; Teasley & Wilder, 1997), and college age (Costanzo, 1992). While we have much to learn from these writings in terms of their applications of transactional theory, the films and related activities suggested by these authors are generally not appropriate for K–6 students. I believe this trend has left those elementary educators who are interested in instructional film use within their classrooms with few places to turn to for supportive information and specific suggestions for film use.

A significant amount of what is available on this topic at the elementary level has been contributed by Carole Cox (1975, 1982, 1983, 1996), who, in conjunction with co-author Joyce Many, was one of the first elementary educator-researchers to make connections between Rosenblatt's theory of reader-response and film viewing (see Cox & Many, 1989). Unfortunately, only within the past five years have others begun to expand upon and add to the body of work created by Cox and her colleagues. In addition, much of this work has centered on the role of technology in education, focusing heavily on computer use and only vaguely addressing the role of film and related response issues.

Therefore, I speculated that, in order for us to begin rethinking the role of film in our classroom literacy instruction, information was needed that immediately addressed the instructional options available to elementary teachers, including sample film titles and activities, and that offered supplementary information which discussed related trends in the field of language arts education. Here, I will focus on the latter of these tasks.

Two recent discussions most immediately applicable to this issue of film use in the elementary classroom are the expanding notions of what qualifies as "text" and the application of reader-response theories to elementary language arts pedagogy. Their relevance and application to film use in the elementary classroom will be discussed in the following sections.

Expanding Notions of What Counts

Currently, film viewing plays a major role in popular culture and in the daily lives of our young students (Costanzo, 1992; Rosenthal, 1997; Witkin, 1994). In short, there are two approaches which may be taken by educators in response to this trend. We can either become resentful and judgmental about frequent home viewing practices, mourning the de-emphasis of written text, or we can look at students' movie experiences and emerging knowledge of films as an opportunity to support literacy development and to make connections with more traditional media (i.e., written text). There are several reasons why the latter of these reactions has proven more effective. First, recognition and use of students' knowledge of movies can open doors for students who have traditionally been thought to be at-risk, as suggested by language arts educator Carole Cox (see also Teasley & Wilder, 1997):

> Media experiences from inside and outside the classroom provide access to learning for all students, drawing on a shared media culture as the basis for classroom exploration. . . . The media culture is available, in some way to everyone . . . different kinds of media provide different kinds of access to a range of students, encouraging those who are sometimes silent because of their social status, race, culture, gender, disability, or language-minority status. (Cox, 1996, p. 486)

In other words, the validation of alternate texts such as photographs, computers, television, film, and videotape, through their emphasis and use in the classroom, may allow those students who are in some way at-risk in their literacy development to participate in classroom discourse, to become a part of the classroom community, and to be validated as learners and people. For example, while only a few children in a given third-grade classroom may have actually read the written version of the book, *Sarah, Plain and Tall* (MacLachlan, 1985), some may have rented the film version from the video store or viewed it on television. Other children may not be familiar with *Sarah, Plain and Tall,* but they may have seen the sequel, *Skylark* (Close & Self, 1993), on television. In addition, several more children may be able to make connections between these texts and titles and others they have encountered which focus on the Westward Movement, farm life, families, death, courage, and other related topics. The possibilities for engaging in complex conversations about these diverse, yet strongly related experiences is staggering. It is the formulation of intertextual connections and personal responses such as these that we strive for as response-based teachers (Short, 1993).

Secondly, the use of film is another avenue by which we can reach second-language learners and others who have not had their home literacy experiences validated through their current literacy instruction. Students who have had limited experiences with English and with written text in their homes and within preschool settings have often had other rich experiences, frequently with film. Therefore, if your immediate instructional goals are to encourage students' personal responses and to build community within the classroom, and these are not dependent on the form or content of a particular piece, this alternate approach may be ideal. For example, both the classic animated tale and the newly released dramatic version of Disney's *101 Dalmatians* (Disney, 1961; Feldman, 1996) are available in English as well as Spanish. Students may have also seen the picture book versions of the title, related games, or news stories. Hence, students may begin by sharing their common experiences with this title, later focusing more on traditional mediums as their classroom and literacy experiences evolve. Therefore, by expanding the notion of what qualifies as "text" we are also expanding the prevailing notions of which literacy experiences are valuable and who gets to participate in classroom conversations.

Students' growing understandings and use of film and other alternate forms of "text" is often referred to as *media literacy.* In a 1994 document prepared for the National Council of Teachers of English Commission on Media, then director Carole Cox defined the term as follows:

> Media literacy refers to composing, comprehending, interpreting, analyzing, and appreciating the language and texts of . . . both print and nonprint media. The use of media presupposes an expanded definition of "text." . . . Print media texts include books, magazines, and newspapers. Nonprint media include photography recordings, radio, film, television, videotape, video games, computers, the performing

arts, and virtual reality . . . constantly interact . . . (and) all (are) to be experienced, appreciated, and analyzed and created by students. (NCTE, 1994, p. 13)

Acknowledgment of the presence and relevance of media literacy has been widespread in recent years, due in part to the rapid development of computers and other forms of technology. While many debate its role, there are few who doubt the relevance of media literacy as we approach the millennium. Indeed, its immediate significance was felt most recently at the annual meeting of the National Council of Teachers of English, where the program offered more presentations than ever before focusing on film use and technology in the classroom.

The benefits are boundless and the groundwork set. Our students are already talking about the Internet, video games, television, and film. We need merely to take advantage of these conversations and experiences. There is much to be lost if we choose not to act. The following section includes examples of instructional opportunities which were missed as a result of a limited view of what types of text count in the elementary classroom.

Missed Opportunities

As I considered the *April Morning* event with Jason, I began to wonder if similar examples existed with other students involved in the study So, I returned to the data. Reading through the piles of transcripts, I found that, for three years, students had been trying to talk with me about their experiences with film text. There were numerous opportunities for the discussion of film elements, as well as for addressing film as an alternative to written text. The following are just a few examples of the "missed opportunities" I found when I reviewed the transcripts of the book conversations I had engaged in with two of the students, Ben and Ellen, with a broader definition of "what counts."

The use of suspense in movies and books was a common theme among the students. In this first example, Ben compares the suspense found in one of the Goosebumps books, by author R. L. Stine, to that found in mystery and horror movies.

BEN: It (R. L. Stine book) was kind of like the movies. What I don't really like about movies is sometimes you know "who did it" all the way through the movie. I like the ones when you think it is one guy,

> then all of a sudden you find out it's the other
> guy . . . That's what this book was (like).

In this second example, Ellen comments on the use of suspense in written
text and film, and her dislike of the latter. Her focus here is on the Nancy
Drew series books written by Carolyn Keen. Ellen stated that, given the
chance, she would tell the author to:

> ELLEN: . . . have more suspense in the stories. I like a lot
>   of suspense (in books). But, in movies, I can't
>   stand too much suspense. Just a little and I'm
>   screaming at the top of my lungs.
>
> MICHELE: I think it is a lot harder to put suspense in books.
>
> ELLEN: It's easier to show it.

Each of these excerpts provides information on the students' individual
abilities to form intertextual references and their ability to analyze the use of
the element of suspense in differing texts. While the term *intertextual
reference* has primarily been applied to comparisons made between two
books, these students have displayed their ability to compare across modes
and mediums, between written text and film text. These comments, and the
many others like them found in the transcripts, have a great deal to say about
the students' individual experiences with film and provide insights into their
literature learning and literacy development. They are, at the very least,
"points of departure" for individualized literary instruction.

Within the book conversations, there was also evidence that Ben and
Ellen had made repeated attempts to talk about the relationships which
existed for them between written texts and films of the same name. In our
first example we see Ben as he talks about his interest in reading books
generated from films. These books, called novelizations, have been written
only after a movie by the same title has been released (e.g., *My Girl,* 1991;
Hook, 1992; *Babe,* 1995; and *Toy Story,* 1995).

> BEN: I like to read the Walt Disney movie books;
>   books that they make from the movies.
>
> MICHELE: Oh. I see here that you read *Honey, I Blew Up
>   the Kid* (Band & Gordon, 1992).
>
> BEN: Yeah. I just finished that.

There is much which could have been done instructionally with this information to expand and extend Ben's experience. In addition to probing further on this topic, finding out what specifically it is about this category of books which attracts Ben, he could also have been encouraged through discussion, journaling, or a Venn diagram to compare the film and written versions of these pairs.

In this related example, Ellen broadly shares her impressions of the "movie versions" of children's books and their relationship to the original story.

> ELLEN: That (the movie version of *My Side of the*
>   *Mountain,* Radnitz, 1968) would be neat to see,
>   but it's probably not the same as the book.
>   They're (movie versions) never the same as the
>   book.

Unfortunately, rather than probing Ellen further on her comment that (movie versions) are "never the same as the book," I attempted to redirect her back to the written text. This sent Ellen the message that it was the book version, rather than the film version, that was the focus.

I have no doubt that interactions similar to those provided here occur in elementary classrooms around the country every day, and they are a result of how we have been enculturated to view the place of books and films in education. One of the easiest things we can do, as teachers, to take advantage of these missed opportunities is to acknowledge the film references made by our students during class discussions and to help them to make connections to *all* related texts.

Integrating Film Viewing and Response Theory

As we begin to acknowledge the instructional value of alternate forms of text, we naturally attempt to bring to them the approaches and theories which have been applied to written text over the years. One of the most popular approaches to have made the transfer from written text to film text has been that of reader-response theory.

The premises of reader-response were first written about by Louise Rosenblatt in 1938 in her book *Literature as Exploration,* and later expanded upon in *The Reader, The Text, The Poem: The Transactional Theory of the Literary Work* (1978). These writings suggest that readers are actively engaged in the reading process and that they construct, rather than merely decode, meaning from written text while they read. Reinforcing this point, Rosenblatt (1994) states:

> Every reading act is an event, or a transaction involving a particular reader, and a particular pattern of signs, a text, and occurring at a particular time in a particular context. Instead of two fixed entities acting on one another, the reader and the text are two aspects of a total dynamic situation. The meaning does not reside ready-made 'in' the text or in the reader but happens or comes into being during the transaction between reader and text. (p. 1063)

Therefore, in any single reading event, there is a reader, text, and context "transacting" with one another to create meaning from the situation. These meanings are generally shared with others in the form of "personal responses." The term *response* suggests a type of personal reaction to what has been read or experienced; a student's individual thoughts and reflections.

Ideally, students in response-based classrooms do a great deal of sharing of their personal responses to text through oral, written, and artistic modes and mediums. In offering a wide variety of response opportunities, teachers ensure that all students will be exposed to the various ways in which we communicate and that each individual may find a comfortable way in which to express their responses. As a result of the "risk-taking" which is involved in the formulation and sharing of personal responses, teachers recognize the importance of a community atmosphere within their classrooms. If students do not feel at ease in their physical environment and valued by those with whom they share the classroom, genuine or unfiltered responses will not be shared.

In recent years, authors who have written about film use at the secondary level, such as Shull (1989), Costanzo (1992), Fehlman (1994), and Teasley and Wilder (1997), have made various connections between Rosenblatt's writings on reader-response and the viewing of films. For example, there has been widespread use of the term "viewer-response," in this literature. Adapted from Rosenblatt's commonly used term "reader-response," this new variation emphasizes the change in focus action from reading to viewing. In addition, authors such as Fehlman (1994) have applied Rosenblatt's popular 'reader, text, context' model for describing how personal meanings and responses are constructed. In both instances, change is evidenced, not only in the action of the student, but also in the implied text preference. In this latter example, rather than focusing on the 'reader, text, context,' Fehlman talks about the *viewer, text, context;* where the viewer is the individual watching the film, the text is the film itself, and the context is the environment in which the film is experienced.

In many ways, these examples appear to be natural applications of Rosenblatt's work. For, it has been suggested by Cox (1989) that,

> Rosenblatt (1985) takes an eclectic view of the various literary forms and their potential as lived-through experiences. She uses the term 'poem' to stand for any literary work of art . . . The formal differences between stories, poems, and plays which she classifies together as literary events are no less great than the differences between literature and film. (p. 289)

The following are additional examples of popular premises of Rosenblatt's writings which have been applied to film viewing and related points which deserve consideration.

Rosenblatt (1938/1976) has written that,

> The reader brings to the work personality traits, memories of past events, present needs and preoccupations, a particular mood of the moment, and a particular physical condition. These and many other elements in a never-to-be-duplicated combination determine his response to the peculiar contribution of the text. (p. 31)

This statement implies that a reader (viewer) brings as much, if not more, information to the literacy event than the text (film). Therefore, as a teacher and fellow reader (viewer), while you might have an idea of the possible responses which could be offered in discussion, it may be impossible to expect certain meanings or responses from students. And, as individuals with unique experiences, the students in our classes will formulate a spectrum of meanings for the same literacy event.

From these teachings, we begin to realize that what is viewed, just like what is read, must be interpreted by the viewer. Only through this personal interpretation can "life be breathed into" the film, so that it can become a *poem* as defined by Rosenblatt (1978). Based on this premise, there can be as many poems for a given text title as there are people who read the written version or who view the film version. Therefore, the goal of finding the "right" interpretation becomes moot (see Teasley & Wilder, 1997). Ironically, films which are adaptations of novels are in essence already in poetic form, since the film is *one* interpretation of the author's and/or screenwriter's original text (Costanzo, 1992). Thus, we are creating a poem from a poem. This adds another dimension to understanding the construction of students' responses.

It is important to note that viewers receive different information while transacting with the film text than readers do with their written counterparts. Films are multisensory experiences which engage our minds differently than books. In some ways, they may "fill in gaps" (Iser, 1989) for us (i.e., in terms of what the setting and/or characters might look like), but they may also prevent us from using our *mind's eye*—the pictures we create in our heads when we read—by providing too much visual and auditory information. We often observe the intersection of the "film's perception of reality" and our own "personal perception of reality" when we engage in multiple encounters with the same text title. The most common example of this is when we watch the movie version of a novel after we have read the written text. The key is in understanding that the nature of students' responses, as well as the manners in which they are created, will differ as we move between these texts, and that engaging students in such a variety of literacy experiences will provide us, as educators, with additional insights into individual students as responders and literate people.

With regard to "how" one approaches a text, Rosenblatt has spoken at length about the stances, efferent and aesthetic, that a reader, or in this case a viewer, may take during a given event. Rarely, she states, is an event solely efferent or strictly aesthetic for the reader, here the viewer. Rather, a given textual experience has elements of both in combinations which vary from person to person. Take, for example, my recent viewing of the film *Emma* (Gigliotti, Weinstein, & Weinstein, 1996). Although I was watching the movie primarily because of my love of Jane Austen's work and the scenery of period English films, I was also looking for specific similarities between this film and *Clueless* (Berg & Shroeder, 1995), a story set in present day which is said to possess many parallels to Austen's novel.

While, in this case, I had a personal agenda for watching the movie which gave my viewing a strong efferent characteristic, we, as teachers, frequently press our efferent agendas upon our students. For example, the students in the secondary classes described in the pieces above were often called upon to take notes or to fill in charts during their viewing of a film. As a result of such activities, students' school experiences with film often become primarily efferent in nature and their main purpose becomes to gather facts. As an option, students may be given the opportunity to engage in "multiple viewings"; first, watching the film as a whole without the task of notetaking or other focused tasks and again later for the purpose of closer examination of particular scenes, characters, etc. This also applies to films which at first glance would appear solely informational or expository in nature, for as is implied by Rosenblatt (1991), you can never tell the extent to which an encounter will be aesthetic or efferent for an individual person.

In closing, through my prior classroom experiences and, more recently, observations in a wide variety of elementary grades and class settings, I have seen firsthand the instructional benefits of response-based pedagogy and the power of personal response as an instructional tool in broadening students' understandings of the forms and functions of written text. However, it is only recently that I have begun to explore the possibilities and the influences of a child's film experiences upon their individual literary growth and literacy development in the elementary grades. Through the fledgling inquiry described here, I have drawn several conclusions. First, additional information is needed which expands on the relationships between film, literacy development, and the premises of response theory as described by Louise Rosenblatt. Second, investigations are needed which link current theoretical discussions of *text* to elementary language arts pedagogy. And, finally, elementary educators would benefit from resource lists providing films and activities which are in keeping with the ideas discussed here.

Conclusion

Today's elementary students come to our classrooms with a great deal of knowledge about films in video form, as well as other types of text and the technology which creates them. When we take advantage of these prior experiences, we open the doors of participation to many children who have been closed off because of the nature of their past life and textual experiences, their primary language, and/or their gender. In addition, we provide expanded and extended learning experiences and opportunities for making intertextual connections for all of our students. In acknowledging students' experiences with alternate texts, in this case film, and using those experiences as a basis for response-based language arts instruction, our students will not only experience personal validation, but also growth in their understandings of the multiple roles of literature and media in our lives.

Films and Children's Books Cited

Adelson, G., Baumgarten, C., Kennedy, K., Marshall, R. (Producers), & Spielberg, S. (Director). (1992). *Hook* [Film]. (Available from Columbia Pictures).

Arnold, B., Guggenheim, R. (Producers), & Lasseter, J. (Director). (1995). *Toy story* [Film—Animated]. (Available from Walt Disney Productions).

Band, A., Brock, D., Feldman, E., Gordon, S., Jones, D., Steel, T. (Producers), & Kleiser, R. (Director). (1992). *Honey, I blew up the kid* [Film]. (Available from Walt Disney Productions).

Berg, B. M., Schroeder, A., Lawrence, R., Rudin, S. (Producers), & Heckerling, A. (Director). (1995). *Clueless* [Film]. (Available from Paramount Pictures).

Close, G., Self, W. (Producers), & Sargent, J. (Director). (1993). *Skylark* [Film]. (Available from Trillium Productions/Sarah Productions/Self Productions).

Comfort, J., Feldman, E., Hughes, J., Mestres, R. (Producer), & Herek, S. (Director). (1996). *101 Dalmatians* [Film]. (Available from Walt Disney Productions).

Disney, W. (Producer), & Geronimi, C., Luske, H., Reitherman, W. (Directors). (1961). *One hundred and one Dalmatians.* [Film—Animated]. (Available from Walt Disney Productions).

Gigliotti, D., Weinstein, B., Weinstein, H. (Producers), & McGrath, D. (Director). (1996). *Emma* [Film]. (Available from Miramax Films).

Goldwyn Jr., S., Halmi Jr., R., Mann, D., Patterson, D. (Producers), & Mann, D. (Director). (1988). *April morning* [Film]. (Available from Samuel Goldwyn Company).

Grazer, B. (Producer), & Zieff, H. (Director). (1991). *My girl* [Film]. (Available from Columbia Pictures).

MacLachlan, P (1985). *Sarah, plain and tall.* New York: Harper Trophy.

Miller, B., Miller, G., Mitchell, D. (Producers), & Noonan, C. (Director). (1996). *Babe* [Film]. (Available from Universal Pictures).

Radnitz, R. B. (Producer), & Clark, J. B. (Director). (1969). *My side of the mountain* [Film]. (Available from Paramount Pictures).

References

Costanzo, W. V. (1992). *Reading the movies.* Urbana, IL: National Council of Teachers of English (NCTE).

Cox, C. (1975). Film is like your Grandma's preserved pears. *Elementary English, 52,* 515–519.

Cox, C. (1982). Children's preferences for film form and technique. *Language Arts, 59,* 231–238.

Cox, C. (1983). Young filmmakers speak the language of film. *Language Arts, 60,* 296–304.

Cox, C. (1994). Media literacy. In A. Purves (Ed.), *The encyclopedia of English studies and language arts* (Vol. 2). New York: Scholastic.

Cox, C. (1996). *Teaching language arts: A student and response-centered classroom* (2nd ed.). Needham Heights, MA: Allyn and Bacon.

Cox, C., & Many, J. (1989). Worlds of possibilities in response to literature, film, and life. *Language Arts, 66*(3), 287–294.

Fast, H. (1961). *April morning.* New York: Bantam Books.

Fehlman, R. H. (1994). Teaching film in the 1990's. *English Journal, 83(1),* 39–46.

Holquist, M. (Ed.). (1990). *Dialogism: Bakhtin and his world.* New York: Routledge.

Iser, W. (1989). *Prospecting: From reader response to literary anthropology.* Baltimore, MD: Johns Hopkins University Press.

Myers, M. (1996). *Changing our minds: Negotiating English and literacy.* Urbana, IL: National Council of Teachers of English (NCTE).

National Council of Teachers of English (NCTE). (1994, Summer). Perspective: Media, performance, and the English curriculum—two views. *The NCTE Standard,* 12–14.

Rosenblatt, L. M. (1938/1976). *Literature as exploration.* New York: Modern Language Association (MLA).

Rosenblatt, L. M. (1978). *The reader, the text, the poem: The transactional theory of the literary work.* Carbondale, IL: Southern Illinois University Press.

Rosenblatt, L. M. (1991). Literature—S. O. S.! *Language Arts, 68,* 444–448.

Rosenblatt, L. M. (1994). The transactional theory of reading and writing. In R. Ruddell, M. Ruddell, & H. Singer (Eds.), *Theoretical models and processes of reading* (4th ed., pp. 1057–1092). Newark, DE: International Reading Association (IRA).

Rosenthal, I. (1997). *Sixth graders interpretive thinking about texts significant to their peer culture.* Unpublished doctoral dissertation, University at Albany, State University of New York, Albany, NY.

Senger, H., & Archer, B. (1989). Exploring *Sounder:* The novel, the screenplay, and the film. *English Journal, 78(8),* 48–52.

Short, K. G. (1993). Making connections across literature and life. In K. Holland, R. Hungerford, & S. Ernst (Eds.), *Journeying: Children responding to literature* (pp. 284–301). Portsmouth, NH: Heinemann.

Shull, E. M. (1989). The reader, the text, the poem—and the film. *English Journal, 78(8),* 53–57.

Teasley, A. B., & Wilder, A. (1997). *Reel conversations: Reading films with young adults.* Portsmouth, NH: Heinemann.

Walmsley, S. A., Rosenthal, I., & Whipple, M. M. (1997). *In betwixt and between: Tracking the literary development from 5th to 7th grade.* (Tech. Rep.). Albany, NY: Center for the Learning and Teaching of Literature.

Witkin, M. (1994). A defense of using pop media in the middle school classroom. *English Journal, 83(1),* 30–33.

3 The Challenge of Change: Exploring Literacy and Learning in Electronic Environments

Charles Kinzer and Donald J. Leu, Jr.

We live during a time when fundamental change is taking place in the nature of literacy and learning as digital, multimedia resources enter our world. Literacy and learning are being redefined by the digital communication and multimedia technologies that are quickly becoming a part of the information age in which we live (Negroponte, 1995; Reinking, 1995a). The many resources available on CD-ROM and the Internet are the beginning of a radical departure in the nature of information available to us and our students. Our response to these important changes will determine our students' ability to succeed in the world that awaits them.

As we look at the technologies that surround us, it is important to consider the challenges we face because of the new tools that are afforded us. We believe these new tools will increase, not decrease, the teacher's central role in orchestrating learning experiences. We will be challenged to thoughtfully guide students' learning within electronic information environments that are more complexly networked than traditional print media, presenting potentially richer and more integrated learning opportunities for both teachers and students.

Our purpose in this article is to describe the potential of multimedia and hypermedia technologies and explain how they can facilitate literacy teaching and learning. We do this first by discussing various software projects with which we have been involved to show how multimedia and hypermedia technologies are changing traditional definitions of literacy and

Reprinted from *Language Arts*, February 1997.

learning. Then, we describe several new challenges for teachers to consider as access to the Internet and the World Wide Web becomes more widely available. We hope this information will help in thinking about the fundamental changes taking place in literacy and learning.

The Reporter Project

Technology can often help mitigate difficult issues that teachers face. The Reporter Project is one such effort. Its goal was to use multimedia technology to enhance sixth-grade students' information-gathering and writing abilities and to help with three problems faced by teachers:

- Teachers face students who bring to the literacy task a wide range of backgrounds and experiences. Background knowledge and experiences affect comprehension in several ways (Alexander, Kulikowich, & Jetton, 1994; Bransford & Johnson, 1973) and teachers often use prediscussion to enhance motivation and to help set expectations for what will be read. But it is difficult to address the wide variety of needs and backgrounds that are found in any classroom.

- There is often little shared knowledge among students in a class or between the teacher/mediator and a respective learner. This makes it difficult to link new, to-be-learned information with what is already known. Teachers who share experiences with learners have a great advantage when trying to provide new knowledge to students in ways that facilitates their understanding.

- Often, what is learned remains "inert" (Whitehead, 1929). That is, knowledge is not used in appropriate situations even though it has been learned to the extent that it is demonstrated on paper and pencil tests. This is often seen across content-domain subject areas, where students may learn something in one class that is relevant to another but do not access or use the relevant knowledge in the second class. It is also seen in vocabulary learning, where students do well in providing definitions on paper and pencil tests but do not use the vocabulary items in appropriate conversational situations.

The above issues were addressed through what is known as anchored instruction using multimedia tools. Anchored instruction has been a major focus of a group of colleagues working through the Learning Technology Center at Vanderbilt University (Bransford, Kinzer, Risko, Rowe, & Vye,

1989; Cognition and Technology Group at Vanderbilt, 1990, 1993; Kinzer, Gabella, & Rieth, 1994). Use of a video (provided through a videodisk or a CD-ROM controlled by the computer) is a way to approximate non-school-based learning for students. We found this preferable to the more decontextualized methods found in traditional schooling. An anchor attempts to address the first issue noted above by providing students with a common experience, generally from a multimedia computer system that incorporates the use of videodisks or CD-ROMs to provide a cohesive program that all participants in the classroom experience. The second issue is confronted through using the anchor as "given knowledge"—as a point of reference—to which new knowledge is linked during instruction. Teachers and students draw on examples from the anchor and incorporate these into discussions. The third issue is addressed by using the technology to integrate curriculum across content areas. This allows students to use new information across domains at the time that it is learned, and it appears to mitigate "compartmentalization" of knowledge.

The Reporter Project used news footage provided by NBC as both anchors and models for writing. It attempted to merge closely both reading and writing through the use of a consistent data set that encouraged students to pose questions, decide on audience awareness through use of point of view, and find relevant facts and separate them from irrelevant or incorrect information, and then, using this information, write a news-based, narrative story. Figure 1 shows the entrance to the newspaper office, where the students are assigned to the Reporter section (collecting facts and making outlines, finding a theme for their story-to-be) or to the Writer section of the newsroom.

One of the benefits of computer technology is the ability of the computer to keep track of students' progress, especially across sessions, and to report their progress to the teacher in various ways. Figure 2 presents part of the progress-tracking system used by this program.

The student assigned to the Reporter area is presented with a series of story options that relate to various departments of the newsroom. The student can choose to work on a story in one of the following departments: news, sports, style, science, or "the American scene." Each of these assignments requires that the student gather facts and collect information. Students have a choice about which area to work in first, but eventually all areas must be completed. Completing all of the areas facilitates the development of audience awareness, one of the goals of this program. For example, a sports story about a game requires a close focus on the game and a peripheral

Figure 1. Opening screen of the Reporter Project software. Students are placed into Reporter or Writer areas depending on their previous work in the program.

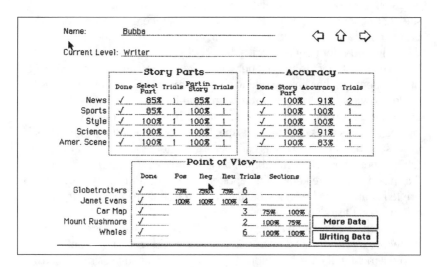

Figure 2. One benefit to teachers and students is the individualized tracking that computers can provide. Here, teachers and/or students can easily see their progress through the program and decide on areas that need additional attention.

focus on the game's surroundings. A reporter covering the same game for the Style section, however, must recognize that readers would expect a greater focus on the spectators—perhaps who was in the luxury boxes and their fashion choices—than do readers in the Sports section. Thus, moving through the various sections of the program builds a recognition that stories must not only have a focus, but the focus must relate to a writer's audience and goals.

Once the student enters the Reporter area, the video anchor is presented, followed by stories and informational material related to the anchor. The technology allows the student to highlight any word in the story and hear it pronounced, to see a video that provides appropriate visual context for content-area words, and/or to read (or have "read" by the computer) a definition. The student must find and choose relevant information, write a main idea statement (an inappropriate main idea results in options to see the video again and to review the facts that were gathered), and move to another story to continue to practice the skills of information collection, point of view, cause and effect, and main idea. After completing stories in the Reporter area, the student may go to the Writers area to write a story (including a headline that reflects the main idea).

Here, too, the capabilities of the technology come into play. The program is customized for each student (because of the tracking that allows each student to choose a different story and to be in a different place within the program), allowing the student to submit his or her story to the "editor," where it resides for peer and/or teacher feedback. As it is submitted, however, the student is asked if he would like to compare the story with that of an expert who has been working on the same story. This option allows the student to view the story delivered by the real-life television news anchorperson on the day that the story aired. This allows novice writers to compare their stories (and the facts that they chose to include) with the real news story as it aired. Students can revise their stories at this point (or at any future time), although each submission is stored for retrieval by the teacher. Submitted stories are kept in the reporter/writer's file and can be revised and printed at any time, by either the teacher or the student, allowing an ongoing comparison of students' work over time.

The Reporter Project was developed and tested in sixth-grade classrooms for two years and showed that students made statistically significant improvement in their recognition and use of elements such as main ideas, supporting details, and cause and effect relationships (Schmidt, Meltzer, Kinzer, Bransford, & Hasselbring, 1990). Their writing was also more cohesive than their control-group peers who were taught using similar materials and sequences but without the use of the technology.

What we learned from this project raises interesting issues. For example, we noticed that students and teachers used the anchor videos as "jumping-off points" to learn new, related things that interested them, raising issues about curriculum and who makes decisions about its content and its sequence. Students followed paths that were undefined at the start of the project and learned more as a result. In addition, we found that issues surrounding revisions, collaboration, and feedback in writing and reading need to be examined. Our readers and writers often interacted with each other about their work and used technology to locate information that could be used almost instantly through a "cut and paste" process. Certain changes in the students' approach to writing and revision were a direct result of the multimedia and technological supports that were available. Students became more literate in terms of their knowledge and their ability to communicate their knowledge than they were before they began the project.

The Young Children's Literacy Project

Intended for use with young children, this project incorporated full-motion, color video, sound, and Internet/World Wide Web access capabilities in addition to the tracking and other functions noted above. The video-based anchor and strong emphasis on student engagement with text across subject-areas that were part of the Reporter Project were retained here. Added was much more capability in terms of students' interaction with text (both in terms of reading and writing), as well as in their use of oral language.

This project used as its basis the notion of the mental modeling that occurs during the comprehension process (Glenberg & Langston, 1992; Johnson-Laird, 1983; McNamara, Miller, & Bransford, 1991). Rather than using multimedia to enhance the understanding of a particular story, the anchor video, together with on-line sequencing and book-making activities, was designed to provide the framework for understanding stories. The goal was to have children understand the power, use, and importance of literacy as well as to enjoy the time spent in literacy activities. For example, students learned plot structure and sequence in addition to the power and purpose of literacy through reading, writing, and making books.

After viewing a video-anchor story, children sequenced and retold the multimedia anchor story (see Figure 3). Later, they used their retelling as a

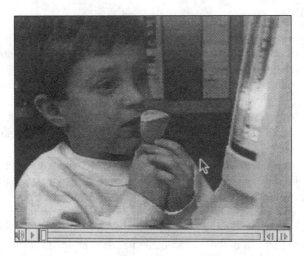

Figure 3. Here, a student uses the computer's recording system to answer a question orally and then to retell the anchor story that was just presented.

basis for writing, illustrating, and adding music to a story (see Figure 4). The capability of adding music to stories was very popular and provided a vehicle for discussing setting and other elements of mood as reflected by the music chosen. Eventually, students wrote and read related stories, published them, and placed them in the classroom and the computer's library for access by others. Access to the stories occurred in many ways, including the Internet. Figure 5 shows the relevant World Wide Web home page. This home page uses as a common background the anchor that students around the country and around the world saw and used in their classrooms and links students' and teachers' common set of experiences to new and ongoing literacy activities. Use of the Internet and the collaborative aspects built into the Young Children's Literacy software maximized the potential for author circles, book-study groups, collaborative learning, and learning communities.

During the developmental stage of this project, Sharp, Bransford, Goldman, Risko, Kinzer, and Vye (1995) found that multimedia environments with dynamic visual supports facilitated language comprehension and provided a framework for understanding and remembering linguistic information. The Young Children's Literacy Project continues to explore the effects that multimedia technology can have on the

Figure 4. One part of the book-making portion of the program. Other sections allow the addition of music and video to a student's story.

Figure 5. A screen-caption showing a portion of the World Wide Web home page available as an outcome of the Young Children's Literacy project.

reading and writing of young children and on classroom environments. It is already clear, however, that anchored instruction and the capabilities of computer technology (random access across databases, communicative links through the Internet and the World Wide Web so that a classroom can become part of a global community of learners, use of full visual and oral/aural multimedia capabilities for learning and presentations, and the storage and record-keeping potential of the technology) will require new methods and new conceptualizations of assessment. Technology provides a powerful means of storing, revising, and presenting work over time, thus facilitating evaluation of more authentic work than is presently possible with traditional measures.

The Hypermedia Design Project

Can hypermedia enable low prior knowledge readers to comprehend challenging material as well as high prior knowledge readers? This was the question explored in the hypermedia design project.

The amount of prior knowledge a reader possesses about a topic has a robust effect on reading comprehension. Readers with high prior knowledge almost always outperform students with low prior knowledge. Increases in prior knowledge lead to increases in comprehension and interest (Alexander, Kulikowich, & Jetton, 1994; Tyler & Voss, 1982), greater frequency and higher quality of self-generated questions (Scardamalia & Bereiter, 1991), and profoundly influence the interpretation of ambiguous passages (Bransford & Johnson, 1973). Moreover, the effects of prior knowledge on reading comprehension increase as students become older (Alexander, Kulikowich, & Jetton, 1994) and as the informational density of texts increases (Tyler & Voss, 1982). Older students with low prior knowledge about a topic are at a tremendous disadvantage compared to older students with high prior knowledge when they read challenging material.

Hypermedia contains at least two characteristics that may be useful in helping readers overcome a lack of prior knowledge about complex and informationally dense texts. Designed appropriately, hypermedia responds immediately to readers' informational needs as they attempt to construct a model of the information they encounter. This makes learning especially efficient for a low prior knowledge reader. For example, one of us has done work with the U.S. Department of Defense (Hillinger & Leu, 1994) and noted that new air force mechanics unfamiliar with different aspects of the "hot section" of a jet engine could regularly seek out the specific information she required by simply clicking locations linked to the appropriate information. Although similar information might be obtained by searching an index, a glossary, or a table of contents in a traditional engine manual, the speed of access and the precision of the information received is often greater in a hypermedia program. This may be especially useful in an informationally dense passage where many items are unfamiliar.

Second, within a hypermedia program a reader has access to multiple media sources of information. In addition to traditional text and graphic information, speech, animation, and video are all available. Moreover, interactive simulations may be used in certain situations to allow users to explore simple cause and effect relationships or more complex relationships between multiple components. For example, in seeking to understand the organization and operation of a jet engine, a reader using hypermedia could take one apart and put it back together again in a simulation. It is likely that each media source contains special advantages when communicating different informational needs. A student using a hypermedia environment might develop different ways of knowing, using different media sources, depending upon which resource was most helpful in clarifying a particular concept. It is also likely that constructing meaning from multiple perspectives, using multiple media sources, provides a richer understanding of complex information (Spiro, Feltovich, Jacobson, & Coulson, 1992), especially if one lacks prior knowledge about a topic.

The Hillinger and Leu (1994) research project noted earlier explored the ability of a hypermedia environment to overcome comprehension limitations caused by a lack of prior knowledge. The researchers converted a complex training manual for the repair and maintenance of a CT7-9 turboprop engine into hypermedia and observed both high prior knowledge and low prior knowledge subjects as they attempted to learn this information. The hypermedia program created for this study allowed users to take the engine apart, read about each of the different sections, view animations and hear audio explaining engine operations, view videos and hear audio of key procedures, and rapidly obtain additional information about unfamiliar concepts.

In this study, high prior knowledge subjects were members of an air force propulsion unit responsible for the repair of F-16 jet fighter planes. They were familiar with high-performance engine systems but unfamiliar with the CT7-9 turboprop engine. Most had several years of college education. Low prior knowledge subjects were university students unfamiliar with high-performance jet engines. The low prior knowledge subjects achieved the same level of understanding with the hypermedia environment as high prior knowledge subjects, a finding seldom reported in the literature on the comprehension of conventional printed texts. This finding held for both specific, targeted information defined in the learning task before treatment (identifying engine components and putting them back in the correct order) as well as for general, non-targeted information unrelated to the learning task. It was sustained when covariate analysis controlled for the slight differences in the amount of education between the two populations.

Thus, the results suggest that hypermedia programs, when designed appropriately, can eliminate comprehension differences between high and low prior knowledge readers. Low prior knowledge readers may comprehend informationally dense structures as well as high prior knowledge readers, probably because they can easily seek out information in an environment that responds to their specific information needs and because information may be presented through multiple media representations to support learning. This result has important consequences for the design of instructional materials, especially when these materials may be dense and informationally rich. Such a possibility is seldom reported in comprehension research with traditional texts. It suggests that hypermedia may make certain information more accessible to a wider variety of readers.

The Classroom Integration Project

Each of these projects has provided useful insights about how appropriately designed software can contribute to literacy and learning. Nevertheless, we face an important paradox with respect to computer use in school classrooms today: Although computer technology is becoming more widely available, it is not becoming fully appropriated by teachers and integrated into classroom learning experiences (cf. Anderson, 1993; Reinking & Bridwell-Bowles, 1991; U.S. Congress, Office of Congressional Assessment, 1995). Often, a classroom computer is placed in a corner and is only available for students after they complete assigned work. Frequently, computer time is devoted to playing an electronic game, one unconnected with classroom learning. Thus, an important problem is how to move computer technology to a more important location in the curriculum where teachers might use it to support central learning tasks.

Undoubtedly, there are many reasons for the failure to integrate computer technology more systematically into the curriculum. Among the reasons are lack of resources, inadequate teacher education, and insufficient time. There may also be another important source of this problem: Software is often designed by technical experts without considering the specific needs of teachers and students (Anderson, 1993; Becker, 1993; Leu & Reinking, 1996). As a result, teachers do not always see a clear match between available software and what they do in the classroom.

Creating software more relevant to teachers was explored in a project wherein a team of sixth-grade teachers at an urban school were provided with all of the programming and media assistance they required to create a multimedia program around their classroom needs (Leu, 1996). They worked as a collaborative team with a multimedia software developer, an educational researcher, and over 20 graduate students to develop a multimedia software program that integrated social studies, writing, and literature in a year-long thematic unit on the ancient civilizations of Egypt, Greece, and Rome. The teachers in this project made all of the content and design decisions, which were then developed into a multimedia program by the software developer. Revisions were continually made to early drafts based on teachers' feedback until the final program reflected their classroom needs as closely as possible. Then, the nature of the design elements favored by classroom teachers and the extent to which this software was integrated into the classroom curriculum were examined.

Figure 6 shows a portion of the program designed by these teachers. The time line at the top allows users to move to different historical periods. Map icons at the bottom allow users to view one of five maps for each period: World, Mediterranean, Egypt, Rome, and Greece. In Figure 6, for example, a student has moved the time line to 1500 B.C. and has selected the map of Egypt. On each map, a number of different content icons appear. Clicking on any icon opens up the information contained there, including a graphic or video clip as well as text information about the item.

In Figure 7 a student has clicked on an "interview" icon (a microphone) to find out about Pericles. Here, the student may read the scrolling information to the right or click on any interview question to the left and view a video of Pericles' response to the interview question. Icons include information about important historical, cultural, and architectural concepts. They also include myths from the different cultures and interviews with famous individuals.

Figure 8 shows an element that teachers viewed as central to the program, a student pack used for response and communication. In the writing space, teachers and students write responses to an assignment or a message to a friend. At the top of the student pack are a series of icons. These

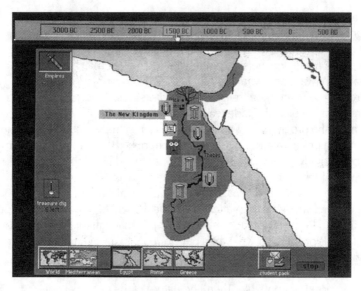

Figure 6. A sample screen from the Classroom Integration Project illustrating the three main navigation features: a time line (top), map buttons (bottom), and content icons (center).

Figure 7. An example of information contained in an interview content icon.

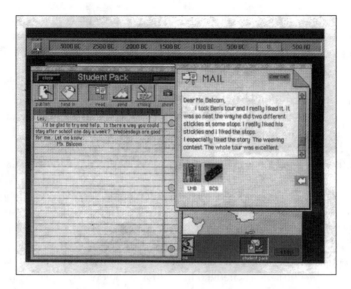

Figure 8. Communication features contained in the student pack.

allow students to publish their work on a bulletin board, hand in an assignment to the teacher, read e-mail in their mailbox, send a message to someone in the class, post a sticky note (an electronic Post-it note for others to read) anywhere in the program, or "shoot" a picture of a video or graphic to include with a message.

In addition to concepts central to their curriculum, teachers wanted a number of "constructivist design features," such as a bulletin board, student- and teacher-generated tours through the program, a response journal, a student-generated dictionary/glossary, an e-mail system, sticky notes, and student-developed interviews of famous or mythical individuals. These constructivist design features enabled students and teachers to construct and communicate their own interpretations of the meaning within the multimedia information structure. They could also use these features to add information from outside sources. This differs from many other software products that contain rich information resources that may be read or printed out but that do not always allow students and teachers to construct their own interpretations of the information within the electronic environment and then communicate this information to others.

In essence, these teachers wanted their multimedia program to perform in the same way that students used more traditional informational resources during regular classroom assignments. Typically, students in these classrooms searched for information in traditional print sources, constructed their own interpretations of the meanings they found in these sources through written reports and projects, and then shared their work with the class. These teachers expected software to do something similar to their on-going classroom program in social studies. The design features teachers included in their program allowed students to construct new meaning and communicate this meaning to others, all within an electronic environment.

Did having a multimedia program designed to meet classroom teachers' needs become more systematically integrated into the curriculum? This appears to be the case. Teachers never gave required assignments in other commercially developed software (20–30 separate titles) even when these were the only software selections available. Typically, these programs were used after students had completed their regular work. In contrast, teachers assigned projects for students throughout the year in the program they designed. Moreover, the percentage of time spent on multimedia software related to the curriculum changed from approximately 10% before this program entered the classroom to approximately 75% after it entered the classroom. These results suggest that multimedia software will become more systematically integrated into the curriculum when it meets the needs of teachers and the nature of their instructional program. Software publishers need to pay greater attention to teachers' instructional needs if they expect their programs to be tightly integrated into the classroom.

Curriculum Challenges and Opportunities on the Internet

Additional challenges await us as graphic browsers, such as Netscape Navigator™ (a program used to access the World Wide Web), allow classrooms to access the rich multimedia resources available on the Internet. The Internet also creates new opportunities for teaching and learning.

A central issue is equity of access. A recent survey by the Department of Education (Heaviside, Malitz, & Carpenter, 1996) reports that although 50% of schools had access to the Internet in the fall of 1995 (up from 35% in 1994), this varied greatly by school. Schools with relatively few students from poor families were twice as likely to have access to the Internet (62%) compared with schools with large proportions of students from poor families (31%). If all children are to have equal opportunity to access the informational resources of the Internet, it is clear that new public policy initiatives must be designed to insure this.

Another challenge we face is one of teacher education. In order to take advantage of Internet access for classroom learning, teachers need support and time to develop an understanding of how the Internet may be integrated into their curriculum. This issue is an important challenge for schools of education that are beginning to integrate Internet technology into their preparation programs. It is also an important challenge for the 1.5 million teachers currently teaching at the elementary and secondary levels; most will require support and time during the next few years to become familiar with Internet use in the classroom.

As we move to integrate these resources into classroom learning it seems clear that strategic knowledge will become even more central to success in electronic environments than in traditional print environments (Leu & Reinking, 1996). Knowing how to navigate through the complex and informationally rich environments possible in electronic contexts requires us to consider new forms of strategic knowledge and to support students as they acquire this knowledge. Knowing how to find the best information in the shortest time will quickly advantage certain students over others who have not developed these skills. We must seek to understand the new forms of strategic knowledge required in electronic literacy contexts as we seek ways to support students in developing this knowledge.

Initially, we might be guided in this effort by encouraging students to support one another as they develop these strategies. That is, multimedia environments, because they are both powerful and complex, often require us to communicate with others in order to make meaning from them. Thus, learning is frequently constructed through social interactions in these contexts (Baker, 1995; Labbo, 1996; Leu, in press), perhaps even more naturally and frequently than in traditional print environments.

The Internet also challenges us to work with parents and students to develop appropriate use policies as we seek to maximize the appropriate use of information available on the Internet and to minimize use of inappropriate sites. Indeed, communities will need to develop mechanisms for determining what is considered inappropriate viewing for students at different developmental levels. Software filters such as Cyber Patrol, SurfWatch, or CYBERSitter, informational sessions for students, and appropriate use contracts may all be part of a community's response. The issue of information use is a delicate one, however. This is especially true in a society that values free speech at the same time it seeks to protect children.

Each of these challenges, as well as others not yet imagined, requires us to rethink traditional notions of literacy and learning as the Internet becomes a more central feature in classroom learning. Following is a list of addresses and descriptions of several sites we have found useful on the World Wide Web.

EdWeb—http://edweb.cnidr.org:90/resource.cntnts.html
If you are unfamiliar with the World Wide Web of the Internet, this is a good place to begin. It contains useful background information to assist you as you start exploring resources on the web.

Global SchoolNet Foundation—http://www.gsn.org
This non-profit foundation with a long history of supporting teachers has developed a rich set of resources for students and teachers. At this location there are many learning projects for your class to join as well as ideas for integrating the World Wide Web into your classroom. You may also talk with other teachers in a discussion group. This is a great site to explore the possibilities of the web for your classroom.

Frequently Asked Questions About Acceptable Use Policies—
ftp://ftp.classroom.net/wentworth/ClassroomConnect/aup-faq.txt
This location, sponsored by Classroom Connect, provides a useful discussion of what acceptable use policies are, why they are important, and how to go about developing one for your school. A sample acceptable use policy is provided so that you can copy and edit it for your school's use.

AskERIC Virtual Library—http://ericir.syr.edu
This is the web site for the Educational Resources Information Center, a federally funded national information system. The site contains many useful resources for teachers, including lesson plans and a location where you may ask questions about teaching and receive a personalized answer back within 48 hours. A rich site with many useful resources for teaching.

Teachers Helping Teachers—http://www.pacificnet.net/~mandel
A location developed by a teacher in California to put teachers in touch with one another. It features a chat area where teachers may talk to one another about common issues, lesson plans, instructional ideas, and a "Stress Reduction Moment of the Week." An especially useful location is a bulletin board with e-mail addresses of teachers around the world who are interested in sharing ideas.

Conclusions and Summary

We have shared some of our experiences with technology in order to describe the challenges multimedia, hypermedia, and the Internet present for literacy educators. Challenges face us in developing new definitions of literacy, in effectively exploiting the potential of electronic resources, and in understanding the information and communication technologies that are available to our students.

Clearly, we are entering a period where traditional definitions of literacy will need to be evaluated for their appropriateness within electronic environments (Reinking, 1995a). Recent work by Baker (1995) and Labbo (1996) raises important questions about traditional definitions of literacy. Baker found that literacy changes in a number of important ways in technology-rich classrooms. Students exchanged meaning through spatial images and auditory products as well as with text. Moreover, students frequently constructed meaning socially through technology. In addition, nonlinear information interactions often took place. In her work, Labbo found technology to redefine the symbols that children generated. Both scholars call for expanded definitions of literacy and literacy development— definitions that include the effects of multimedia on teaching and learning.

There are also challenges associated with the non-linear nature of hypermedia. Hypermedia allows readers to move through documents in multiple dimensions as they seek information. They may cut and paste information into their own writing and they may explore in greater depth or skim as they determine the optimal path through any information structure. This raises challenges not only in terms of copyright issues (see Reinking, 1995b), but also in terms of our understanding of text construction and revision. Rouet and Levonen (1996), Dillon (1996), and others have pointed out that the linear structure of text provides support for readers and writers and that this might be lost when we move to a hypermedia environment. On the other hand, some of our work suggests that hypermedia, designed appropriately, supports readers, especially those who lack prior knowledge about a topic. In the rich and nearly limitless informational resources available on the Internet, however, users may find themselves seduced by interesting information that leads them far afield from their original purpose (Birkerts, 1995). This suggests there will be an even greater need in the future for students to glean the relevant from the irrelevant and to synthesize central knowledge across sources (Leu, in press).

Finally, there are issues that deal with teachers' roles and actions in the teaching and learning of literacy. Although multimedia technologies and the Internet provide access to rich information resources, they also require that teachers become more knowledgeable in their roles as guides and facilitators of learning. Teachers will need to become even more insightful about literacy learning in order to evaluate the software that is becoming available and to understand how this software might support literacy instruction. Most importantly, they need to seek out software experiences consistent with their best insights about learning and incorporate these into their curriculum.

Whenever a new tool arrives it becomes important to use it wisely and appropriately for the task at hand. This requires a clear understanding of both the tool and the task. This may be the greatest challenge we all face as we seek to understand both the many new electronic tools becoming available for literacy and the ways in which these tools redefine literacy tasks. Our answers will largely determine the success our students experience during the information age in which they live.

References

Alexander, P. A., Kulikowich, J. M., & Jetton, T. L. (1994). The role of subject-matter knowledge and interest in the processing of linear and non-linear texts. *Review of Educational Research, 64,* 210–252.

Anderson, R. E. (1993). The technology infrastructure of U.S. schools. *Communications of the ACM, 36,* 72.

Baker, E. A. (1995). *The nature of literacy activities in a technology rich fourth grade classroom from a meaning making perspective.* Unpublished doctoral dissertation, Vanderbilt University, Nashville, TN.

Becker, H. J. (1993). Computer experience, patterns of computer use and effectiveness: An inevitable sequence or divergent national cultures? *Studies in Educational Evaluation, 19,* 127–148.

Birkerts, S. (1995). *The Gutenberg elegies.* New York: Ballantine Books.

Bransford, J. D., & Johnson, M. K. (1973). Consideration of some problems of comprehension. In W. Chase (Ed.), *Visual information processing* (pp. 383–438). New York: Academic Press.

Bransford, J. D., Kinzer, C. K., Risko, V. J., Rowe, D. W., & Vye, N. J. (1989). Designing invitations to thinking: Some initial thoughts. In S. McCormick & J. Zutell (Eds.), *Cognitive and social perspectives for literacy research and instruction* (38th NRC Yearbook, pp. 35–54). Chicago: National Reading Conference.

Cognition and Technology Group at Vanderbilt. (1990). Anchored instruction and its relationship to situated cognition. *Educational Researcher, 19,* 2–10.

Cognition and Technology Group at Vanderbilt. (1993). Anchored instruction and situated cognition revisited: A response to Tripp. *Educational Technology, 34,* 28–31.

Dillon, A. (1996). Myths, misconceptions, and an alternative perspective on information usage and the electronic medium. In J. F. Rouet, J. J. Levonen, A. Dillon, & R. J. Spiro (Eds.), *Hypertext and cognition* (pp. 25–42). MahWah, NJ: Lawrence Erlbaum.

Glenberg, A. M., & Langston, W. E. (1992). Comprehension of illustrated text: Pictures help to build mental models. *Journal of Memory and Language, 31,* 129–151.

Heaviside, S., Malitz, G., & Carpenter, J. (1996). *Advanced telecommunications in U.S. public elementary and secondary schools, 1995.* Washington, DC: Office of Educational Research and Improvement, U.S. Department of Education.

Hillinger, M. L., & Leu, D. J. (1994). Guiding instruction in hypermedia. *Proceedings of the Human Factors and Ergonomics Society's 38th Annual Meeting* (pp. 266–270). Santa Monica, CA: Human Factors and Ergonomics Society.

Johnson-Laird, P. N. (1983). *Mental models.* Cambridge, MA: Harvard University Press.

Kinzer, C. K., Gabella, M. S., & Rieth, H. J. (1994). An argument for using multimedia and anchored instruction to facilitate mildly-disabled students' learning of literacy and social studies. *Technology and Disability Quarterly, 3,* 117–128.

Labbo, L. D. (1996). A semiotic analysis of young children's symbol making in a classroom computer center. *Reading Research Quarterly, 31,* 356–385.

Leu, D. J., Jr. (1996). *Supporting reading comprehension in social studies and response to children's literature using multimedia software designed by teachers and students: Exploring a new model of software development and use (Final Report).* Washington, DC: Office of Educational Research and Improvement, U.S. Department of Education.

Leu, D. J., Jr. (in press). Sarah's secret: Social aspects of literacy and learning in a digital, information age. *The Reading Teacher.*

Leu, D. J., Jr., & Reinking, D. (1996). Bringing insights from reading research to research on electronic learning environments. In H. van Oostendorp & S. de Mul (Eds.), *Cognitive aspects of electronic text processing* (pp. 43–75). Norwood, NJ: Ablex.

McNamara, T. P., Miller, D. L., & Bransford, J. D. (1991). Mental models and reading comprehension. In R. Barr, M. Kamil, P. Mosenthal, & P. D. Pearson (Eds.), *Handbook of reading research,* vol. 2 (pp. 490–511). New York: Longman.

Negroponte, N. (1995). *Being digital.* New York: Knopf.

Reinking, D. (1995a). Reading and writing with computers: Literacy research in a post-typographic world. In K. A. Hinchman, D. J. Leu, & C. K. Kinzer (Eds.), *Perspectives on literacy research and practice* (44th NRC Yearbook, pp. 17–33). Chicago: National Reading Conference.

Reinking, D. (1995b, December). *Ownership and dissemination of electronics texts: Is a new ethics needed?* Paper presented at the 45th National Reading Conference, New Orleans, LA.

Reinking, D., & Bridwell-Bowles, L. (1991). Computers in reading and writing. In R. Barr, M. L. Kamil, P. B. Mosenthal, & P. D. Pearson (Eds.), *Handbook of Reading Research, vol. 2* (pp 310–340). New York: Longman.

Rouet, J. F., & Levonen, J. J. (1996). Studying and learning with hypertext: Empirical studies and their implications. In J. F. Rouet, J. J. Levonen, A. Dillon, & R. J. Spiro (Eds.), *Hypertext and cognition* (pp. 9–24). MahWah, NJ: Lawrence Erlbaum.

Scardamalia, M., & Bereiter, C. (1991). Higher levels of agency for children in knowledge building: A challenge for the design of new knowledge media. *The Journal of the Learning Sciences, 1,* 37–68.

Schmidt, C. R., Meltzer, L., Kinzer, C. K., Bransford, J. D., & Hasselbring, T. S. (1990). *The effects of video and oral media on story comprehension and writing.* Paper presented at the Biennial Conference on Human Development, Richmond, VA.

Sharp, D. L., Bransford, J. D., Goldman, S. R., Risko, V. J., Kinzer, K., & Vye, N. J. (1995). Dynamic visual support for story comprehension and mental modeling by young, at-risk children. *Educational Technology Research and Development, 43* (4), 25–42.

Spiro, R. J., Feltovich, P. J., Jacobson, M. J., & Coulson, R. L. (1992). Cognitive flexibility, constructivism, and hypertext: Random access instruction for advanced knowledge acquisition in ill-structured domains. In T. M. Duffy & D. H. Jonassen (Eds.), *Constructivism and the technology of instruction: A conversation* (pp. 57–75). Hillsdale, NJ: Lawrence Erlbaum.

Tyler, S., & Voss, J. F. (1982). Attitude and knowledge effects in prose processing. *Journal of Verbal Learning and Verbal Behavior, 4,* 331–351.

U.S. Congress, Office of Congressional Assessment. (1995). *Teachers and technology: Making the connection.* Washington, DC: U.S. Government Printing Office.

Whitehead, A. N. (1929). *The aims of education.* New York: Macmillan.

4 Integrating Technology in the Classroom

Linda McMillen, Sherrell Shanahan, Kathleen Dowd, Joyce MacPhee, and Jennifer Hester

Technology holds the tantalizing promise of tools for learning and easy access to a vast treasury of information from around the world. The Internet—the so-called electronic superhighway—CD-ROM technology, and a growing abundance of software packages offer challenging new ways for students to practice and extend their literacy. The horizons of previous generations of elementary students were limited to the resources available in their local schools or libraries. Now they can zip off to the Smithsonian or the Louvre for a quick visit, ask a question of their favorite author, read a story written yesterday by a fourth grader who lives on the other side of the world, listen to a book with animated pictures, and still have time for buddy reading or recess. It sounds wonderful—and it is—but there is a catch. There is so much electronic information, and it is growing so fast that it becomes overwhelming. Teachers and students can waste a lot of time fumbling among the wealth of technology; it's enough to make you throw up your hands and go read a good old-fashioned book! To help busy teachers make some sense of this, we waded through a plethora of material and reviewed a representative sample of language arts–related software and web sites for this month's column.

Resource Books

As a resource for children, Preston Gralla's book *On-line Kids: A Young Surfer's Guide to Cyberspace* (John Wiley and Sons, 1996, 282 pages,

Reprinted from *Language Arts*, February 1997.

$14.95) offers a thorough overview of Internet basics. This book is a good resource for the classroom or home. The author translates "techie" talk into user-friendly language for children from third grade through middle school. Included are clear definitions of terms from CD-ROM to *Yahoo,* explanations about bulletin boards, downloading, netiquette, the World Wide Web, and e-mail. There is also an abundance of addresses to visit on the Internet. Gralla considered his audience well as he includes "usefulness" and "coolness" indices (on a 1 to 10 scale) for site summaries, although these reviews do not necessarily consider the instructional value of the material.

Using this book as a guide, young surfers have many opportunities to read and develop technology referencing skills. Gralla suggests ways of choosing on-line services and reviews on-line and software resource materials, including encyclopedias and dictionaries. Instructions on creating a home page are spelled out. Web sites of interest to kids are highlighted including the Michael Jordan home page, the Louvre tour, the Ultimate Band list with videos and music clips, and so on. Of particular interest to teachers of language arts is Chapter 13, "Writing and Reading." On-line writing and publishing and booktalk sites, as well as many other language arts addresses, are reviewed.

Gralla's book makes the young person's trip into Cyberspace a more comfortable journey. Each time we picked up the book, we found something new to learn or try out. The only negative is its non-technological format; information in this field changes so rapidly that this hardcopy is likely to become obsolete quickly.

Grade: A

Computer Conversations: Readers and Books Online (National Council of Teachers of English, 1996, 194 pages, $16.95) is a resource for teachers, grades three and up, who wish to use technology in the classroom and aren't sure how to begin. The authors, Marilyn Jody and Marianne Saccardi, consider their work to be a travel guide into computer literacy and ". . . believe, in fact, that computers can become a powerful force, one as powerful as books themselves became with the advent of printing, in creating the universally literate community of our dreams" (p. xvii). The first chapter describes the BookRead Project of the early 1990s. The authors summarize the use of technology in the classroom to promote reading and writing. E-mail conversations about books among students and between students and authors (e.g., Gary Paulsen and Jean Craighead George) take place, increasing the motivation of reluctant readers because of the opportunity to have discussions about the books. The next five chapters show almost step-by-step how teachers can incorporate technology in their reading and writing activities. Nothing is assumed about the initial expertise of the readers of this work. The authors explain everything from choosing an author and organizing the classroom to equipment, funding, staff development, and administrative support. Electronic books, hypertext and digital texts, and on-line activities are surveyed. Some web sites are recommended.

Nearly half the book is appendices. "Author Chats on BookRead" is an excerpt of computer conversations with three authors. "Reader-Response Workshop" gives examples of students' computer conversations about a short story. "Computers in the Language Arts Curriculum" has a useful chart from the North Carolina Department of Public Instruction showing how technology is part of their literacy curriculum. In "Student Research," the authors have included three essays written from student perspectives on the basics of adding technology to the classroom, descriptions of hypertext and hyperfiction, and an explanation of the electronic discussion group "Lit List." Recommended organizations and guides that could assist the teacher are listed, as is a bibliography with annotated lists of children's literature, professional materials, and guides and resources for using the computer in the classroom.

Teachers who wish to use technology as an instructional tool will find this book to be a practical guide. The examples are clear, engaging, and relevant. Suggestions are profuse. Jody and Saccardi have attempted to reach teachers at many levels of computer literacy, which means that the book was written neither for novices nor the technologically proficient. One computer-savvy reviewer had difficulty maintaining interest in the book and novices may have trouble understanding some of the terminology and descriptions. Overall, however, the authors give educators a reasonably handy guide for making technology an integral component of the reading and writing classroom.

Grade: B

While *Computer Conversations* entered quickly into how to use telecommunications in the classroom, *Technology, Reading, and Language Arts* by Jerry W. Willis, Elizabeth C. Stephens, and Kathryn I. Matthew (Allyn and Bacon, 1996, 256 pages, $25.00) offers a unique combination of information and application. The book links technology to the classroom in an interesting and readable way, but it may not be for everyone. Reviewers disagreed on how teachers would respond to the book because the beginning chapters discuss the conceptual foundation of learning theories, their impact on classroom instruction, and specifically, the use of technology in the classroom. One reviewer thought that busy teachers might not persevere through the initial approach before getting to the "good stuff." This reviewer, however, felt the introductory "discussions" between a particular teacher and noted educational psychologists like Piaget and Vygotsky helped emphasize the importance of understanding your own theory of learning and how it impacts what goes on in the classroom as interesting, relevant, and readable.

The text flows easily from theory to example to technological impact in the classroom. Many classroom situations are described with practical applications of how technology can be incorporated into literacy activities. The stated purpose of the book is to inspire teachers and to relate learning theories to practice. It is neither a "how to" book nor a book that believes that technology is the only way to do things. As such, the title seems to limit the scope of the book.

Learning theories from the cognitive constructivist approach and the social constructivist and skill-based instruction perspectives are presented with accuracy and application. There are chapters dedicated to discussing technological tools for teachers, electronic resources, publications, organizations, and microteaching. Lists of software suggestions, reference addresses, and current books are also included. Numerous graphics show pages from cited software programs as well as computer dialogue between students. Each chapter concludes with a list of references and software citations but may not give a current source, stating that programs are sold "primarily through mail order distributors and retail stores." Perhaps a main phone number of the distributing company would have eased locating the software of particular programs.

Overall, however, *Technology, Reading, and Language Arts* offers a comprehensive approach to combining technology and literacy from the perspective of an informed educator.

Grade: B+

Classroom Connect (Wentworth Worldwide Media, 1996, $39.00 for one year) is a valuable resource for teachers who may be overwhelmed by the amount of information in cyberspace. The magazine is published nine times a year, and each issue contains lists of educational web sites (grades K–12), a helpful glossary, and features dealing with lesson plans, media centers, websites of the month, and other useful information. Although *Classroom*

Connect's pink and gray print and illustrations are not visually pleasing, it succinctly presents information about the Internet. An issue may contain handouts, such as an explanation of the Internet for parents, or an Internet Challenge activity for students. A useful item throughout the magazine is the "Helpdesk," a diamond-shaped symbol next to words in the text that directs the reader to a definition of the words at the bottom of the page.

Even for newcomers to the information age, the magazine is easy to use and understand, offering brief and clear explanations and suggestions for integrating the Internet's resources with the classroom. The table of contents at the back is divided by subject area, topic, or applicable grade level. At least three entries for language arts appeared in each of the 20-page issues we reviewed. One reviewer liked the periodical format because it helps teachers to stay current. The magazine offers a snapshot of up-to-date Internet information and sites. It is three-hole punched for placement in binders and has an annual index; both features make it easy to review specific sections in issues.

The only drawback to the magazine is having to look past the full-page color ads for other offerings of the publisher. However, since these are printed on separate pages, they can be removed relatively easily. Although most of the information in this periodical may be more beneficial for intermediate level or above, primary teachers will find it both helpful and time-saving as they surf the net. We found it to be extremely valuable.

Grade: A

Scholastic's *Software Club* is a resource for teachers who want to encourage students to use educational software at home or who are looking for classroom-appropriate software for their own use. Scholastic has capitalized on the ubiquitous computer market by offering two software clubs: "Software Club Jr." for pre-kindergarten through third grades and "Software Club" for third through eighth grades. Clubs are similar to the popular, and probably more widely known, Scholastic Book Clubs (Seesaw, Lucky, Arrow, etc.). Software can be selected from over a dozen publishers, with programs in math, reading, writing, basic concepts, problem solving, art, and music. The titles represent bestsellers and award winners chosen by a review board of educators from all over the United States. Like the book clubs, there is a summary for each item that suggests an appropriate age level, and there are discounted prices. The summaries indicate the type of computer (Macintosh, IBM) that can run the program and basic memory and hardware requirements. There is a toll-free number and operators available to answer teacher questions and a liberal return policy to guarantee customer satisfaction. The clubs have become so popular since their inception five years ago that Scholastic has established separate phone lines to take orders and answer questions.

As with the book clubs, teachers obtain bonus points for every item ordered. Points may be redeemed for products including computers, software, classroom equipment, and books. Although software prices begin at an enticing $4.95, teachers need to decide if the prices are affordable for their students. Of course, with more families owning computers, this club offers a relatively inexpensive and easy way of obtaining software.

Grade: A

Instructional Software

Increasingly, we hear the insistent cries of "back to basics," and in reading this often means teaching phonics. We reviewed four programs that purport to teach phonics including *Learning Ladder Phonics Adventure with Sing-Along Sam, Wiggleworks, 'Tronic Phonics,* and *Word Munchers Deluxe.*

Learning Ladder Phonics Adventure with Sing-Along Sam (Panasonic Interactive Media Company, 1996, $39.99) is an interactive software program for the primary grades. Using songs, the program takes students through 12 lessons at three levels. The lessons include letters and sounds, consonants, vowels, blends, digraphs, and sight words in isolation and context. The program does not direct players on how to access it. Although we were using a high-speed computer, the music and speech were slow, and the first character's whiny voice was annoying. Some of the graphics may be unfamiliar (igloo, ostrich) or ambiguous (the cab could be a truck) to children. The vowel song is neither catchy nor rhythmic. For the most part, words are introduced in isolation, appearing only in context at the highest level. A word identification game promoted violence by showing pirates blasting cannons, complete with the sound of gunfire and a bird yelling, "You missed me!" and "I'm going to get you." This is not exactly the best message for young children. Students are kicked out of the game after one wrong answer, a feature that is too stringent. The program's basic idea seems to be "to learn to read, just sing." If only it were that easy. Although the reviewers do not recommend this product, the children who we asked to sample it enjoyed the music and games.

Grade: D

Wiggleworks (Scholastic, 1994, $1750) is an interactive software program designed for grades K–2 and is available on CD-ROM or floppy disc for

Macintosh or Microsoft Windows. The program offers 72 children's books divided into three developmental stages and is available in English or Spanish. The book selections are both fiction and nonfiction and contain predictable patterns, rhymes, and themes that reflect children's lives. For each book, there are five instructional activities that encompass reading, writing, speaking, and listening. In the Read Aloud section, children listen to a story with the words presented on the screen for them to follow along. In the Read section, they can read the book at their own pace, clicking on unknown words for the narrator to read for them. Students and teachers appreciated the recording feature that allows users to record and listen to themselves read for immediate reinforcement. Words of interest can be stored on a word list for future review.

In the Write section, students write their own stories and draw pictures. If they need assistance, students can click on a light bulb icon and a story starter idea based on the reading selection will be provided. A computer voice reads back the child's story. In the My Book section, children customize any book in the program by changing the text and illustrations. They become the author, illustrator, editor, and publisher of their own story. The Magnet Board or phonics section of the program provides practice in working with letters and sounds. Unlike a worksheet, the computer reinforces these sounds by reading them to the child. The teacher or student decides what to review in this program, unlike in the other programs that we reviewed.

Wiggleworks offers a management system enabling the teacher to keep track of each student's progress. Teachers can also record messages for students telling them what to focus on during that day's lesson. The program offers lesson plans for each book including objectives, ESL notes, assessment ideas, and activities for integration within the curriculum.

Students liked the program and found it easy to use, but as one kindergarten teacher told us, "There are only a few books [in the program] that the children enjoy. Some of the books just aren't that interesting." Other teachers, however, liked the program and said that they used it as a tool to reinforce their teaching. A second-grade teacher said that she likes that the computer can read and emphasize the words for struggling students. She also appreciates how the program reinforces mechanics, sight vocabulary, and fluent reading, something an audio tape cannot do. For all of its positive features, the entire *Wiggleworks* program is an expensive $1750, although literature packets can be purchased separately.

Grade: A

'*Tronic Phonics* (Macmillan/McGraw-Hill, 1997, the cost is approximately $400 for a class pack of eight disks and 55 books. Additional disks can be purchased separately and range from $49.00 to $59.00.) is a software program that offers interactive phonics practice in English or Spanish for first and second graders. Each disk includes 3 to 5 stories and emphasizes 6 to 10 rimes or phonograms (/at/, /an/, /ip/, etc.). The program is user-friendly and includes a directory of activities featuring Spot the Spider, who helps students use the program. Each lesson contains reading, phonics, and writing activities. In the reading section the children hear a story with sound effects and music. Slower reading with word highlighting is available to help the lowest readers to follow along. When words with the targeted phonogram are clicked, sound effects and word pronunciations are given, and these words are reviewed at the end of the story. Phonics activities emphasize listening, decoding, blending, and writing to focus on the featured rime. The program gives immediate feedback to student responses. At the end of a lesson, children are encouraged to rewrite the story or to write and illustrate their own stories.

We reviewed a sample program from this set that emphasized the phonograms /ay/ and /old/ and the stories, *Molly May* and *Old Jack Fold.* The books were bright and attractively illustrated, but the stories were contrived. What else would be expected when a book is written to present specific word patterns rather than to tell a story? '*Tronic Phonics* includes a management system for keeping track of students' progress and parent goals for home use.

'*Tronic Phonics* reminded us of *Wiggleworks* (Scholastic) and *Phonics Adventure with Sing-Along Sam* (Panasonic). The program, like *Wiggleworks,* contains reading and writing along with the skills material. Both programs contain a recording system, too, although *Wiggleworks is* more extensive. '*Tronic Phonics* seems more appropriate for the teacher interested in providing analytic phonics practice in context, while *Wiggleworks is* for the holistic teacher who wants to combine authentic text, writing, and word study. *Phonics Adventure with Sing-Along Sam* uses a more synthetic approach, teaching each sound separately, and its presentation of words is out of context.

Grade: B

Word Munchers Deluxe (MECC, 1996, $69.00 for one CD. Prices vary for packages with teacher's manual and multiple CDs.) is an entertaining software program that makes practicing word recognition skills fun for students, yet it contains some confusing elements. The feedback that we received from teachers about this program varied depending on grade level. Although the program is intended for use in the first through fifth grades, it seems better suited for grades three and up. Upon entering the program, the user is given a list of topics and grade levels to choose from. These topics include classification, phonics, vocabulary, grammar, and sentence completion. For younger students, this opening screen is overwhelming and hard to use. Many first graders were unable to read the choices and needed teacher assistance to continue with the program. Although many attempted to have the choices read to them by clicking on the words, they quickly found out that this wasn't a feature of the program.

On the other hand, older students enjoyed selecting the skill and level of the program that was right for them. Once inside the game, the player uses a "muncher" to move around a three-dimensional game board and devour the shapes or words that match the targeted skill. Each game screen contains a scoreboard, game level, pause and play button, extra munchers, and two cute commentators. The commentators tell the player what skill is being targeted and briefly describe the game's rules. Students at all levels enjoyed the actual game but were confused by some of the choices. For example, in one phonics section, the player must munch all of the words that begin with *b*. If a child clicks on the picture of a football, thinking of the word *ball,* he is wrong. Instead of giving assistance or clarification for an incorrect answer, the muncher simply says "ick." As one child told us, "It's like a fun video game, but I think they should help you when you get it wrong."

Word Munchers Deluxe comes with supplementary activities that include writing ideas and word games. Some of the classroom ideas are helpful and could easily be used to extend the lessons. For students in third through fifth grades, *Word Munchers Deluxe* provides a lively and enjoyable way to independently review basic word recognition skills, although such learning issues are often resolved by these grade levels making this a less useful program. For younger children, *Word Munchers Deluxe* could be a beneficial way to practice with words, but they will need teacher assistance and guidance until they become familiar with the program.

Grade: C (1st & 2nd grades)
Grade: B (3rd–5th grades)

Interactive Literature on CD-ROM

Software publishers now offer a variety of interactive literature on CD-ROM. We reviewed three programs of this type: *Multimedia Literature, Magic Tales,* and *Living Books.*

Multimedia Literature (Macmillan/McGraw-Hill, 1995, cost varies from $100 for individual titles to $1800 for the school pack.) is a wonderful interactive program in English and Spanish that uses video, photography, audio, and sound effects to support students in grades three to six. The program is available in Macintosh and Windows versions, and it contains 24 modules that include six literature selections—fiction and nonfiction—for each grade level. The titles are the same as those in the publisher's reading series. The story modules can be purchased individually, in a class pack-variety pack, or as a school pack including all grade level titles. The teacher's guide offers suggested times for each activity, ideas for integration with the curriculum, additional resources, and activities for family involvement. Student activities emphasize the development of background knowledge and the reinforcement of key reading strategies and study skills.

We reviewed a fourth-grade nonfiction selection, "Do Not Disturb" and found it user-friendly, age appropriate, and academically oriented. The CD contained a multitude of activities involving reading, writing, note-taking, categorizing, fact versus opinion, encyclopedia and index use, and research. The activities are interactive, involving the student in decision-making, with immediate feedback. The program doesn't take students through entire books but highlights the first chapter to get them going. Students are encouraged to take the book from the library to finish it. The included chapter can be read to the student or it can be read independently. Key words are underlined and when clicked a definition appears. Management and assessment systems are included. *Multimedia Literature* would be an excellent addition to any classroom's software library.

Grade: A

Davidson Publishers offers "interactive storybooks" for primary level children. The series, *Magic Tales,* includes the Russian folktale *Baba Yaga,* the African folktale *Imo and the King,* and the Asian story *The Little Samurai* (Davidson, 1995, $79.95 for the collection). Each kit includes a paperback storybook and CD for Macintosh or Windows 3.1 or 95. The material is geared more for general use than for classroom activity, but some teachers might want to incorporate it as a part of their classroom libraries, especially as additions to the multicultural selections. The publisher has also released a collection of Irish, Native American, and Italian folktales.

Grandpa Mouse narrates each story in an engaging manner, complete with folk music. Each page appears on the monitor, and the words light up, one at a time, as they are spoken. The dialogue often does not appear as text but is voiced by the characters as they are momentarily animated. The user may click on a word to have it repeated aloud. A child may also click on items in the illustrations to have them "come alive." The graphic animations move, speak, sing, or dance. There are no clear directions as to whether the sound can be turned off so children can read aloud alone, nor is it obvious where to click for animation. Although the story itself does not have a humorous tone, these added "interactions" often are. The animations are interesting; click on an open window and a goat reaches in and eats something off the table, or click on a cat and it jumps atop a fireplace ledge. Unfortunately, these actions have little to do with the context of the story. Another drawback is that the paperback story has different words and sentences than those that appear on the CD; for kids just figuring out the nature of text, this could be perplexing.

We had some first and second graders review *Imo and the King* and *Baba Yaga*. The students enjoyed the entertaining stories twice, once while Grandpa Mouse read the story to them and again while playing with the graphics. Although they liked the colorful and detailed illustrations, they were disappointed that the illustrations had only one action. An occasional question such as "I didn't know foxes lived in Africa?" arose about the stories. However, in *The Little Samurai,* details of the Japanese culture are highly stereotyped and images are inaccurately portrayed. For example, the characters wear their kimonos backwards. In the words of a children's literature expert, "No one in Japan would recognize these characters as being Japanese." Although the storybooks help children to develop word identification strategies and knowledge of text features, $80 would be better spent on materials that teach these skills through rich multicultural experiences.
   Grade: C

Living Books CD-ROM is another collection of quality literature accompanied by clever sounds and eye-catching graphics that would be a welcome addition to any primary classroom. This program lets students select well-known books from a library, including Jack Prelutsky's *New Kid on the Block* and Mercer Mayer's *Little Monster Goes to School.* Most books are available in English and Spanish, and a few in Japanese. At the beginning of the program, a friendly bird prompts the user to select a book and offers clear and helpful directions. Once inside the story, the text is highlighted as each page is narrated by children's voices. The highlighted text is especially helpful to beginning readers. The child narrators add a delightful touch to the stories. After the text is read, students can "play" with the engaging graphics by moving the cursor to a particular image. Each image reacts to a mouse click with an animation or short song. The text can be examined in the same way; when a word is clicked, it is read aloud to the student and, sometimes, a graphic definition is provided. We could find no research on the effectiveness of this feature, but it seems like it could help students learn new words. This feature was not available in the *Davidson Magic Tales* series.

Although its primary purpose is to expose students to quality literature in an enjoyable and entertaining manner, *Living Books* also provides classroom teachers, parents, and reading specialists helpful teaching opportunities. Teachers can use these CD-ROMs as springboards for author studies, creative writing projects, partner reading, and drama activities. The program includes—for an additional charge—teacher support materials, "The Living Books Framework." Each framework includes, along with other resources, classroom activities that focus on reading, writing, math, language arts, and science.

We had ten students try out the *Living Books,* and all voiced positive opinions of the material. For example, one child told us, "They had nice pictures and the animals' voices were funny. I hope I can read it again." Another responded, "The sounds and clicking are great! I really liked the stories." They even focused on some of the instructional benefits, "It's good because if a kid didn't understand a word, they could click it and they'd say it back to you."

If you want to turn your students on to quality literature electronically, *Living Books* would be a worthwhile and useful part of your classroom CD-ROM library.

Grade: A–

Assessing Reading Comprehension on CD-ROM

That's a Fact, Jack! (TFJ) (Follett, 1996, $750 for game engine, 25 games [5 games/disc], and User's Manual. Additional title discs are $39.95 each.) is an interactive, multimedia CD-ROM program available for students in fourth through tenth grades. Students are certain to be motivated by this computerized reading game show in which they compete with their classmates to answer comprehension questions about popular children's and young adult books. The game is designed for single or multiple players and the catch is: You must read the book before playing. To run the program, you need a Macintosh computer System 7.0 or greater with at least an 040 processor, a double CD-ROM drive, 2.8 megabytes of available RAM, 30 megabytes of free hard disk space, and a monitor capable of displaying at least 256 colors.

An outstanding feature of *TFJ* is the interactive graphics. At the beginning of the program, the realistic Learn Television Studio appears awashed in fluorescent lights and accompanied by a catchy tune. Seconds later, a security dial tone is heard and students are at the studio's door awaiting entrance. Life-like voices invite them to sign in and select the book of play. Once inside the studio, the students are greeted by *TFJ's* host, Jack Patterson, whose facial expressions and body movements are so natural that it seems impossible for them to be computer-generated.

Although *TFJ* captures students' attention and inspires them to read, which is extremely important, the quality of the comprehension questions, the length of time needed to play, and Jack Patterson's attitude are problematic. Comprehension questions developed by anyone other than those familiar with the particular classroom are always suspect, and those asked by *TFJ* are no exception. Students respond to five different types of questions—literal, inferential, hypothetical, dialog, and writing—in fill-in-the-blank or multiple choice format. The literal and inferential questions are self-explanatory, asking students to recall text explicit information and to demonstrate an understanding of text implicit information, respectively. The writing questions, perhaps more appropriately named questions about literary terms, present a situation from the text and ask students to identify the appropriate literary device. For example, the following question asks students to identify the climax in *A Wrinkle in Time:* "What's the literal name for the scene where Meg rescues Charlie Wallace?"

In general, we felt that literal, inferential, and writing questions were appropriate and relevant to the content of the books. However, teachers may want to edit some of the dialog and hypothetical questions out of the game. Hypothetical questions "require students to make comparisons, and find relationships among facts and ideas and draw conclusions on their own" *(TFJ* manual, p. 114). Many of these questions are irrelevant to the development of characters and story elements. They ask the reader to explore insignificant information unworthy of critical thinking. For example, on the *Bridge to Terabithia* disc, this hypothetical question is asked about Jess' keen interest in art:

> "If he had more encouragement, what college would Jess try to get into?"
>
> 1. Lark Automobile Institute
> 2. The Lark Academy of Music

3. Lark College of Japanese
4. The Lark Art Institute

Although Jess's artistic talent is an integral part of his personality, he is only a fifth grader and speculating about his college preference does not ask the reader to think critically about his behaviors in relation to events in the story.

The dialog questions are challenging. Usually, a quote is given, and the students identify the speaker. The quotes relate to major themes and critical points in the plot; however, the dialog questions would be more valuable if they focused on the meaning of the quotes and not who said them.

Jack Patterson will most likely appeal to students but not to teachers. His responses are funny and quick but, unfortunately, tactless and obnoxious. Patterson responds whenever a player or group of players answers questions, providing some encouragement such as "If at first you don't succeed, you shall try again"; "That's like the totally right answer dude"; and "Feeling good? Well, start thinking about this next one." However, many of his responses to incorrect answers are inappropriate and derogatory as in the following examples: "Are you wrong! Huh!"; "Do the words *no points* mean anything to you?"; "You got it wrong, but look on the bright side. Well actually it is a little cloudy"; "Well, obviously you're a little confused" (The correct answer was *confused.*). Also, Jack's comments are sometimes followed by a belch. The prospect of 30 students adopting Jack Patterson's attitude is quite frightening.

Depending on the number of students and the time taken to answer the questions, it takes 25 to 45 minutes to play one complete round. Follett offers several ways to shorten playing time such as randomizing the questions. With this option, multiple choice questions are not read aloud and appear in a different order every time the game is played. Questions can also be edited from the game to save time. Unfortunately, both of these options eliminate questions. Randomizing questions omits challenging fill-in-the-blank questions, and obviously, editing questions decreases the number and types of questions that students will encounter.

As we mentioned in the beginning, *TFJ* has kid-appeal; it will motivate students to read. However, teachers are capable of developing effective instruction that motivates students to read quality literature without adding more than $700 to the budget.

Grade: C

The Internet: World Wide Web Sites

We spent several days navigating the Internet and felt that we barely scraped the surface. There is an unbelievable wealth of information that is easily attainable to anyone with access. Unlike the static books and software packages we have already discussed, Internet sites change day to day and are linked in such complicated ways that we were uncertain how to review them in a useful manner. An Internet site usually includes a specific collection of information or activities, but it also might provide hyperlinks to other sites. For example, if books were formatted in the same way, when you turned to the reference list you wouldn't only get information about how to locate the specific reference, but the reference would actually be there. This overabundance of information can lead to complications. What do you count as being part of a site? How far do you follow the chain?

We decided the best way to review some sites would be to let teachers eavesdrop on our conversations as we cruised the net. What follows is a discussion of three of the language arts sites we visited.

UBS for Kids Online (http://www.ubs-for-kids.com/)

Sherry: This site, the University Book Store, is an actual store in Madison, Wisconsin, complete with store hours. I like the look of the homepage. It's easy to use and has a lot of different titles to view.

Kathleen: The Online Book Club looks interesting. Every month a new book is selected for the children to read. The students can order the book on-line through the University Book Store and receive it in the mail.

Linda: That's the commercial part of this site, although the staff does mention that the students can also find the book on their own.

Joyce: The paragraph about the author is okay, but I especially like that his e-mail address is listed so the student can ask him questions and receive answers.

Linda: The book contest is an interesting idea, too. Teachers can use it in their classroom by entering their students' written or artistic responses to the book of the month. If a student's work wins, it's published on this site for the world to see.

Joyce: This really validates a student's opinion about a book.

Sherry: Another way students can use this site to engage in authentic literacy events is to submit their own reviews of favorite contemporary books. If their review is accepted for publication, they get a 10% discount on any item in the UBS.

Linda: Again, that's the commercial part of this site.

Kathleen: But look at the review of Dr. Seuss's *Wacky Wednesday*. It's by a 4-year-old. That's great that these children are writing at such an early age. The graphics are outstanding.

Joyce: I like the selection of books reviewed, including *Tuck Everlasting, The Devil's Arithmetic,* and *The Giver,* to name only a few. Books for all age levels are included, too.

Kathleen: Teachers could download the reviews appropriate for their grade level and hang them on a bulletin board as teasers to encourage reading.

Sherry: The review style could be used by the students when writing their own reviews.

Linda: The Kids' Creations section of this site encourages children to send in their written and artistic creations for publication. Teachers could have their students submit their work as the final step in the writing process.

Sherry: This site seems a lot less overwhelming than some of the others we have seen.

Joyce: I like that students can focus on one aspect of the site and not feel that they should be in another area. As a principal of a small private school, I like that students can interact with other students when they use this site, expanding their horizons and allowing them to communicate with children from around the world.

Linda: But students in a large school would also benefit from this site. Sometimes these students feel lost in the crowd because they don't always have a chance to share their ideas. This site gives them the chance to express their views, and if they have an e-mail address, they may receive responses from all over the world.

Kathleen: I really like this site because it shows the students that reading is important everywhere.

Sherry: One more link worth mentioning on this Web site is the virtual tours you can take on-line. You can view the White House, Museum of American Art, and the Rock and Roll Hall of Fame, to name just a few. The site is great for students researching information for social studies or art reports.

Grade: A

KidPub (http://en-garde.com/ kidpub/intro.html)

Joyce: Using the Internet and various Web sites offers numerous possibilities for the classroom teacher, and *KidPub* presents one of the most comprehensive sites.

Sherry: *KidPub* was created by a parent so his 9-year-old daughter would have an outlet for her creativity, a place where she could share her work with other people.

Joyce: That really fits into the idea of authentic writing and writing for a purpose. *KidPub* supports the idea of making children's writing real to them.

Kathleen: What began as a personal quest to validate a child's writing has turned into a network for children from around the world to share their creativity.

Linda: Do you see all the countries represented? Sweden, Malaysia, Japan, Australia, New Zealand, and, of course, many states in the U.S.

Sherry: I like that each story lists how many times it has been read. Like this one has been read 33 times.

Joyce: It is like an extension of children's Writer's Workshop, but it gives children an opportunity to "talk" with other people about what they wrote. It fits perfectly with an ongoing classroom activity.

Kathleen: Here is a poetry collection, so it accepts stories and poetry from children.

Joyce: Look, each child has the option of listing his or her own personal Web site so other children can respond to the story or poem written.

Linda: I'm wondering, does it have any kind of screening? Or does everything that comes in have an automatic audience?

Sherry: The introductory information states that the originator doesn't normally edit stories, but only occasionally makes a few spelling or punctuation corrections.

Linda: I'm sort of concerned about the safety factor or inappropriate stories getting on the Web.

Kathleen: I agree, but there does not seem to be anything here that is at all suspect. But still I am concerned. With the amount of e-mail being sent, I wonder how the homepage manager can keep up.

Sherry: Oh look, here at the end of this section, it states: "Inappropriate paragraphs will be deleted without notice." I guess that's our answer.

Kathleen: I like this section called KidPub Collaboration where a kid can read a story and add a paragraph. That would be great for a school where one class starts a story and it is added onto by other classes in the school and then shared.

Joyce: What a great idea! It makes writing with a purpose really easy to understand by all the students.

Linda: *KidPub* lists participating schools and locations so it is easy to expand this project.

Kathleen: The section on the statistics of the program could work nicely with a math project as well. You could have students do ratios, graphs, or simple addition and subtraction.

Sherry: This program really focuses on its purpose: writing. It allows writing to be used across many areas of the curriculum.

Joyce: I like the KidPub Key Pals section where students can select a penpal from a list of students also interested in "talking" on the Internet. Look, each child lists his or her age, interests, and location. What fun for children.

Sherry: Here's a part that could be better organized. When I select a story from the geographical listing, I can't easily find it in the overall listing because it is not organized alphabetically by title or author. It might be helpful to be able to cross-reference it.

Kathleen: Overall, I really like the format and how it allows students to send their own creations.

Linda: Yes, and it even accepts pictures electronically, so even young learners can participate.

Joyce: Because of the reviews of the submitted stories written by the author of *KidPub* children see good models for peer critiquing and conferencing.

Sherry: Even the children have biographies so they really feel like an author, plus they have an opportunity to get feedback from children from all over the world.

Grade: A

The Children's Literature Web Guide (http://www.ucalgary.ca/~dkbrown/)

Linda: This Web site is a guide to Internet resources
            related to books for children of all ages. There's
            quite a lot of information here. The homepage
            currently has 25 different sites put together by
            David K. Brown, a Canadian librarian. This is a
            collection of resources related to books for
            children and young adults including discussion
            groups, book award lists, movies based on
            children's books, and resources for teachers,
            parents, storytellers, authors, and illustrators.

Sherry: I think it could be very useful for teachers. This
            links to many sites.

Joyce: You can link to *KidPub,* which we reviewed. It
            also summarizes the BookRead Project that was
            in *Computer Conversations.*

Kathleen: The Reader's Theater link could encourage a class
            to write its own scripts and perhaps share with
            other classes on this site. It includes the grade
            level, genre, number of readers, and the average
            time to present the play. There are quite a few
            scripts to choose from.

Sherry: These plays would be useful for teachers
            interested in improving their students' fluency.
            The plays could be downloaded and used over
            and over again.

Linda: The Contemporary Stories site contains on-line
            books. The Bemelmans site includes the first page
            of the children's books, *Madeline,* and the entire
            text of *Rosebud.* Teachers could use these in the
            classroom as extra reading material. The graphics
            are great.

Kathleen: There's an address to send mail to story
            characters. That would be fun for my first-grade
            students.

Joyce: There's also a picture of the author and a short
            biography. Students can even write to the author.

Sherry: Look at all of this information in the Resources for Teachers site. There are teaching ideas about many different subjects from all over the world.

Joyce: Teachers can even find lesson plans for these subjects.

Sherry: You can spend all day in this Web site.

Kathleen: Teachers may want to give their students a day of exploration, but after that they should have a purpose for entering this site.

Linda: Or any other site, for that matter.

Kathleen: Otherwise, like Sherry said, they could spend hours and hours here.

Grade: A

Conclusion

As enlightening and enticing as we found our trek through technology, we were left with some feelings of disquiet. When we examined a $1000 software package, it was hard not to think about how many books could be purchased for children with this money. Even with the least-expensive choices, we found ourselves wondering how children from poor families would ever keep up, or how school districts in urban areas or poor rural communities could afford these resources. At one time, books were considered an expensive luxury, but free lending libraries and the invention of inexpensive paper helped make books somewhat more accessible to all children.

Cyberworld has yet to become accessible in this way, and everyone should be concerned. We doubt that students will miss out on much if their storybooks aren't animated or if the skills instruction they receive isn't electronic. But we can be less sanguine about the division of resources that make it possible for some to take a virtual visit to Ellis Island, publish their book reviews nationally, and engage in e-mail conversation with penpals in Australia while their disadvantaged peers are left behind.

II Second Language Learners

Most educators today are faced with the challenge of meeting the special educational and social needs of students who don't speak English. This section recounts the stories and methodologies of four teachers of second language learners. While the scenarios may be different, their successful approaches reveal the common theme of providing a supportive, social environment in which to learn language within a meaningful context.

The first two articles illustrate success within integrated, predominantly English-speaking classrooms. Suzette Abbott and Claudia Grose's article describes an exciting year in Abbott's first-grade classroom. Abbott perceives the challenges faced by her three non-English-speaking students not as a hindrance but as an opportunity to enrich the language experiences of the entire class. By incorporating bilingual stories and employing support from community volunteers and parents, not only did she foster confidence and language skills in her three ESL students, but she also opened the doors of inquiry and discovery for all her students.

Like the students in Abbott's classroom, Xiaodi, a seven-year-old Chinese boy, was immersed in a predominantly English-speaking classroom. In addition to formal language instruction, Jane S. Townsend and Danling Fu attribute his success to a supportive classroom environment in which his contributions were perceived as purposeful, and in which he was given the freedom to make meaningful connections.

The remaining two articles offer perspectives from classrooms where literacy is first taught in the students' native language. In "Finding the 'Right Measure' of Explanation for Young Latina/o Writers," the authors follow a teacher-researcher's use of classroom talk to include skills instruction in the context of a meaning-centered approach. Margaret Mulhern's article points to the value of using students' stories and experiences to foster literacy development in culturally diverse students, stressing the importance of building a smooth transition between home and school literacy experiences by actively involving parents in their children's education.

5 "I Know English So Many, Mrs. Abbott": Reciprocal Discoveries in a Linguistically Diverse Classroom

Suzette Abbott and Claudia Grose

After we sang Happy Birthday to Andreas, Jeannette suggested we sing it in Chinese! Ming and Yen helped her lead the class. Mrs. Lopez had just come in to pick up her daughter Maria, and she promptly taught us to sing "Cumpleanos Feliz" in Spanish. For four months, I had featured the linguistic diversity brought to our class by three ESL children, striving to turn that diversity into enrichment for us all. With the spontaneous enjoyment at Andreas' birthday party, I saw the effort was paying off.

From early in the school year, Suzette realized the primary challenge of her Inclusion first-grade class: how to integrate into her program three children who spoke little or no English. As a daycare and public school teacher in New York City for 20 years, Suzette had already enjoyed the richness of a multiethnic student body. And years ago, she said, "I was a new immigrant myself—when I arrived from South Africa, I was surprised at how foreign I felt, even though I spoke English. I have always tried as a teacher to draw into the class those children who are potentially 'outsiders,' to assure that they are not seen as less knowledgeable or capable because they are different or speak another language."

This time the challenge went further, beyond the three ESL learners, to encompass *all* the children. How could Suzette build on the opportunity of fortuitous language diversity to enrich the language experiences of the whole class?

Reprinted from *Language Arts*, March 1998.

The literature is full of evidence that a rich curriculum and a positive group environment support and enhance the learning of individuals, both first- and second-language learners (Altwerger & Ivener, 1994; Fox, 1980; Peregoy & Boyle, 1993). Further, as Lim and Watson (1993) write, "effective language learning, either native or second language, depends not on direct teaching of identified skills, but rather on a sound philosophy of learning and teaching, underlying a meaning-filled curriculum" (p. 393). Part of Suzette's philosophy, thus, included giving "children windows through which to see *many* worlds" (Kiefer & DeStefano, 1985, p. 171).

This is the story of Suzette's classroom. The elements described bring to life a theoretical basis for understanding how a rich language arts curriculum serves as fertile ground for the development of both first- and second-language learners as they are actively involved in constructing their deepening knowledge of English (Hudelson, 1994; Peregoy & Boyle, 1993). It also highlights the unanticipated benefits for all learners that emerge from the reciprocal learning in the classroom (Edelsky, 1989; Kiefer & DeStefano, 1985; Moll & Greenberg, 1990). We illustrate the range of scaffolding techniques (the temporary instructional supports—personal, curricular, and social) that help emergent language learners move beyond what they could do on their own (Cazden, 1992; Boyle & Peregoy, 1990; Peregoy & Boyle, 1993), and we show the importance of teacher autonomy, which allows flexibility to respond to children's funds of knowledge (Moll 1988; Moll & Greenberg, 1990).

Suzette's Story

I teach at a small public school in an urban community. The student body is predominantly White and middle class. It includes the children of academics and professionals associated with the many colleges and universities in the area. We also have a number of families recently arrived from China, Africa, Central and South America, and the Caribbean.

When school started, my first grade, one of two in the building, had fifteen children, four of them new to the school. Among the newcomers was Maria, dark bangs framing animated, brown eyes, who came from Venezuela during the summer. Then in early October, two new children appeared: Yen, quiet and serious, two years in America but speaking Mandarin Chinese at home, and Ming, slight in build, mischievous in his smile, who had just arrived from China. Yen could speak some English; Ming and Maria spoke no English at all.

Resources and Routines

Getting started, I knew I was not alone; I could muster the resources at hand—if I could figure out how to use them. First, naturally, there were the parents and caregivers of the children. I was also fortunate to be in touch with a volunteer literacy support program directed by a friend and former colleague. When Claudia heard of my Chinese students, she introduced me to a new volunteer, Mrs. Lu, born in China, educated at Wellesley, now aged 80 and interested in doing something new and worthwhile. As soon as this sprightly little woman came into my classroom, in blue jeans and cropped white hair, she plopped down on a tiny chair to engage Ming and Yen—but she quickly became a point of interest to the whole class.

Finally, there were the children themselves. I decided to address the challenge of the three second-language learners directly with the whole class. Just because these children spoke little or no English, I said, did not mean that they did not know anything. I asked the class to help Yen, Ming, and Maria learn the routines, just as they would help any of their classmates.

From the start, I sought to establish a relationship with the parents of my three second-language learners (Cummins, 1994), to show them my interest in their children's special qualities, to allay their concerns, and to gather information. I found that telephone calls or face-to-face encounters, before or after school, were more useful than sending notes home. Fortunately for me, all the parents spoke some English. In addition, Mrs. Lu was effective in helping me communicate with Ming and Yen and their parents. In my initial contacts, I sought feedback about how their children were talking about their school experiences. Ming's parents related that he liked "English school" because he could play. During this talk, I also learned that Ming was attending Chinese school where he was learning to read and write in Chinese, a useful bit of information for the future. Maria's mother, Mrs. Lopez, arranged her work schedule to spend time each week in the class, helping her daughter but also making books and materials for all of us.

Language arts in my classroom are integrated throughout the day and across the curriculum to give children experience with a variety of reading and writing activities in various pleasurable and comfortable ways. In the first weeks of school, I felt it important to establish the class routines. Knowing that there is a plan for the day and assuming responsibility for different jobs in the room helps all children build independence; it also supports the idea of a community that works together. These established routines and procedures serve as particularly valuable scaffolds for

second-language learners who are struggling to make sense of their new
environment and language (Peregoy & Boyle, 1993; Sutton, 1989).

We begin with a morning meeting to lay out the day's plan and engage in
interactive chart reading and various opportunities for children to share ideas
and personal information. A written schedule shows the times each day for
focused reading and writing activities, in large and small groups and
independently. An important activity is reading the illustrated job chart
which directs individual children's responsibilities. Mrs. Lu translated the
words so that Ming and Yen could understand how they could participate
alongside their classmates in this fundamental aspect of the community.

Fortunately, within the broad mandates of our district frameworks, I had
the autonomy to develop my own curriculum, an essential component for
making reciprocal learning work. Thus I could seize targets of learning
opportunity, to build upon each child's knowledge and abilities. I sought
ways to include and highlight the languages of the three ESL children. One
morning, I invited Mana and her mother to teach all the class to count in
Spanish. As they began, another child, Estella, whose father is Puerto Rican, I
learned, joined in. We made a class chart with the English and the Spanish
words, and from then on we often counted in Spanish as part of our math
time. A few days later, Yen's mother came in to help him and Ming teach the
children the numbers in Chinese. Jeannette, whose mother is Chinese
American, was so intrigued with the Chinese numerals that she copied them
all from the chart into her own writing folder.

Other children asked if their parents or relatives could visit too, and one
thing led to another over coming weeks as children shared stories about
hearing different languages in their extended families and contributed more
samples to our growing collection of multilingual charts. Andreas often had
a hard time settling into school, but his first moment of pride and success
came as he, his mother, and little brother stood in front of the whole class
and counted in Greek. Following another counting lesson, inspired by Liza
whose mother is Korean, an interesting discussion developed as the children
studied and compared the Chinese and Korean number words written on
two charts hanging next to each other. Some children commented on the
intricacy of the individual Korean characters, wondering if it was more
difficult to learn than Chinese.

In those early weeks, I relied on Mrs. Lu and Mrs. Lopez to translate
during meetings and to make sure the children understood the schedule and
special activities. Mrs. Lu also wrote the Chinese words alongside the English
and Spanish words for the months of the year. Then we added the days of the

week in Spanish and Chinese to the English word cards in our class pocket chart, making the daily calendar activity more accessible to everyone. Ming, Yen, and Maria could remind us how to read the Chinese or Spanish, and the rest of the class felt proud at reading another language besides English. Many times in those early weeks, I noticed Maria copying English words from around the room, or Ming referring to the daily schedule. Other children liked to copy the Chinese or Spanish or Haitian Creole number words as well.

Risks and Rewards: A Rich Language Arts Curriculum

Routines established, we set about creating a supportive classroom environment in which all the children, those who knew English and those who did not, would feel comfortable taking risks and working together to build their language and literacy proficiency. Reading aloud to the class was central to my language arts program. The children looked forward to this time each day when they could stretch out on the rug or curl up against the cushions, and enter the world of literature. I combed libraries and discount book sales for a variety of literature that would entrance the children while reflecting and extending their diverse experiences and linguistic knowledge (Natarella, 1980; Nurss & Hough, 1992).

Moon Rope (Ehlert & Prince, 1992), a beautifully illustrated Peruvian legend, is published in a bilingual format with Spanish and English texts side by side. I invited Mrs. Lopez to join me, asking her to read the Spanish text in turn, as I read the English. On another occasion, the two of us read alternate parts of Lynn Reiser's Margaret and Margarita (1993), about two girls speaking their own languages and finding a connecting point.

Some children became restless during the reading of the unfamiliar language parts. I initiated a discussion eliciting children's reactions. Maria expressed her delight at the chance to hear the familiar Spanish language. Estella beamed with pride and pleasure at her ability to understand both the Spanish and the English. Other children talked about the difficulty of paying attention, when it sounded so different. As the year progressed, we came back to this topic several times, as children thought more and more about what it was like not to understand what was being said, and what little devices or strategies would help.

Next, I found two books, At the Beach and Snow, by Huy Voun Lee (1994), in which a mother teaches her child to write in Chinese calligraphy. Ming and Yen read the Chinese characters to the class. Later, during independent reading time, I noticed two of the English speaking girls

carefully copying Chinese characters from the two books. They asked Ming
and Yen for help when they ran into difficulty.

Jeannette brought in *Jingwei Filling the Sea* by Feng Jiannan (1991), which
had Chinese and English texts side by side. "You can read the English and
Mrs. Lu can read the Chinese, just like Maria's mother and you did," she
proposed. At the conclusion of that reading, the children commented on
how different the Chinese language sounded from English, and I overheard
some of them experimenting with the tones—a nice variation on the usual
first-grade language play (Cazden, 1992).

In the late fall, one of the children asked me to read *My Father's Dragon*
(Gannet, 1948). Conscious of the wide variation in linguistic sophistication
in the class, I wondered how to make this engaging series of chapter books
accessible to all. First, I gathered together all the animals and related objects
I could find. We made the eighteen crocodiles with lollipops, for instance,
from photocopies but with real lollipops taped to their tails. This use of
artifacts and dramatization not only helped Yen, Ming, and Maria, it
delighted all the children, as each reading was full of unexpected surprises.
The children loved taking turns manipulating the characters as the stories
unfolded. The experience was such a success that it led to a sustained
interest in dragons that became central to our curriculum, culminating many
months later in a grand celebration of the Chinese New Year.

Several times a week, I read poetry aloud, usually writing the poems on
large charts, and encouraging the children to join in. Sometimes for the
children, I found it useful *to* ask their parents or Mrs. Lu to translate the
poems I read in class. Once they understood the gist, they could enjoy the
other elements of rhyme, and rhythmic patterns and imagery.

Pursuing the dragon theme, I found Lillian Moore's poem, "Dragon
Smoke" (Prelutsky, 1986), a lovely example of metaphor on the idea of
seeing your breath in the cold winter air. The children joked about breathing
"dragon smoke" and quite literally showed Ming and Maria what was meant
in the poem. A few days later, as we walked outside, Ming pointed to the
exhaust from the cars driving by and, with a twinkle in his eye, said "Dragon
smoke!" and then blew his own. He had truly understood the figurative and
literal language, and along with the others, could enjoy the fun of it.

Poetry also inspired other connections. One morning, Jeannette came in
to school grinning broadly as she displayed a large gap in her upper gum.
Tim, who often had trouble staying involved during shared reading, recalled
two poems about teeth that we had read before. Someone pointed out that
the title of one of the poems had the Spanish word for tooth written next to

it. I then asked for the Chinese word. Yen and Ming each responded, but with different words. After we tried to say both, Makeda offered to find Mrs. Lu to ask her which word was correct. We now had the word for tooth in three languages: Chinese, English, and Spanish, and we saw that there can be several words for the same meaning.

After finishing the books in the Dragons of Blueland series, we wrote and practiced reading a group message to send home asking for any dragon books, toys, or pictures. This request led to the engagement of even more parents in the curriculum and opened new experiences and connections.

In February, Tim, a monolingual English-speaking child, brought in *Vejigante Masquerader* (Delacre, 1993), a bilingual story about a Puerto Rican boy who dresses up in a special mask and costume as part of the Fiesta during Carnival in Ponce. Estella was bobbing up and down with excitement. She said that she had a Vejigante mask at home, given to her by her father. When she brought in her mask, the children kept trying it on, and we made plans to make our own.

Talking about the mask, I started to say the word in my normal South African accent, but caught myself and changed my mouth into the American pronunciation. Sabrina, a child who rarely contributed to language arts discussions, looked up in fascination. "I know what you did. You started to say 'mah . . .', and then you changed and said 'mask'." Eric quickly explained, "She talks like that because she comes from South Africa." Sabrina had picked up the nuanced accents, and Eric could explain why. I wondered if this kind of metalinguistic thinking would have happened without our ongoing focus on the rich language differences in the classroom (Moll, 1988).

In my class, writing and reading go hand in hand, each helping to reinforce the other. Whenever possible, I enlisted Mrs. Lu and Mrs. Lopez in helping the three emergent English learners with their writing. I explained that there were many ways to write and spell, and all were acceptable. Maria initially wrote in Spanish, sometimes dictating first to her mother and then translating with help. Ming and Yen drew many pictures, and labeled them using both English and Chinese. Some children wrote stories based on published books, or on personal experiences. Tim, a most resistant writer, was inspired one day by Yen's presentation to each child of a folded paper boat. Clutching the creation, he recalled a trip he had taken to Venice with his parents, and he struggled to produce a series of picture stories about gondolas—a first for him and the start of a collection of boat stories in the class.

Most children started using invented spelling and we had several class discussions, collecting suggestions for ways to figure out spelling. At first, Ming, Yen, and Maria hesitated to experiment in their writing. I realized that they were concentrating on gaining command of vocabulary to convey their ideas. It was premature for them to focus on the details of the sounds (Nurss & Hough, 1992). Instead, I helped them use picture dictionaries and other books, as well as the environmental print in the room. Our evergrowing Word Wall of common sight words was especially valued by the two boys, and at one point Ming actually added some Chinese translations. I was confident that as they wrote more and gained confidence in their English language, they would eventually experiment with spelling, too.

Ming was a child who immersed himself in what interested him—mice, whales, outer space. Sometime in late October, I noticed that he was drawing pictures of mice in his writing folder day after day. One day during Writing Share, he showed everyone his drawings. The children were fascinated both by the humorous way he drew the mice and his delight in sharing. For Show and Tell on another day, he produced a photograph of himself in his mother's laboratory, wearing a surgical gown. Here was an outside resource that I could not have foreseen, for as he showed the photograph, he spoke one English word, "mice." Sure enough, there behind him were stacks of cages full of mice for the laboratory experiments.

For our next shared poem I chose one about mice and encouraged the class to write or draw a response to the last line, "I think mice are nice." The children studied Ming's stylized and whimsical mice, and learned from his technique as they made their own illustrations. He was now the expert! The children were so pleased by the results that two girls volunteered to arrange a display of the large poetry chart and all the children's writing and drawings to hang outside our room for all the school to see.

In preparation for a trip to the science museum to see a movie about whales, we poured over the pictures in whale books. Ming became fascinated and his enthusiasm was contagious; soon his classmates recognized him as the Killer Whale expert. Thereafter, anyone coming across a picture or book relating to whales rushed over to show it to Ming for his assessment.

After I read William Steig's (1971) *Amos and Boris* to the class, Ming sat with the book, studying the illustrations and diligently copying the opening sentences describing the little mouse who loves the ocean. He highlighted the word "ocean" on his paper, as he drew his beloved mouse. A few days later, he drew a picture of himself watching the mouse happily riding on the whale's back. All three of his characters had speech bubbles: the Ming and Amos characters announced, "I like whales," and the whale replied, "I like Ming." I was not surprised at his picture, but very impressed that he had incorporated the dialogue format which we had only recently introduced in class.

One day during Writing Share time, the usually taciturn Yen spoke up shyly, "I want to show you something." He produced his writing assignment from Chinese School, marked with a large grade A. As his classmates scrutinized the unfamiliar Chinese characters, Yen's confidence grew and he told everyone that he has to "write them pretty." To my astonishment, he further explained that when he sometimes forgets a line or mark, "the phonics help me to remember how to write the Chinese." Later Mrs. Lu explained to me that many Chinese schools now use an alphabetic phonetic approach to teach reading and writing (Ho & Bryant, 1997). Here was a whole new discovery for me to pursue!

We studied Yen's writing sheet, noticing special accent marks, and discussed how these marks told Yen which way his voice should go. The children tried to follow, using their own voices. Seeing this homework sample, I suddenly understood how strange our writing process must have seemed, compared to his experience in Chinese School (Anderson & Gunderson, 1997). I was gaining insights at the same time as my children.

For Valentine's Day, the children had spent days planning a sale of art and baked goods. Maria noticed when she came in that day that the morning message had not yet been written. "I know what to write," she announced. With my help sounding out some words, and by looking around the room for others, she happily wrote on the chart: "Get ready for the Sale."

Risks and Rewards: The Social Environment

In the normal course of their interactions and play, the children were experimenting and making discoveries about language. As the second-language learners were taking risks and experimenting with English for the purpose of communication and social interaction, the other children were making discoveries about the nature of language, their own and others (Peregoy & Boyle, 1993).

Yen became entranced with the earth-moving machines, trucks and other vehicles in our gravel box which I had set up because of the children's interest in the road building going on outside the school. One day as he and several other children were playing, I overheard him asking, "What is 'worse'?" After a moment, I realized that Andreas had told Yen that he was "making it worse," an abstract concept, difficult for Yen to grasp. It also became clear that Andreas did not want Yen and the other children to play in the box. I stepped closer to hear what the problem was, and to see if the children could come up with a solution. They did: a bigger gravel box, so Yen and Andreas could work in parallel—a fine example of the children's problem solving, but also a social breakthrough for Yen.

Maria's language development was very much involved with her social relationships. In September and October, I would see her by herself in the playground, watching the other girls. She stayed on the fringe of small groups, using her drawing skills to communicate, at one point writing a wordless book about the weather. Soon she found Estella, whose Puerto Rican heritage and fluent Spanish made her a special ally. They often wrote and did other projects together. Maria was a keen observer of the social patterns in the class, often getting ideas from other children, and mimicking English phrases which she heard; a favorite was "cool . . . it's cool." One morning in midyear, Mrs. Lopez reported Maria's comment that "there are so many troubles" in the class, referring to the ebb and flow of relationships among the girls. Her parents reassured Maria that it was nothing new; it was just that Maria now understood enough English to follow the squabbles. On another day, Maria and Estella were playing near three other girls. The three were commenting that Ming and Yen were "so lucky, because they can tell secrets," since they spoke Chinese together. At that point, Estella spoke up, pointing out that she and Maria could tell secrets too, in Spanish.

Large group meetings were particularly difficult times for Maria and Ming in the early part of the year. They would wriggle and fidget, and I could see their frustration as they tried to make sense of all the English language around them. Ming would often lie down and tune out. Sometimes he seemed exhausted (Freeman & Freeman, 1993). Yen took it upon himself to confide in Mrs. Lu his concern that Ming turned his head away in the big group activities. During one whole-group math class, Yen saw that Ming was not understanding the task at hand. To the surprise of his classmates, he spoke up. "Let me explain to Ming," and proceeded to do so in Chinese. Without prompting, Yen had learned how he could help others, and set a fine example for the class (Forman & Cazden, 1994).

One day during Meeting Time, as we were looking at the ubiquitous dragon toys, it became clear that Ming had something to say about a particular little green winged dragon. He raised his hand and tried to speak, haltingly pronouncing the word "dragon," but trying to say something else as well. It happened to be a day when Mrs. Lu was there, sitting behind him. The children were used to hearing Ming and Yen speak together in Chinese.

Now they heard Ming explaining his thoughts to Mrs. Lu. From their facial expressions, and their quiet attentiveness, it was clear that they were very eager to hear what "secrets" Ming had to convey. Mrs. Lu duly reported Ming's observation about the similarity between one little dragon and another animal, a dinosaur. The other children accepted his point with interest, and many agreed with him. They realized for themselves that Ming's difficulty in expressing himself in English did not mean he did not have knowledge to share.

Not too long afterwards, Ming's confidence allowed him to risk taking the next step. In a math discussion about different coins, he started to say something while pushing his hand back and forth in front of him. Listening very carefully, I made out the words, "quarter, my mother." He was enacting placing quarters in the washing machine coin slot! Once the other children understood his idea, and his participation was validated, he sat back with a smile of satisfaction.

From halting single words like "mice," to overgeneralizations—"I love that book . . . I love that whale . . . I love poems," he began to formulate spontaneous sentences, and ask about words he did not understand. Following my reading of a story about a doctor giving a child a shot with a needle, Ming asked, "What's a needle?" Dora immediately responded, "It's when you get a shot. A shot with a needle, not shooting." As she spoke, she acted out receiving a shot with a needle. A chorus of children began explaining to Ming, and Yen added a further explanation in Chinese. Ming was able to ask for clarification and, at the same time, the other children recognized the potential semantic confusion that was posed.

A climactic moment came one day when I reentered the room; Ming looked up at me and asked in a matter-of-fact tone, "Where have you been?" After telling him, I commented on how much more he was speaking in class now. He beamed and replied, "I know English so many, Mrs. Abbott!" I could only smile back in full agreement.

Building on the Children's Experiences

In December, Yen went to China for a month. That gave us an excuse to study the globe—from Boston, Yen had traveled across the whole United States and the Pacific Ocean to China. Everyone was excited to receive a letter from Yen from China. The stamps were of special interest, but the important news was that he had lost a tooth, information that was quickly added to the classroom tooth chart. On his return, Yen and his parents showed photos and traced on the globe the places they had visited and the route of the airplane. This discussion helped Yen reenter the class, and all the children began to see themselves in relation to the greater world in a way that made sense to them.

Just before the December vacation, the two first grades planned a joint Peace Breakfast, inviting all the families to bring samples of their holiday foods to share with everyone. Using the children's dictated language, we typed a simple reminder which they could read themselves and which they illustrated individually, showing the foods reflecting their different celebrations. For the occasion, we learned "The Sharing Song" in English and "De Colores" in Spanish. The songs were written on large charts which the children illustrated to help them remember the words. We also practiced along with an audio tape to make sure we pronounced the Spanish correctly. Later Mrs. Lopez confided to me Maria's comment: "Mrs. Abbott is doing well with Spanish. But her accent—I need to work with her on her mouth." It must have been reassuring for her to see her teacher also struggling with another language.

In early January, at Estella's suggestion, we read *Three Kings' Day* (McConnie Zapater, 1992), in acknowledgement of her celebration of that holiday. The children in the book eat *arroz con leche* (sweet rice with milk) as part of their celebration. Estella told us how delicious this is, so I asked her family for the recipe (cooking was a regular part of our curriculum and we often cooked recipes inspired by stories we read together). Not only did Estella's family send in the recipe, but also all the ingredients! I wrote the recipe up on a big chart, with clear illustrations and few words so that all the children could read it as we cooked. As always, some children loved it, and others did not even want a taste—but everyone enjoyed the cooking.

In early February, our dragon theme reached fever pitch as we began to prepare for the Chinese New Year. I read aloud *Lion Dancer* (Waters & Slovenz-Low, 1990) about a Chinese American child who learns to dance as part of the dragon. Jeannette's mother brought in a videotape of street dances in Beijing and some audio tapes of Chinese songs. Mrs. Lu picked a short, simple song to write out on a big chart, with small copies for the children's poetry folders. She wrote the Chinese characters on the top line over a phonemic transcription in English to help with the pronunciation. The third line of print was an English translation of the text. As we looked at the song on the big chart, I used the phrase "Chinese characters"; this led to a wonderful discussion about "characters" in books we'd read and how Chinese writing is made up of "characters."

Under Mrs. Lu's instruction, we practiced singing, and Yen and Ming helped us as well. Now they were the ones who were more language proficient than the rest of the class! As we worked to learn the Chinese words, a discussion arose comparing the sounds with those of the Spanish song we had learned earlier. Many children concluded that Spanish was easier for them because it sounded more like English. This led to further comments about how hard it must have been for Ming and Yen to learn English. By the looks on their faces I could see that this experience of trying to learn another language, especially one that is very different from one's own, had given many of the children their first clues about the complexity of language.

As the New Year approached, our preparations became more concentrated. Jeannette's mother came in twice to teach us the simple street dance. The other first grade made a large dragon of papier-mâché to hold over their bodies during the parade. We arranged with all the other grade-level teachers to let us parade through their classrooms on the Festival Day. As we continued reading our book about Ernie Wan's celebration of Chinese New Year, we discussed costumes and colors, and all the preparations that had special meaning: for instance, that red signifies good fortune.

On the long-awaited day, the children came to school dressed in red, as requested in the note we'd sent home. All the families were invited. The other first grade assembled under their elegant dragon, and led the parade. We followed close behind, waving our fans and scarves, dancing in and out of the classes, down the stairs, through the kindergartens, and to the cafeteria.

After catching our breath, we sang "Xiao Hu Die" (Little Butterfly) to the wonder of the assembled company. Then we dined on dumplings and oranges, traditional New Year's food donated by a parent, and Mrs. Lu shared her memories of New Years in China seventy years ago.

The diverse contributions of the second-language learners had become the property of us all. As all the children gathered themselves together, and opened their New Year's envelopes, (a traditional feature contributed by a parent) they beamed and chatted all at the same time, tired, proud, and happy.

Discussion

Teachers are pushed and pulled in all directions, urged to try one approach here, another technique there. Nowhere is this more apparent than in the current debate about teaching English as a second language or, more generally, the challenges faced by the teachers in a classroom with diverse language learners (Nieto, 1996; Hudelson, 1990, 1994). Good teaching emerges from the teachers' solid convictions, identification of a goal, and adherence to that goal through the flow of classroom life.

Believing that language learning "is an active, constructive holistic process, [that is] inherently social in nature" (Strickland & Strickland, 1997, p. 203), Suzette's goal was creation of a classroom environment that would nurture the integration of first- and second-language learners for the reciprocal and profound benefit of both groups (Hudelson, 1990; Nurss & Hough, 1992). In her regular visits to the classroom as supervisor of literacy volunteers, Claudia brought a fresh perspective that helped them both reflect on all that was really going on in that lively setting.

The developing linguistic facility of the three second-language learners over the year was obvious, from Ming's risk taking in uttering the single word "mice," to, just three months later, his casual enquiry, "Where have you been?" (Urzua, 1980). Equally apparent, though not as expected, were the spontaneous initiatives of the other first-graders that demonstrated growing awareness of their own language and, at the same time, their interest and confidence in exploring the other languages around them. Sabrina, an English monolingual speaker, found nothing strange about choosing to take home *Margaret and Margarita*, fully confident of her ability to read both the Spanish and English texts.

Suzette's class worked as a case study of the benefits of reciprocity in multilingual elementary education. Far from distracting from the teaching of monolingual learners, the presence of the ESL children in a curriculum and environment that acknowledged and engaged their contributions, enhanced the learning for all. The "emphasis on substance and content facilitated the frequent occurrence of . . . metalinguistic and metacognitive events: the conscious examination of other's and one's own use of language and thinking" (Moll, 1988). The children's ability to talk about the elements of language grew; they became aware of the role of sounds, visual characteristics, intonation, and semantic flexibility. They learned to explain words like "worse" and "shot" in context (Cazden, 1992).

At another level, the children came to understand more deeply the purpose of language, both oral and written, and the way people across cultures use language to organize information, communicate meaning, make sense of the world. As he tried to understand his new land, Yen was alert to comparisons and differences. By spring, as he became more comfortable in English in a classroom that encouraged examination and celebration of diversity, he could comment on the different physical features of Chinese and American people (Nieto, 1996). Ming, forever quantifying objects, proudly announced his love of Chinese history because it is "10,000 years old."

Creation of such an environment in which all children—second-language learners and primary English speakers—are challenged and encouraged to work together for reciprocal benefit, depends on three broad circumstances:

1. The teacher's belief, demonstrated in matters large and small, that all children have funds of knowledge to share (Moll & Greenberg, 1990), are capable of communicating their information and can be understood, by one means or another, whatever their spoken language (Nieto, 1996; Urzua, 1989);

2. The deployment of multiple forms of language and literacy scaffolding that encourage risk taking and that support experimentation, discovery, and communication (Boyle & Peregoy, 1990; Hudelson, 1990; Peregoy & Boyle, 1993);

3. An educational philosophy across the whole school that supports teacher autonomy in making curricular and pedagogical choices in response to the dynamic personality of the class (Moll, 1988).

Scaffolding in Suzette's class took many forms, from direct translation provided by parents, volunteers, and other classmates, to the establishment of set routines, to the use of pictures and multilingual print on the wall, to the dramatization of whole texts to make them vivid and memorable (Boyle & Peregoy, 1990; Peregoy & Boyle, 1993; Sutton, 1989). Important, too, was the way in which children sought out and found their own resources, turning to each other or asking others for clarification (Chomsky, 1980; Forman & Cazden, 1994).

Ming's successful struggle to convey his understanding of the use of quarters marked a big step toward community participation. It was Suzette's scaffolding, her close attention, her belief that she could understand, and her restatement for the class of Ming's message, that propelled him forward into other attempts at communication in English (Hudelson, 1990; Urzua, 1980).

At the same time, her modeling of careful listening, patient attending, and clarifying comments was noticed and unconsciously appreciated by many others in the class. The shared experiences, discussions, and investigations encouraged all the children to explore differences, draw comparisons, and appreciate the variety and richness of their world. In a climate of mutual support and respect, they took steps toward understanding diversity and developing empathy (Nieto, 1996).

Routine displays of environmental print in several languages and sharing of bilingual texts were further forms of scaffolding. They served the vital purpose of validating the first languages of the ESL children, providing them with a place to show their own expertise and broadening the linguistic awareness of the whole class (Ernst & Richard, 1994/1995; Freeman & Freeman, 1993).

From parent participation came a more subtle process: their sharing of their family language and culture emphasized for the children (their own included) the positive view of "knowing" something, rather than the negative point of "not knowing" English (Moll & Greenberg, 1990). Invitations to share language and culture conferred "official" status upon them (Nieto, 1996; Quintero & Huerta-Macias, 1990). For some of the children, this paralleled their own emerging feelings of having something positive to contribute, not just of being deficient in something that everyone else seemed to know. Maria thus expressed confidence that she could play the teacher role in helping Suzette improve her Spanish pronunciation.

Teachers have long known that parental participation is a key factor in children's success in school. Too often, though, parents feel uncomfortable or unwelcome in a vibrant classroom society; work or family commitments, or different cultural understandings about school and learning may also deter direct participation in school activities (Nieto, 1996).

Suzette's success in this endeavor came from her ability to show flexibility and creativity to accommodate potentially interested and interesting relatives, or other representatives of the community, finding materials and activities appropriate for different families (Mrs. Lu was a special resource, of course, but hardly unique). Bilingual shared reading was a natural way to engage parents who might have felt uncomfortable otherwise: the spontaneous dragon curriculum opened other avenues; cooking and arts projects, preparations for the various celebrations, and simple requests for information or artifacts that reflected home cultures offered other ways for parents to participate. These opportunities strengthened the home-school connection, and gave parents a closer view and better understanding of classroom life (Anderson & Gunderson, 1997; Quintero & Huerta-Macias, 1990).

Recognizing that "writing, speaking, listening and reading all nourish one another" (Rigg & Allen, 1989, p. xiii), Suzette provided opportunities for children to engage individually and together in a wide variety of meaningful activities, providing the "warm bath of language" (Rigg & Allen, 1989, p. xii) for the new English learners and allowing all children to construct their own understandings of how oral and written language works.

For this, teacher autonomy is the key. Ever mindful of the district-mandated curriculum frameworks, Suzette still was free to make choices that responded to who her students were, as individuals and as a group, choices that allowed them to "act as thinkers . . . not as passive givers and receivers of prepackaged curriculum" (Moll, 1988, p. 468). By following up on the children's interests and taking advantage of their experience outside the classroom, she helped the class make connections that enhanced their global awareness in ways that were appropriate to their developmental stages.

Late into the spring, the number charts and birthday songs labeled by the children were displayed outside the classroom, attracting interest from students of all ages, as well as their parents. By all measures, the total of this first grade's language experience amounted to far more than the sum of its parts.

Children's Books Cited

Delacre, L. (1993). *Vejigante masquerader.* New York: Scholastic.

Ehlert, L., & Prince, A. (1992). *Moon rope.* New York: Scholastic Inc.

Gannet, R. (1948). *My father's dragon.* New York: Random House.

Jiannan, F. (1991). *Jingwei filling the sea.* Beijing: Dolphin Books.

Lee, H. V. (1994). *At the beach.* New York: Henry Holt & Co.

Lee, H. V. (1994). *Snow.* New York: Henry Holt & Co.

McConnie Zapater, B. (1992). *Three kings' day.* Cleveland, OH: Modern Curriculum Press.

Prelutsky, J., & Brown, M. (Eds.). (1986). *Read-aloud rhymes.* New York: Alfred A. Knopf.

Reiser, L. (1993). *Margaret and Margarita, Margarita Y Margaret.* New York: Scholastic.

Steig, W. (1971). *Amos and Boris.* New York: Farrar, Straus and Giroux.

Walters, K., & Slovenz-Low, M. (1990). *Lion dancer.* Ernie Wan's Chinese New Year. New York: Scholastic.

References

Altwerger, B., & Ivener, B. L. (1994). Self-esteem: Access to literacy in multicultural and multilingual classrooms. In K. Spanenberg-Urbschat & R. Pritchard

(Eds.), *Kids come in all languages: Reading instruction for ESL students* (pp. 65–81). Newark, DE: International Reading Association.

Anderson, J., & Gunderson, L. (1997). Literacy learning from a multicultural perspective. *The Reading Teacher, 50,* 514–516.

Boyle, F. E, & Peregoy, S. F. (1990). Literacy scaffolds: Strategies for first- and second-language readers and writers. *The Reading Teacher, 44,* 144–200.

Carger, C. L. (1993). Louie comes to life: Pretend reading with second language emergent readers. *Language Arts, 70,* 542–547.

Cazden, C. (1992). Play with language and metalinguistic awareness. *Whole language plus: Essays on literacy in the United States and New Zealand* (pp. 59–74). New York: Teachers College Press.

Chomsky, C. (1980). Developing facility with language structure. In G. S. Pinnel (Ed.), *Discovering language with children* (pp. 56–59). Urbana, IL: National Council of Teachers of English.

Cummins, J. (1994). The acquisition of English as a second language. In K. Spannenberg-Urbschat & R. Pritchard (Eds.), *Kids come in all languages: Reading instruction for ESL students* (pp. 36–62). Newark, DE: International Reading Association.

Edelsky, K. (1989). Putting language variation to work for you. In P. Rigg & V. G. Allen (Eds.), *When they don't all speak English: Integrating the ESL student into the regular classroom* (pp. 96–107). Urbana, IL: National Council of Teachers of English.

Ernst, G., & Richard, K. J. (1994/95). Reading and writing pathways to conversation in the ESL classroom. *The Reading Teacher, 48,* 320–326.

Forman, E. A., & Cazden, C. B. (1994). Exploring Vygotskian perspectives in education: The cognitive value of peer interaction. In R. B. Ruddell, M. R. Ruddell, H. Singer, (Eds.), *Theoretical Models and Processes of Reading* (4th Ed.) (pp. 155–178). Newark, DE: International Reading Association.

Fox, S. E. (1980). Promoting growth in oral language. In G. S. Pinnell (Ed.), *Discovering Language with Children* (pp. 46–47). Urbana, IL: National Council of Teachers of English.

Freeman, D. E., & Freeman, Y. S. (1993). Strategies for promoting the primary languages of all students. *The Reading Teacher, 46,* 552–558.

Ho, C. S. H., & Bryant, P. E. (1997). Learning to read Chinese beyond the logographic phase. *Reading Research Quarterly, 32,* 276–289.

Hudelson, S. (1990). Bilingual/ESL learners talking in the English classroom. In S. Hynds & D. L. Rubin (Eds.), *Perspectives on talk and learning* (pp. 267–283). Urbana, IL: National Council of Teachers of English.

Hudelson, S. (1994). Literacy development of second language children. In F. Genesse (Ed.), *Educating second language children* (pp. 129–158). New York: Cambridge University Press.

Kiefer, B. Z., & DeStefano, J. S. (1985). Cultures together in the classroom: "What You Saying?". In A. Jagger & T. Smith-Burke (Eds.), *Observing the language learner* (pp. 159–171). Newark, DE: International Reading Association.

Lim, H. L., & Watson, D. J. (1993). Whole language content classes for second language learners. *The Reading Teacher, 49,* 384–393.

Moll, L. C. (1986). Writing as communication: Creating strategic learning environments for students. *Theory into Practice, 25,* 102–108.

Moll, L. C. (1988). Some key issues in teaching Latino students. *Language Arts, 65,* 465–475.

Moll, L. C., & Greenberg, J. B. (1990). Creating zones of possibilities: Combining social contexts for instruction. In L. C. Moll (Ed.), *Vygotsky and education* (pp. 319–348). New York: Cambridge University Press.

Natarella, M. (1980). Sharing literature with the young child. In G. S. Pinnell (Ed.), *Discovering language with children* (pp. 48–51). Urbana, IL: National Council of Teachers of English.

Nieto, S. (1996). *Affirming diversity.* White Plains, NY: Longman Publishers.

Nurss, J. R, & Hough, R. A. (1992). Reading and the ESL student. In S. J. Samuels & A. E. Farstrup (Eds.), *What research has to say about reading instruction* (pp. 277–313). Newark, DE: International Reading Association.

Peregoy, S. F., & Boyle, O. F. (1993). *Reading, writing and learning in ESL.* New York: Longman.

Quintero, E., & Huerta-Macias, A. (1990). All in the family: Bilingualism and biliteracy. *The Reading Teacher, 44,* 306–312.

Rigg, P., & Allen, V. G. (1989). *When they don't all speak English: Integrating the ESL student into the regular classroom.* Urbana, IL: National Council of Teachers of English.

Strickland, D. S., & Strickland, M. R. (1997). Language and literacy: the poetry connection. *Language Arts, 74,* 201–205.

Sutton, C. (1989). Helping the nonnative English speaker with reading. *The Reading Teacher, 42*(9), 684–688.

Urzua, C. (1980). Doing what comes naturally: Recent research in second language acquisition. In G. S. Pinnell (Ed.), *Discovering language with children* (pp. 33–38). Urbana, IL: National Council of Teachers of English.

Urzua, C. (1989). I grow for a living. In P. Rigg & V. Allen (Eds.), *When they don't all speak English: Integrating the ESL student into the regular classroom* (pp. 15–38). Urbana, IL: National Council of Teachers of English.

6 A Chinese Boy's Joyful Initiation into American Literacy

Jane S. Townsend and Danling Fu

When seven-year-old Xiaodi (Sh-ow-dee) was reflecting on his first published story from his first year in an American school, he exclaimed, "I was so excited that I jumped and jumped because I could do just like the others!" Over the course of one school year, Xiaodi had emerged from being a quiet, shy second-grader who spoke little English to a popular classroom member, demonstrating Chinese writing to fascinated American students, drawing illustrations for eager classmates, and mentoring other, newer Chinese students. His confident, smiling demeanor and his easy, congenial interactions with friends and teachers had developed in less than a year.

What happened to support Xiaodi's joyful initiation into American literacy? How was this young language-outsider welcomed into full participation in multiple discourses of English? And what does his experience tell us about helping other newcomers? We studied Xiaodi's journey and discovered multiple sources for his achievement.

Our Research

The purpose of our research was to explore the ways in which students with diverse linguistic and cultural backgrounds develop a new literacy. To examine the process in detail, we conducted a case study of one Chinese boy's entry into an American community of readers and writers. Some may argue that a "process approach" to reading and writing is only suitable for students from middle-class, mainstream American families (Cope &

Reprinted from *Language Arts*, March 1998.

Kalentzis, 1993; Delpit, 1995; Martin, 1989); we wanted to find out if that was so.

The setting we chose—the teacher, the classroom, the school—was one that had demonstrated its effectiveness in helping students develop their abilities in both reading and writing (Hansen, Newkirk, & Graves, 1985). The school population was predominantly middle class with only one or two children at each grade level from non-mainstream cultural and linguistic backgrounds. We chose the second grade for our research focus because children at this age tend to do more sophisticated reading and writing than do first-grade and kindergarten students who are largely at an emergent literacy stage. Yet, second graders are still developing their concepts of reading and writing.

At the beginning of one school year, Xiaodi was the only foreign student in the second grade who was a language newcomer, so we selected him to be a case study. To examine Xiaodi's experiences, we observed him in both his regular classroom and his ESL room. We collected samples of his work and conducted regular, periodic interviews with him, his teachers, and his mother.

What Happened to Xiaodi?

Xiaodi came to this country to join his mother who was a graduate student from the People's Republic of China. Xiaodi had completed first grade in China. He came to this country without knowing any English, and his ideas about reading and writing were very different from what many of us take for granted. He was immediately labeled as a "speaker with limited English proficiency" when he enrolled in the second grade. Even so, he was placed in a regular classroom with American students, except for a 45-minute period each day when he received help from an ESL teacher and interacted with other foreign students.

Xiaodi's work in the ESL class involved mostly explicit instruction and directed exercises. However, in his regular class, he participated in reading and writing workshops and made choices about what activities to pursue. For example, he chose to draw when he didn't understand the teacher's out-loud reading during storytime. During the reading workshop, the teacher arranged for students to work in pairs, and, at first, other students read stories to Xiaodi (no doubt increasing their own fluency) and, later, they read together with him. As he began to understand more English, he stopped drawing during storytime and, along with all the other children, paid rapt attention to the teacher's out-loud reading. Very soon after that, he began reading on his own. By December, he was reading books in English every night for 20–30 minutes (mostly stories as well as nonfiction about animals), and he also wrote two or three lines in English for his assigned reading response journal.

Taking turns at the front of the class to talk about their home reading was a favorite part of the students' classroom activity. For a few months, Xiaodi observed his peers share their reading, but he wasn't able to participate. He said: "I want to sit on the table like them, swing my legs like the other kids holding books, and read to the class." (Xiaodi's comments throughout are translated by Fu.) He seemed charmed by his classmates' easy casualness, so different from the expectations for students' behavior in China. One day in December, Xiaodi prepared an elaborate drawing of a story he had read and volunteered to talk about it. All the students and the teacher gave him great applause. This event marked a turning point for Xiaodi. Rather than correcting *his* nonstandard English, the teacher asked the class to celebrate Xiaodi's accomplishment. She said to the class: "We all know that when Xiaodi first came to us, he couldn't speak much English. Now see what Xiaodi can do!"

Xiaodi's progress in writing English was as remarkable and rapid as his reading development. He told us that when he saw all the other children writing, he wanted to write too. He began his participation in the writing workshop of his regular classroom by writing a letter in Chinese to his father who was still in China. In his letter, he described his new life in the United States, his friends, and his school. He told his father that he liked the American school very much, the children were nice, and the teacher was much nicer than the teachers in China, who seldom smiled. Xiaodi also told his father that he was allowed to do things in school that were fun and that he didn't need to sit straight with his hands folded in front of him, listening to the teacher lecture all the time, as he had had to do in his Chinese school.

Over time, with the help of his teachers and classmates, Xiaodi learned to work through several drafts of his writing to reach a finished product that could be published in a small foldover book. He developed his ability to reflect and review. At the end of the year, he explained that he wanted to work more on one of the published stories: "Some kids asked me a question about the bear and shark story. They asked me how the bear could kill the shark when he was already in the shark's mouth. I want to revise that part, though it is already a published one." It's interesting that he considered his classmates' advice about a published story and wished to revise and make his work better. According to his mother, students in China, especially those at Xiaodi's age, are never encouraged to share their writing with their peers. They take advice only from teachers, the authorities. Further, substantive revision is not an issue for young learners in China (Fu, 1992). Instead, the focus is on correcting errors (editing) and using "set phrases" from previously published literature to "sound beautiful" (Fu & Townsend, 1997).

At the end of that year, in May, he identified his favorite pieces of writing, and he said he was most proud of a draft for the story, "The Dog and his Frend" (see Figure 1).

When asked about his choice, he responded:

> It is long, the longest story I ever wrote, and longer than some other kids' stories in the class. I like the title and words I used in the story. I also like the ending. It's a happy ending, and funny too. This is the first story I did on the computer. I was proud of myself; I really like it.

He thought this story was even better than the two published ones—"it is longer than them, the words are better . . . and the title is better than those stories too."

"The Dog and his frend"

Once upon a time there was a dog. He wanted a friend, but his mum didn't want her own son to go by himself. But the dog cried all day, so his mum let him go.

So there he was in the woods. And he saw a wolf. He got so happy because he saw that was a friend. So they both got to the wolf's house. The wolf said:"you can stay here." So the dog stayed there for a year. But he missed his mum.

So he went home, and he saw his mum crying. Because he was not home for a year. Then he forgot to go back to wolf's house. The wolf was so angry, and the wolf wrote a letter to the dog. The letter said: "you have to come before the weekend is coming. If you don't, then we are going to have a fight".

And the dog saw the letter, but he forget to go back.So they are going to have a fight.The fight was start,dog's mum was there too.the wolf bite dog's tail:"you bite wolf's nick.And the wolf die.and the dog still finding the frend.And his mum got home.

Now the dog find a grold dog.Then they get married.they had a boy puppy.They was haply ever after.but he miss the wolf too. Because the wolf is his frend too.
                        THE END

Figure 1. "The Dog and His Frend."

Yet, his excitement about publishing reveals another aspect of Xiaodi's development. He explained:

> Other kids in the class published stories, and I can do the same. I am Chinese and can publish stories like them. I am very, very happy about it and very proud of myself. Some kids published one, some two, some five, six, and even ten, but I only got two. That is okay. My stories are long, longer than some of the kids', and my pictures are great.

In reflecting on those two stories, Xiaodi stressed the fact of their publication more than any specific quality of the writing. For him, publishing his writing showed that he could do "just like the others," and that gave him a sense of belonging—in essence, a feeling that he had become a member of the American literacy club (Smith, 1988).

Even though Xiaodi started the second grade knowing little English, he told us he never felt handicapped. Rather, he felt recognized and respected for what he could do. And indeed, in a variety of ways, he used his prior knowledge of Chinese to join, and contribute to, his newly developing American literacy. He used his understanding of written and visual symbols to communicate his ideas, he drew on his knowledge of two different cultures to create stories that entertained his classmates and teachers, and he developed insight into his own abilities and accomplishments. By the end of his first year in an American school, his teacher could say, "He is a second-grade reader and writer just like the others in the class."

What Helped Xiaodi?

What supported Xiaodi's initiation into American literacy? What helped him become an active member of his new school community? We believe it was only in a language-rich environment that Xiaodi could possibly have developed into such an effective reader and writer within one year. Communicative competence comes from opportunities to use language in real ways for real reasons with real people. Xiaodi's teacher offered him many such opportunities and the time to explore them. He had personal reasons to talk with a variety of people in a variety of contexts, his peers and teachers recognized and applauded his unique knowledge and abilities, and he had choices about what to read and write. In these ways, he developed a facility for using multiple discourses in English, a facility for communicating with a range of people for a range of purposes.

Multiple Discourses

Xiaodi's ESL class provided explicit language instruction—sentence structures, vocabulary, reading comprehension exercises, phonics (using music and song). His regular class made Xiaodi feel immediately welcome in his new literacy community. The reading and writing workshop gave Xiaodi a chance to watch his peers develop over time as readers and writers. He listened to their life stories. His classmates provided the language models and the specific vocabulary that he needed to enter this new childhood culture. He also had many chances to talk about his own ideas, in small-group conversations with other children who were in a similar situation in his ESL class, with peers in workshop contexts, in conversations and whole-group discussions with teachers. He got help from his classmates in his reading, writing, and talking. And his teachers (regular and ESL) structured their classrooms to encourage such conversations (Perez, 1996).

Inviting Xiaodi into discourses that were new to him, his teacher demonstrated other important facets of being literate in American society. When she read out loud during storytime, she revealed the sounds of fluent reading in a new language that held a whole set of different stresses and cadences than the Chinese language Xiaodi was used to. Also, by encouraging students to write in the genres they were reading, she made explicit a powerful reading/writing connection. And finally, in class discussions and individual conferences, Xiaodi's teacher showed, in her openness, kindness, and honest curiosity, just what it can mean to be a literate learner in Western society.

In October, as part of the writing workshop, Xiaodi wrote a letter to an American friend and mailed it. He also made a card for his mother. By December of his first year in an American school, Xiaodi had made great strides in his writing. He had started to write stories in English, influenced by his reading as well as by the other students' work. He had also collaborated with his friend Rungu from Zimbabwe in composing a piece for children, "How to Make a Secret Hiding Place" that they dictated to a teacher's aide who printed their words. In January, he wrote a teaching book for other children learning English. About the book, he explained, "This is a picture book I made for small kids, with pictures and a few words on each page. This book can help them learn language." In April, he published his first fiction book, then another later that year.

We believe Xiaodi developed a sense of audience in his various communications because the work he was doing made personal sense, and his developing literacy nurtured the relationships he so valued with classmates. Indeed, the stories he wrote and the pictures he drew were enormously entertaining to his friends, and he received affirmations that were surely instrumental to his growth and success.

Personal Recognition

A significant support to Xiaodi's development was that his language and personal skills were recognized and respected, and he could use what he already knew to join and make contributions to the class and school community. His native language became a great asset when his classmates responded with enthusiasm to his Chinese writing.

His friends all admired his ability to write in Chinese and were fascinated by the Chinese characters he used. He also drew illustrations along with his Chinese writing, explaining, "I know people can't understand my Chinese, so then they can look at the pictures." Classmates clamored for him to decorate their published book covers with Chinese writing. And later on, in the spring, when he could speak more English, he was invited to an upper-grade class to talk about China and to demonstrate on the blackboard how to write Chinese characters.

Xiaodi worked out his own strategies for writing in English and continued to include drawings as supports for others to understand his ideas. He loved to draw, and his artistic skill so impressed his teacher and his friends that he was asked to draw the cover for the grade-wide published collection of writing and for the class newsletter. He was often asked by his peers to illustrate their books and to design and draw the covers of their published books and writing folders. Indeed, he became so busy drawing for his friends that some children paid money to get his time!

As further evidence of Xiaodi's emergence from a quiet newcomer to an active class member, he began to be called on to escort *other*, newer Chinese students around the school, becoming for a time a mentor who helped and advised them. In this way, he became an insider, drawing on his knowledge of both Chinese and English to offer guidance to those who were less experienced. He was able to use his native language comfortably and in a way that affirmed his growing competence as a student in an American school (Kutz, Groden, & Zamel, 1993).

By recognizing his talent, his teachers and classmates made Xiaodi feel like a valued member of his new class community even before he could communicate fully in English. His native abilities acknowledged, Xiaodi was able to find the courage to enter new territory with an openness and an ardor that served his learning well.

Time and Choice

What was especially helpful for Xiaodi was having choices to make and being given the time to make them. At the beginning of the school year, he was left alone to find his own pace and his own points of entry to the new culture. Of course, he was in a friendly and supportive environment. Indeed, he joined the reading and writing workshops as well as other learning activities the first day of school along with the rest of his classmates. And he was allowed to take his own time pursuing various activities.

Just as important, Xiaodi was allowed the freedom to use his native language as he moved into new language realms, employing an "interlanguage" as a bridge to new discourses (Kutz, 1997). Kutz explains: "At any moment, a person who's acquiring a new language has a perfectly regular grammatical system—an interlanguage—which represents her working hypothesis about the structure of the new language" (p. 129). Xiaodi was able to sequence his own development so that he could learn what he needed to know *when* he needed to know it as well as when he was able to learn it (Lindfors, 1987).

For example, early in September, when Xiaodi began to write in English, he used invented spellings that reflected his accent and the only English sentence structure he knew: "I like . . . ," filling in the space with the words he cared most about: "pekhr" (picture), "fruand" (friend), "man" (mom), "cat," "fadr" (father), "mang ke" (monkey), "tehr" (teacher), "dog," and "shrk" (shark). Xiaodi wrote the words that were salient to him, and he arranged them neatly alongside the Chinese orthography and accompanying illustrations (see Figure 2). When asked, later in the year, to reflect on this early work in English, Xiaodi explained:

> They are my early writings—the first time I learned to sound out words. Though they were all wrong, they were still good. That was my first try. And I wrote the Chinese words and drew pictures there too. If people couldn't understand my spellings, they could read Chinese and look at pictures.

At that point, Xiaodi was shifting from the Chinese practice of writing characters from memory to spelling out words by sounding them out, a big step in his learning a new literacy (from an ideographic language system to an alphabetic one). And he was conscious that he had learned something

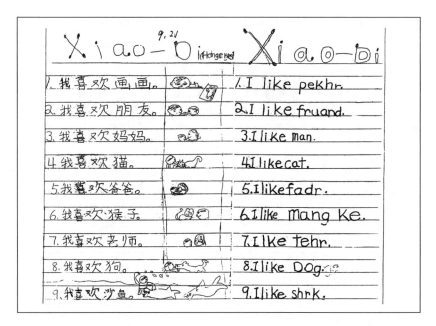

Figure 2. Xiaodi's bilingual writing with illustrations.

entirely new. He said that he felt he was really writing, not just spelling out words, because he wanted people to understand him. And because he knew that his sounded-out words were hard to understand, he added Chinese characters and drew pictures to help his audience. He was proud of his work, excited to have learned a new skill, excited to be communicating with classmates, excited to be expressing himself in a new language.

Xiaodi had both the time and the freedom to learn to read and write at his own pace for his own reasons. He was able to read and write about topics that mattered to him personally, and he could draw on his previous knowledge of Chinese for help in making sense of the new literacy (Smolkin & Suina, 1996).

Late in September, Xiaodi tried writing only in English, using the "I like . . ." sentence structure to name his friends and make more complicated sentences that showed his developing "interlanguage": "I like plaus sgu fruand" (I like play with school friend) and "I liike wrhe book us sgu fruand" (I like write book with school friend). We can see in these examples (see Figure 3) that Xiaodi leaves out grammatical morphemes (the infinitive form "to," plural "s,"

Figure 3. Xiaodi's early writing.

and articles "a" and "the") precisely because the Chinese language doesn't include these linguistic features. We can also see in these examples that Xiaodi cared a lot about his friendships with classmates. Indeed, from the first day of school, when the principal called on other students to show him around, Xiaodi turned most eagerly to his peers for help and information.

Also helpful for Xiaodi was the freedom to select his own writing projects. When he saw his classmates writing about their friends, he tried to write a piece about his best friend, Rungu. However, he only wrote two sentences and then quit. When we interviewed him and asked him why, he told us he didn't like to write personal experience narratives. Xiaodi thought there was no room for his imagination (the part of writing he enjoyed most) in what he saw as a simple retelling of factual events. He explained his view: "I can't write this kind of story. I don't know how. I just can't do it. I like to write fantasy better. But I want to try this kind of writing later."

Without the opportunity to choose his own topics and genres, Xiaodi might have felt restricted and discouraged. Instead, his teacher encouraged him to experiment with different forms of writing, a practice which allowed him to embrace some, like stories, and reject others, at least for a time. It's unlikely that Xiaodi would have tried writing in new ways, accepting so wholeheartedly the risk of potential failure, without knowing that he could change his mind and do something else, should *he* decide to. By publishing only self-selected pieces, Xiaodi maintained control of his progress and lowered his anxiety about new endeavors (Krashen, 1982). Not only did he have choices about what to read and write, he could also take as much time as he needed to complete his projects.

What Might Help Other Language Newcomers?

It's clear that the classroom environment—the sense of community—had a tremendous impact on Xiaodi's joyful initiation into a new literacy. However, we're afraid that this kind of language-rich classroom may be unusual. For example, several years later, when Xiaodi moved to another American community and entered a new school in the fifth grade, he had a very different experience than the one he'd had in the three years he spent at his first school. Xiaodi went from reading 20–30 books in the fourth grade to reading only the three books assigned to him during the entire fifth-grade year. When his mother asked him to read those three books at home, he told her that he had already read two of the books. His teacher spent six weeks on one book, and he was sure he would be "bored to death." Indeed, in his mother's words, "His fifth-grade year killed his interest in reading."

Spelling was the main focus in his fifth-grade language arts program, and his assignments involved identifying antonyms and synonyms and composing paragraphs from his weekly 20 spelling words. Both his mother and visiting grandparents (who were writers in China) struggled to help Xiaodi, who had a hard time making sense of such a senseless (purposeless) assignment. Xiaodi also had to complete 26 worksheets a week in language arts alone and spend months analyzing ("to death") the few books he did read. He wasn't reading or writing outside of school and never mentioned books or writing projects at home. Xiaodi's opportunities for language growth were shut down, and his mother became so alarmed she transferred him to a private school the following year.

Xiaodi's experiences can shed light on how we might best help (or hinder) language outsiders in our schools, but it's crucial to remember that Xiaodi was a unique individual. His interests and abilities were his own. We must be wary of thinking that all second-language learners are the same, unintentionally stereotyping children on the basis of one "single dimension of likeness" (Allen, 1991, p. 356). Although second-language learners may share the desire to learn English, their interests and abilities vary.

Each student in our classrooms—whether native speaker or second-language learner—is unique in his or her approach to learning. As Fillmore (cited in Lindfors, 1987) has pointed out, "There is more than one way to learn a new language" (p. 456). However, what we found from studying Xiaodi's experiences leads us to believe that the kind of real communicative purposes embedded in a process approach to reading and writing can indeed benefit not only middle-class American children but also students from linguistically and culturally diverse backgrounds.

Even though Xiaodi came from a literate family, what helped him would surely help all language learners. Hudelson (1990) asserts that "good teaching for native speakers is equally appropriate in the bilingual/second language context" (p. 282). From what we saw of Xiaodi's experiences, we can identify three dimensions especially important for all students: freedom, purpose, and support.

Freedom

Fu (1995), a second-language learner herself, studied four Southeast Asian refugee students' entry into a new culture in an American school and concluded: "Students need not only more time and space, but also more freedom in their learning. They should be instructed to try different ways to learn and to express themselves" (p. 204). It was important for Xiaodi that he was allowed the freedom and time to make his way in his new, second-grade classroom. He wasn't pressured to do prescribed tasks that made little sense to him. Instead, he chose to join classroom activities when they did make sense, and he was also able to choose multiple modes of expression to communicate his ideas. Sometimes, well-meaning instructors can provide too much structure in the way of prescribed topics and forms of response.

Also, for children who are developing their competence in a second language, demanding standard-language forms in their talk and writing creates barriers to exploration, risk-taking, and motivation. Kutz (1997) explains that it is crucial for teachers and learners

> to see how multiple discourses, many varieties of language and languages informal and formal, public and private, distant and personal—merge and mingle in the world around us, and to understand that our

schooled notion of a single, standard, authoritative discourse leaves
out most of the actual language of the worlds we inhabit. (p. 275)

In the second grade, Xiaodi was allowed to choose the forms and content
of his work. He could choose to talk and write about ideas that were
important to him. Xiaodi was also free to use what he had already learned
about literacy in his native language. He understood from his year of school
in China that visual symbols can represent meaning, that readers interpret
those symbols, and that both reading and writing are ways to communicate.
He was able to use this understanding *to figure* out the demands and
expectations of a new literacy. And, happily, he was given the time he
needed to make sense of a very different way of using language than the one
he knew.

All second-language learners bring their considerable knowledge of their
native language to learning a new tongue. However, it's not in all situations
that their native language will be allowed in the classroom, much less
celebrated, as was Xiaodi's in the second grade. We could see Xiaodi both
relying on what he knew about Chinese to add to his linguistic store and
using his Chinese writing as a communication bridge in his early English
writing.

Perhaps most helpful for second-language learners is the chance to
choose what they want to do when they want to do it. In Xiaodi's second-
grade class, the teacher encouraged her students to experiment with different
genres. She provided guidance, suggestions, and reading materials that gave
students ideas for their writing projects. She provided the explicit instruction
in writing conferences and mini-lessons that her students needed *when* they
needed it. And her students were allowed to choose the topics that mattered
to them personally in both their reading and writing.

The inquiry styles of individual children vary (Lindfors, 1997). Xiaodi
turned to peers for most of his information and interaction. And as we could
see from his fifth-grade experience, without the freedom to inquire about
what he wanted to know from the people he cared most about, without the
freedom to express and explore the ideas he found most interesting, Xiaodi's
language growth, like any other child's would be, was (momentarily)
stymied. Though he continued to make excellent grades in his school work,
he lost his interest in literacy endeavors.

Purpose

For Xiaodi, the focus of all the activities in his second-grade class was
communication and connection. Indeed, what's most striking about Xiaodi's

work are the real communicative and expressive purposes embedded in each example. He wrote a letter in Chinese to his father, a letter to a friend, and a card to his mother in English. He also wrote a series of "I like . . . " statements that were Xiaodi's way of expressing and finding his identity in his new language community. Personal communications came early. One-to-one communications with known others were probably the easiest discourses—both written and oral—to manage because contextual variables such as status differences and questions of shared background knowledge didn't pose a big challenge.

As he broadened his sense of audience, he composed a teaching book for other young language learners. Later, as he learned more about the new culture, he could move to writing stories that he knew would entertain his classmates. In each case, we can see Xiaodi shaping and controlling his own language activity to serve his own chosen communication purposes and audiences. A desire to make friends, to learn, to feel competent in his new culture, fueled his development. In talking about his reading and writing with classmates, in publishing his work, and in demonstrating his expertise, he had compelling reasons to stretch his capacities. He was nurturing his relationships and establishing his stature. What's apparently most helpful for all language learners—in developing both communicative and grammatical competence—is the opportunity to construct language in personally meaningful ways that serve real communication purposes (Kutz, 1997; Lindfors, 1989).

It's certainly true that second-language learners, like other students with special needs, benefit from extra help. For Xiaodi, a small part of his day (45 minutes) was spent in his ESL class, and the explicit instruction he received in English language forms and vocabulary was surely helpful to his development. However, what was most important, in our view, was that that instruction served the real communicative and expressive challenges he faced in his regular classroom.

Many language newcomers are isolated in self-contained classrooms designed only for second-language instruction. Usually, instruction for students with special needs focuses on what they lack, such as vocabulary, conventional grammar, and basic reading and writing skills. Yet, we believe that what benefited Xiaodi most was his immersion in a rich language environment, where he was given plenty of opportunities to interact with his peers and use the new language for his own chosen purposes. His achievement was demonstrated by what he could do as a reader and writer in the new language.

Purpose must be in some measure personally shaped to have any significance to the learner. Although the audiences that Xiaodi chose, as well as the content of his talk and writing, were unique to him, all language users require some sense of audience, some sense that language serves a communicative function. How any of us compose our ideas and messages depends on whom we're addressing and why. That sense of audience and purpose may be even more crucial for students entering a new culture and learning a new language.

Support

Kutz (1997) discusses the ironic bind that so many newcomers to our culture and schools face:

> We are all at different times, insiders or outsiders to different discourse communities. Our successful participation in those communities will have a lot to do with whether we're invited into the conversation and treated with tolerance and respect as we gradually acquire a new discourse, or whether we're kept outside of the conversations that would support that acquisition until we demonstrate a mastery that we can't achieve without that participation. (p. 137)

In discussing what helps someone gain the courage to enter new language territory, Kutz, Groden, and Zamel (1993) emphasize a classroom environment that makes it "safe to take the necessary risks to learn new strategies and new ways" (p. 12). For Xiaodi in the second grade, social support networks were immediately available. From the moment the principal called on other students to show him around, Xiaodi was enveloped in a warm and supportive community. His teachers and his classmates encouraged Xiaodi to take the risks necessary for his learning.

Consider what made Xiaodi feel safe: He had choices about pacing. He had time to think. His classmates, his teacher, and his mother read to him until he was ready to begin reading on his own. He could use his native language to establish his competence. He found the people around him friendly, encouraging, respectful, and his conversations with them gave him a sense of belonging and identity in the new culture and provided a chance to practice his new, developing English. He wasn't expected to be perfect in his use of English. His invented spellings and Chinese writing were welcomed as useful bridges to more conventional English literacy. His abilities in drawing and in Chinese writing were spotlighted. He was never embarrassed by what he didn't know.

For other second-language learners, who are in different circumstances and who have different interests and abilities, a supportive classroom environment must be equally important. Though support can take various forms, one of the great benefits of schooling is that it presents the chance to create the kind of social contexts that welcome diverse perspectives and help everyone learn. What teachers know about language, especially its purposeful and developmental nature, will surely have a tremendous impact on the kind of instruction they plan and implement (Townsend & Harper, in press).

The most persuasive evidence of Xiaodi's accomplishments was his ability to reflect on his own development, to recognize his strengths and weaknesses. When he examined his portfolio of writing, for example, thinking he must find "the one piece that can represent me," he struggled to find only one that would best reflect his achievements. When he was reassured that he could choose as many as he wanted just so long as "you think that those pieces show your growth as a reader and a writer in English," Xiaodi breezily replied, "Oh, I can do that. That's easy." He knew that his development was multifaceted.

It matters what schools and teachers do. To see linguistic diversity as a resource is to invite all our language newcomers to full participation in our classrooms (Eldridge, 1996). Though it's impossible for a teacher to understand all the nuances of any culture, one need only be aware that differences in modes of learning and literacy exist. We can't expect the learner to be the only one open to new cultural perspectives. As Hudelson (1990) has remarked, "adjustments must work both ways" (p. 279). To develop welcoming classroom environments requires openness, sensitivity, and flexibility, among all class members.

References

Allen, V. G. (1991). Teaching bilingual and ESL children. In J. Flood, J. M. Jensen, D. Lapp, & J. R. Squire (Eds.). *Handbook of research on teaching the language arts* (pp. 356–364). New York: Macmillan.

Cope, D., & Kalentzis, M. (1993). The power of literacy and the literacy of power. In D. Cope & M. Kalentzis (Eds.), *The power of literacy: A genre approach to teaching writing* (pp. 63–89). Pittsburgh, PA: University of Pittsburgh Press.

Delpit, L. (1995). *Other people's children.* New York: New Press.

Eldridge, D. (1996). When the shoe won't fit: Sizing up teachers' concerns about and responses to diversity in the language arts classroom. *Language Arts, 73,* 228–304.

Fu, D. (1992). One bilingual child talks about his portfolio. In D. Graves & B. Sunstein (Eds.), *Portfolio Portraits* (pp. 174–184). Portsmouth, NH: Heinemann.

Fu, D. (1995). *"My trouble is my English": Asian students and the American dream.* Portsmouth, NH: Heinemann.

Fu D., & Townsend, J. (1997). Cross-cultural dilemmas in writing: The need for transformations in learning and teaching. Manuscript submitted for publication.

Hansen, J., Newkirk, T., & Graves, D. (1985). *Breaking new ground: Teachers relate reading and writing in the elementary school.* Portsmouth, NH: Heinemann.

Hudelson, S. (1990). Bilingual/ESL learners talking in the English classroom. In S. Hynds & D. L. Rubin (Eds.), *Perspectives on talk and learning* (pp. 267–283). Urbana, Illinois: National Council of Teachers of English.

Krashen, S. (1982). *Principles and practice in second language acquisition.* Oxford, UK: Pergamon.

Kutz, E., Groden, S. Q., & Zamel, V. (1993). *The discovery of competence: Teaching and learning with diverse student writers.* Portsmouth, NH: Heinemann.

Kutz, E. (1997). *Language and literacy: Studying discourse in communities and classrooms.* Portsmouth, NH: Heinemann.

Lindfors, J. W. (1987). *Children's language and learning* (2nd ed.). Englewood Cliffs, NJ: Prentice-Hall.

Lindfors, J. W. (1989). The classroom: A good environment for language learning. In P. Rigg & V. G. Allen (Eds.), *When they don't all speak English: Integrating the ESL student into the regular classroom* (pp. 39–54). Urbana, Illinois: National Council of Teachers of English.

Lindfors, J. W. (1997). *Listening to children's inquiry.* Manuscript submitted for publication.

Martin, J. (1989). *Factual writing: Exploring and challenging social reality.* London: Oxford University Press.

Perez, B. (1996). Instructional conversations as opportunities for English language acquisition for culturally and linguistically diverse students. *Language Arts, 73,* 173–181.

Smith, F. (1988). *Joining the literacy club: Further essays into education.* Portsmouth, NH: Heinemann.

Smolkin, L. B., & Suina, J. H. (1996). Lost in language and language lost: Considering native language in classrooms. *Language Arts, 73,* 166–172.

Townsend, J. S., & Harper, C. (in press). What future teachers know and don't know about language diversity. *The Professional Educator.*

7 Finding the "Right Measure" of Explanation for Young Latina/o Writers

Liliana Barro Zecker, Christine C. Pappas, and Sarah Cohen

Learning has been compared to an apprenticeship in which the more experienced members of a social group share their expertise with novice learners to support their progress into more advanced levels of performance or understanding (Bruner, 1983; Vygotsky, 1978). However, the exact form that this sharing takes, or should take, is still puzzling to many educators. How much expertise is to be shared, when, and how? What are the best ways to build on learners' previous experiences so that they can construct new knowledge? Deciding what to make explicit for learners and finding the right balance between giving specific assistance and letting learners reshape knowledge through discovery is no easy task (Edwards & Mercer, 1987).

Apprenticeship in Literacy Learning: Two Dimensions of the Challenge

A major problem in supporting apprenticeship in literacy learning stems from the fact that reading and writing are mental processes, silent and not obvious in many ways. Wells and Chang-Wells (1992) have argued that there are many possible ways for readers and writers to relate to texts but it is a certain kind of engagement with text—which they call "epistemic"—that fosters truly literate ways of thinking. Epistemic modes of engagements are ones in which "meaning is treated as tentative, provisional, and open to

Reprinted from *Language Arts*, September 1998. The research reported in this essay has been supported by grants to Christine C. Pappas from the Spencer Foundation and the Center for Urban Educational Research and Development at the University of Illinois at Chicago. The views expressed are solely the responsibility of the authors.

alternative interpretations and revision" (Wells, 1990, p. 369). Thus, teachers of young children face the challenge of modeling the idea that meaning can be transformed and reformulated.

Classroom talk, what is said and how it is said, can then be considered *oral text* and as such it is a most effective vehicle to make explicit to young children the covert aspects of literate thinking. In other words, classroom talk provides an opportunity for teachers to model epistemic kinds of engagement with text.

But, as they support young writers in their apprenticeship, teachers face the challenge of having to balance the focus on meaning with the focus on form, since young children are also attempting to tackle the complex conventions of written language as a coded medium of communication. In recent years, literacy instruction has taken a more constructivist or collaborative tone, one that is more inclusive of students' interests and previous experiences (Hiebert, 1991; Willinsky, 1990). Within this framework, the mechanics of writing—punctuation, capitalization, spelling, etc.—are not taught in isolation via drill activities but, rather, in the context of students' needs as they *use* literacy to communicate. But teachers who have attempted to adopt this philosophy have often found it hard to decide *what* should be learned at different grade levels. Many tensions arise as teachers try to integrate form (i.e., written language as a code to be learned) and meaning (i.e., the ideas to be communicated). As a result, instruction in specific skills can sometimes become casual and random (McIntyre, 1995a, 1995b). Many questions still remain about how teachers can most effectively incorporate skill instruction in the context of meaning-centered approaches (Atwell, 1991; Labbo, Hoffman, & Roser, 1995; McIntyre, 1995b). This issue is particularly relevant as teachers prepare to teach the growing number of linguistically diverse students in American schools. It has been argued that these students need explicit and systematic instruction in the Standard English code in order to have access to better socioeconomic opportunities (Delpit, 1995; Reyes, 1992).

Sarah as a Teacher-Researcher

This article describes a second-grade teacher-researcher's efforts to foster her Latina/o students' growth in writing. Sarah, for whom Spanish was a second language, was teaching for the first time in a bilingual classroom in a Midwestern inner-city public school. All of her students were Spanish-speaking children, mostly from Mexican families who had recently immigrated to the United States. Sarah's reading and writing instruction was conducted predominantly in Spanish since her students had varying but, in general, very limited command of English.

Sarah participated in a school-university collaborative research project that explored teachers' self-selected inquiries on how to implement changes that would make their literacy curricula more effective and student centered. University and teacher-researchers met weekly as a group to discuss the teachers' successes and struggles. Videotapes and field notes collected by university researchers were shared with teacher-researchers, individually and as a group. These ongoing discussions provided opportunities for the teachers to examine and reflect on the observations of their classroom work related to their inquiries (See Pappas, 1997, and Pappas & Zecker, in press a & b, for more details about the larger collaborative school-university project in which Sarah's inquiry was embedded).

"¡Pero yo no escribo!": The Impetus of Sarah's Inquiry

At the beginning of the school year, Sarah had been surprised and saddened by the children's reluctance to engage in writing activities. When, soon after classes started, Sarah encouraged one of her students to write a story to accompany her picture, the girl simply responded, "¡Pero yo no escribo!" ("But I don't write!") Having experienced a first-grade year during which writing had been limited to the completion of phonics worksheets and handwriting exercises, the children did not see themselves as writers or believe they could become writers. Thus, the focus of Sarah's inquiry was to find possible ways to scaffold her students' development as writers. She set out to present a variety of possible writing invitations for them so that they could experience writing for communication. As the school year progressed, the ways in which she tried to make explicit for her students many of the not-so-obvious what's, why's, and how's of written language and authorship became especially salient.

Two facets of the challenge to support an appropriate apprenticeship in writing were present in Sarah's inquiry: she struggled to balance meaning and mechanics and made efforts to provide opportunities for her students to engage with texts epistemically. In this article, we focus on the latter as we reflect on Sarah's strategies—sometimes successful, sometimes not—to make the tacit aspects of writing explicit to her students via classroom talk. In two areas especially—fostering revision and making genre distinctions—Sarah tried to find the "right measure" of explanation so her students might begin to see how meanings can be tentative and transformed.

Note that, due to space restrictions, only some examples include both the original Spanish and its English translation. The other talk samples in the paper are translations only.

Invitations to Write and Revise

Sarah started by setting up a variety of opportunities for her students to write, share, and reflect on texts. She had whole-class, teacher-led mini-lessons and student-sharing activities similar to "author's chair" sessions (Calkins, 1994; Graves, 1994; Graves & Hansen, 1983). She also set up a system that enabled her to have individual writing conferences with her students. Within these various routines, she frequently "put into words" the many tacit aspects of writing.

Because her students did not see themselves as writers, Sarah was careful to articulate in detail for them the rationale and goals of their writing engagements. For example, she explained to Felipe, a student who joined the class later during the school year that *"The journal is where we put our thoughts, what we did during the day, on the weekend, how you feel, what your family is like. You can make drawings about what you have written. If you have questions, you can ask your classmates, okay?"*

When introducing readers' logs, Sarah explained *"Write your name and the date. You have to write the title of the book that you read. Then I want you to write about what the story was about, if it was a story, what happened? If it was a science book, about nature, what did you learn?"* Thus, Sarah talked about the communicative functions of these two kinds of writing, making explicit for the children their content as well as their form.

Sarah approached the teaching of the mechanics or surface aspects of writing from the same perspective. She included detailed explanations about spelling, punctuation, and capitalization rules during group and individual conferences. Sometimes, she would conduct whole-class spelling lessons explaining to the students, *"Estas son palabras que usan mucho y que escriben mal,"* ("These are words that you use a lot and you often misspell.") In that sense, Sarah was able to achieve some balance in her teaching as she was able to address both the message and the medium of written language in the context of her students' own writing.

Talking the Talk of Revision

Sarah paid special attention to the revision process as she felt it was important for the children to experience ways in which they could transform their writing and thus their thinking. As she explained the goals of whole-group conferences, she said:

> We are going to give our comments, suggestions, questions . . . and we are going to talk as a group . . . how those comments can be used to change the story, to develop the story . . . the stories that the authors write. You are the authors already . . . listening and giving suggestions, asking questions on the story. Later, we are going to think together about how the person who reads the story . . . can improve it, or how she or he can develop her or his story. What happens is that, often, we write a story and we think that it is already finished, but sometimes it is missing details in some parts, or it could be developed much more.

Often, Sarah capitalized on the students' comments to help them reflect on the role of audience feedback from the author's vantage point. For example, at the end of October, after Raul had shared his Halloween story with his classmates and responded to some of their questions, Sarah closed the session by saying: "These questions, they make me think, Raul, that sometimes it is good to give more details. The audience wants more information. Maybe next time you can give more details." Thus, in promoting revision, Sarah was helping students to understand that initial meanings can be re-examined and retold.

Sometimes, Sarah modeled through talk the possible ways in which students could incorporate changes in their stories. During one of these sessions, Lorena volunteered to read one of her stories to the class. Sarah explained she would write the audience questions on the board as a way to provide Lorena with assistance during the revision to follow. Lorena read a story about Julia, a girl who liked to draw, color, and make books. Julia had a friend who also liked to engage in drawing, coloring, and book making. After finishing her reading in front of the group, Lorena answered questions from her peers using short, succinct responses and not elaborating on details. Afterward, Sarah explained how Lorena could use the feedback to revise her story. She modeled some possible changes for Lorena to consider:

Example 1

SARAH: Estas preguntas pueden ayudar. ¿Okay? Te preguntaron, "¿Por qué le gustaron los cuentos a la niña?" y "¿Por qué le gustaban los dibujos?" Eso es una cosa que no está en el cuento. Podrías poner estos detalles en tu cuento. Parece que a la gente que lea tu cuento le gustaría saber mas sobre la niña. ¿Me entiendes, Lorena?

LORENA: Si, entiendo.

SARAH: Y si pones esos detalles, sería mas complete. ¿Entiendes? También te preguntaron, "¿Por qué los coloreó, los cuentos y los libros?" Y si lo hacía sola o con su amiga. Si su amiga la ayudaba. ¿Okay? Parece que tus compañeros, Lorena, están diciendo que quieren saber mas; podrías darnos un ejemplo. Podras darnos una escena entre la niña y su amiga haciéndolo . . . lo que hacían. ¿Entiendes? Eso es diferente que decir, "A la niña le gustaban los dibujos." Podrías decirnos, umm, "Una niña, Julia, y su amiga un día estaban haciendo unos dibujos. Julia hacía eso y . . . después dijo su amiga, ¿Por que no ponemos el color rosa en el conejo en el cuento?"

BOY 1:   (***)[1]

SARAH: Uh-huh. Puedes darnos una perspective sobre cómo se portan las niñas. ¿Entiendes?

LORENA: *[Nods.]*

SARAH: Hay otras cosas que podrías decir sobre la niña. ¿Cómo es su vida? A parte de que le gustaba hacer dibujos y cuentos, podrías decirnos si va a la escuela, si sale, cómo es su familia, cosas así. ¿Verdad? ¿Okay? Entonces, si tu crees que te gustaría hacer el cuento mas grande, cambiar un poquito, contesta algunas preguntas que te hicieron tus compañeros. ¿Okay? Esas preguntas, Lorena. *[As she is pointing to the board.]*

Translation

SARAH: These questions can help, okay? They ask you, "Why did the girl like stories?" and "Why did she like the pictures?" That is something that is not in the story. You could put those details in the story. It seems as if the people that read your story would like to know more about the girl. Do you understand me?

LORENA: Yes, I understand.

SARAH: And if you put in those details, it would be more complete, do you understand? They also asked you, "Why did she color the stories and the books?" And if she did it alone or with her friend. If her friend helped her, okay? It seems that your classmates, Lorena, are saying that they want to know more; you could give us an example. You could give us a scene between the girl and her friend doing that . . . what they did. Do you understand? That is different than saying, "The girl liked pictures." You could tell us, umm, "A girl, Julia, and her friend, one day were drawing pictures. Julia was doing that and . . . then her friend said, "Why don't we color the bunny in the story pink?"

BOY 1:   (***)

SARAH: Uh-huh. You can give us a perspective about how the girls behave. Do you understand?

LORENA: [Nods.]

SARAH: There are others things that you can say about the girl. What's her life like? Besides liking to make drawings and stories, you could tell us if she goes to school, if she goes out, what her family is like, things like that, right? Okay? Then, if you think that you would like to

make the story bigger, change a little, answer
some of the questions that your classmates
asked you, okay? Those questions, Lorena.
[As she is pointing to the board.] (Field notes,
11/02/94)

Sarah used the questions asked by Lorena's classmates to provide her with
specific examples of how to incorporate more information into her story and
then orally "revised" Lorena's story to model for her a possible new final
product. She was using classroom talk as "text," as the canvas on which to
make explicit the need to treat written texts as tentative and provisional,
always having the potential for revision. But when Sarah later reminded
Lorena to use the audience response to revise her story, Lorena looked
puzzled and her response consisted of copying from the board all the
questions that Sarah had written. For her, that was revision.

Thus, Sarah experienced difficulty in "handing over" her expertise in
revision. Like other teacher researchers have discovered, Sarah realized that,
more often than not, students seemed to talk the talk of revision but did not
actually revise their writing (Calkins, 1994; Labbo et al., 1995). Students in
Sarah's class, like other young writers, seemed to write for the here and now.
Despite her efforts, they seemed to translate revision strategies into very
concrete operations, writing more for the sake of the activity than for the
creation of a final product that would consider the needs of the audience
(Calkins, 1994). Near the end of the school year, Sarah encouraged Raúl to
use Pablo's feedback to improve his story, reminding him to "take notes" on
Pablo's comments so that "you can remember what he tells you." Later Raúl
approached Sarah and asked: "And now, what do I do with this? He gave me
all this." He showed Sarah his "notes" which were parts of his story copied
verbatim on a new piece of paper. As Sarah mentioned that the notes could
help him revise his story, Raúl responded: "But I already copied all the parts
he liked!" Frequently, during whole-class conferences, Sarah highlighted that
praising the good parts of a story was very important. Apparently, Raúl had
focused only on that part of the discussion, and his "revised" product
consisted of the audience's favorite parts copied unchanged from his original
story.

Despite Sarah's explanations and other attempts to scaffold the revision
process more explicitly, some of her students never realized these new ideas
in their final products. However, the mismatch between what is "talked
about" and what "gets written down" is not atypical (Calkins, 1994; Pappas,
Kiefer, & Levstik, 1994). Sarah found that it was hard to find what she called

the "right measure" of explanation and keep individual children's focus of interest and understanding. At times, it seemed as if she might have unintentionally made writing too complex by *forcing* writing into being too much of a process (Labbo et al., 1995). Beginning writers need time to incorporate flexible revising strategies into their repertoires (Calkins, 1994). They use oral language as a bridge to many aspects of literacy learning (Dyson, 1986; Gundlach, 1982) and talking the talk of revision may be sufficient as an initial, emergent step into more conventional authorship.

Explaining Genre Distinctions

As the year progressed, Sarah's students began to participate more actively in the discussions around their writing. In example 2, Sarah's uses Felipe's writing to launch a discussion about the differences between fiction and nonfiction.

Example 2

[Sarah is standing in front of the class, addressing the students while holding Felipe's piece.]

1 SARAH: Felipe no está haciendo exactamente un cuento.

2 BOY 1:   (***)

3 SARAH: Está escribiendo algo—algo que no es ficción; es sobre la ciudad de Chicago.

4 BOY 2:   ¿Cómo?

5 SARAH: ¿Mande? ¿Cómo? Dice cómo es Chicago . . . es lo que está escribiendo. Eso no es un cuento; no es ficción.

6 BOY 1:   Yo no quiero hacer eso.

[Sarah is interrupted by students telling her what they are writing about. There is lots of overlapping talk.]

7 SARAH: Umm, lo que estoy diciendo es que no tiene que ser un cuento. Si quieren hacer . . . escribir otra cosa, otro tipo de cosa, cómo

son los animales, las plantas . . . otra cosa
que no es—que no sea ficción Kara, tú
pronto vas a Puerto Rico. Podrías escribir
cómo es Puerto Rico; hacer no exactamente
un cuento sino una descripción, como hemos
estado haciendo descripciones sobre
monstruos, sobre tu persona, sobre tu casa;
podrías hacer otro tipo de descripción sobre
otra cosa, animales, o lugares, lo que sea. . . .

*[Children talk about the "cuentos" they have
written.]*

8 SARAH: ¿Mario? ¿Entienden la diferencia entre
ficción. . . .

9 BOY 2:   *[Completing Sarah's sentence]* Y cuentos?

10 SARAH: Cuentos y cosas que no son cuentos, que no
son ficción. ¿Qué entiendes, Vicente?

11 VICENTE: Que no debo hacer cosas de ficción.

12 SARAH: No, no . . . no que no debes sino que—no
que no tienes que hacer cosas de ficción.
Puedes hacer cosas de ficción pero también
puedes si quieres hacer cosas que no son
ficción. ¿Qué es ficción, Alma? ¿Qué es
ficción, Raul? ¿Franco?

13 FRANCO: Como de eso de . . . de brujas

14 SARAH: Okay, brujas sí, si escribes sobre brujas
generalmente . . . generalmente es ficción.
¿Por que? *[Addressing the class.]*

15 BOY 3:   Porque es mentira . . .

16 SARAH: Mentira . . . o también se puede decir que no
exactamente es mentira sino que no es real.
¿Okay? Una cosa que . . .

*[There is an interruption as a child yells at
Mario and Sarah needs to spend some time
asking them to quiet down. Then she goes
back to her discussion.]*

17 SARAH: Una cosa que escribes sobre algo que no es
              real es, es como ficción. ¿Entiendes?

18 FRANCO   ¿Como básquetbol?

19 SARAH: ¿Mande?

20 FRANCO: ¿Como básquetbol?

21 SARAH: Como básquetbol? Bueno, puedes hacer un
              cuento de ficción sobre básquetbol pero . . .

22 CHILDREN:(***)

23 SARAH: Un cuento, por ejemplo, de ficción es como
              diciendo cosas que no, que realmente no han
              pasado. ¿Okay? Inventado una historia.

24 CHILDREN:(***)

25 BOY 1:   (***) cuento de básquetbol (***)

26 SARAH: ¡Claro! Un cuento sobre cualquier cosa, de
              básquetbol, de pescados, todas esas cosas
              son reales. Solamente cuando hacen cuentos,
              usan esas cosas pare inventar una historia.
              ¿Entiendes, Vicente?

27 VICENTE: Sí.

28 SARAH: ¿Bien? ¿Sí? ¿Pablo? *[He is raising his hand.]*

29 PABLO: ¿Cómo un pescado que juega básquetbol?

30 SARAH: ¿Cómo qué?

31 PABLO: ¿Un pescado que juega básquetbol?

32 SARAH: Bueno, eso seria como muy, muy irreal,
              como fantasia. Ficción no tiene que ser
              fantasía. Ficción puede ser un niño jugando
              básquetbol; o un hombre, o una mujer
              jugando básquebol . . . Ficción no tiene que
              ser fantasía, Pablo. ¿Okay? Solamente la
              diferencia entre ficción y fantasía es que—si
              no es ficción, tiene que haber pasado . . .
              haber pasado en la vida . . . umm, por
              ejemplo, una descripción sobre la vida de
              Michael Jordan es una historia sobre su vida,

		es real. ¿Okay? Pero si tú quieres escribir un cuento sobre . . .

33 BOY 1:   ¿Michael Jordan?

34 SARAH: Sobre tu—siendo una estrella de básquetbol, no seria real . . .

35 CHILDREN: (***)

36 CHILDREN: Sería algo que estás creando en tu imaginación.

37 PABLO: (***) pero (***) puede ser real.

38 SARAH: Puede ser en el futuro. *[Turning to Franco.]* Franco, me molesta que estés haciendo ruido! *[Returning to the class.]* Puede ser real en el futuro pero ahorita no es real. ¿Okay? Es algo que estás imaginando, Pablo, para escribir como un cuento. ¿Okay? ¿Felipe?

39 FELIPE: Maestra, lo que escribí ¿Que es? *[Pointing to his piece, which Sarah is holding up.]*

40 SARAH: ¿Esto? Lo que estás escribiendo, algo sobre Chicago, de cómo es Chicago en tus ojos, verdad? ¿Es algo real o irreal?

41 CHILDREN: Algo . . . real

42 SARAH: Real? Sí . . . es algo muy real . . . estás haciendo como un librito explicando cómo es la ciudad . . .

43 FELIPE: *[Interrupting]* Como (***).

44 SARAH: No estás inventando una ciudad. ¿Verdad? Entonces es real, no es ficción. ¿De acuerdo? *[To the entire class]* ¿Otras preguntas?

Translation

		[Sarah is standing in front of the class, addressing the students while holding Felipe's piece.]

1 SARAH: Felipe is not writing a story, exactly.

2 BOY 1:   (***)

3 SARAH: He is writing something—something that is not fiction; it's about the city of Chicago.

4 BOY 2:   What?

5 SARAH: Pardon? What? He tells what Chicago is like . . . that's what he is writing. That's not a story; it's not fiction.

6 BOY 2:   I don't want to do that.

[Sarah is interrupted by students telling her what they are writing about. There is lots of overlapping talk.]

7 SARAH: Umm, what I'm saying is that it does not need to be a story. If you want to do . . . write something else, other type of thing, what are animals like, plants . . . something else that is not—that would not be fiction. Kara, you are going to Puerto Rico soon. You could write about what Puerto Rico is like; write not exactly a story but a description, like we have been doing descriptions about monsters, about yourself, about your house; you could do a description about something else, animals, or other places, whatever . . .

[Children talk about the stories they have written.]

8 SARAH: Mario? Do you understand the difference between fiction . . .

9 BOY 2:   *[Completing Sarah's sentence.]* And stories?

10 SARAH: Stories and things that are not stories, that are not fiction. What did you understand, Vicente?

11 VICENTE: That I should not do fiction things.

12 SARAH: No, no . . . not that you shouldn't, but—it's not that you shouldn't do fictional things. You can do fiction things, but also, if you want, you can do things that are not fiction. What's fiction, Alma? What's fiction, Raúl? Franco?

13 FRANCO: Like that about . . . about witches.

14 SARAH: Okay, witches yes, if you write about witches,
             in general . . . in general it's fiction. Why?
             [Addressing the class.]

15 BOY 3:   Because it's a lie . . .

16 SARAH: A lie . . . or we can also say that it is not
             exactly a lie but it is not real, okay?
             Something that . . .

             *[There is an interruption as a child yells at
             Mario and Sarah needs to spend some time
             asking them to quiet down. Then she goes
             back to her discussion.]*

17 SARAH: Something that you write about something
             that is not real, it's like fiction. Do you
             understand?

18 FRANCO: Like basketball?

19 SARAH: Pardon?

20 FRANCO: Like basketball?

21 SARAH: Like basketball? Well, you can make a fiction
             story about basketball but . . .

22 CHILDREN:(***)

23 SARAH: A fiction story, for example, it's like saying
             things that, that have not really happened,
             okay? Making up, a story.

24 CHILDREN:(***)

25 BOY 1:   (***) basketball story (***).

26 SARAH: Right! A story about anything, about
             basketball, about fish, all those are real
             things. It's only that when you write stories,
             you use those things to make up a story. Do
             you understand what I am saying?

27 VICENTE: Yes.

28 SARAH: Good. Yes? Pablo? *[He is raising his hand.]*

29 PABLO: Like a fish that plays basketball?

30 SARAH: Like what?

31 PABLO: A fish that plays basketball?

32 SARAH: Well, that would be like very, very unreal,
              like fantasy. Fiction does not have to be
              fantasy. Fiction can be a boy playing
              basketball; or a man, or a woman playing
              basketball. Fiction does not have to be
              fantasy, Pablo, okay? It's only that the
              difference between fiction and fantasy is
              that—if it's not fiction, it has to have
              happened . . . have happened in real life . . .
              umm, for example, a description on Michael
              Jordan's life is a story about his life, its real,
              okay? But if you want to write a
              story about . . .

33 BOY 1:   Michael Jordan?

34 SARAH: About you . . . being a basketball star, that
              wouldn't be real . . .

35 CHILDREN:(***)

36 SARAH: It would be something that you are creating
              in your imagination.

37 PABLO: (***) but (***) it can be real.

38 SARAH: It can be in the future. *[Turning to Franco.]*
              Franco, it bothers me that you are making
              noise! *[Returning to the class.]* It can be real
              in the future but now it is not real, okay? It is
              something that you are imagining, Pablo, to
              write as a story, okay? Felipe?

39 FELIPE: Teacher, that what I wrote, what is it?
              *[Pointing to his piece, which Sarah is holding
              up.]*

40 SARAH: This? What you are writing, something about
              Chicago, about what Chicago is like in your
              eyes, true? Is it something real or unreal?

41 CHILDREN:Something . . . real.

42 SARAH: Real? Yes . . . its something very real . . .
                  you're making like a flyer explaining what the
                  city is like . . .

43 FELIPE: *[Interrupting]* Like (***).

44 SARAH: You are not making up a city, true? Then it's
                  real, it's not fiction. All right? *[To the entire
                  class.]* Other questions? (Field notes,
                  06/02/95)

The above conversation shows how Sarah would respond to the
children's initiations by using their comments to extend their budding
understandings (Wells, 1986; Wells & Chang-Wells, 1992). Sarah used
Felipe's text on Chicago (lines 3 and 5) and other students' ideas about
writing on basketball, Michael Jordan, and witches to be explicit about the
distinction between fictional and informational writing. She built upon their
prior work on "descriptions" and provided other possible informational
topics, such as Puerto Rico for Kara (line 7). In her responses, Sarah provided
additional information that clarified some of the children's current ideas, as
was the case when she told them about the difference between fantasy and
realistic fiction (line 30), or when she explained that writing about witches is
generally considered a work of fiction (line 14). The students eagerly
participated, venturing possible answers even when, as illustrated by Felipe's
remark near the end of the discussion (line 39), they were not fully sure of
how Sarah's explanations applied to their own writing.

But collaborative classroom discussions, because they are not scripted,
can become more complicated than teachers have anticipated, precisely
because they are spontaneous. When Sarah responds to Pablo's comment
about a fish playing basketball (line 31), she moves into an apparent
unplanned discussion of the differences between fiction and fantasy. Her
explanation becomes somewhat tangled when she talks about what could
happen in *real life,* and what is *very, very unreal* (line 32). The discussion
might have also been confounded by Sarah's use of the word "story" to
describe both nonfiction and fiction: " . . . a description of Michael
Jordan's life is a *story* about his life, it's real. . . . But, if you want to write a
story about . . . you being a basketball star, that wouldn't be real" (lines
32 & 34).

Nevertheless, Example 2 shows how much classroom talk was
co-constructed. Jointly, Sarah and the students examined a set of very
implicit ideas that writers often apply as they compose different kinds of

texts. Sarah was able to build upon the students' genre conceptions, however partial they were, by helping them consider new aspects of the fiction/nonfiction differentiation. She was successful in assisting her students see the potential and possibilities of making meaning.

Summary

Sarah's inquiry shows how difficult it can be to realize the apprenticeship perspective in literacy learning. Finding the right measure of explanation is not always easy. Meeting students at their developmental levels to provide the right amount of assistance at the right time is a complex, multifaceted endeavor. Not all attempted scaffolds work, and they need to be constantly readjusted if they are to be truly collaborative. Bringing the writing process into practice in the reality of the classroom requires constant retooling (Lensmire, 1994; Sudol & Sudol, 1991, 1995). And, certain aspects of written language learning can be made explicit more easily than others. But Sarah's teaching also illustrates the power of classroom talk as a tool for literacy instruction. It demonstrates that it is possible to include skill instruction in the context of a meaning-centered approach to the teaching of literacy.

All children are likely to benefit from instructional strategies like the ones that Sarah used to promote epistemic literacy engagements. The teaching described here, however, is quite different from what is usually provided for low-socioeconomic and ethnic minority children. Too frequently, students' existing knowledge bases are not valued or considered in their literacy instruction (Moll & Gonzalez, 1994) and as a result, they experience unchallenging, rote learning (Bartolomé, 1994). Sarah's students certainly had the cognitive and the linguistic resources to become literate, to understand, and to use writing meaningfully.

Note

1. Text marked with (***) indicates speech that was indecipherable.

References

Atwell, N. (1991). *Side by side: Essays on teaching to learn.* Portsmouth, NH: Heinemann.

Bartolomé, L. I. (1994). Beyond the methods fetish: Toward a humanizing pedagogy. *Harvard Educational Review, 64,* 173–194.

Bruner, J. (1983). *Child's talk.* London: Oxford University Press.

Calkins, L. M. (1994). *The art of teaching writing.* Portsmouth, NH: Heinemann.

Delpit, L. (1995). *Other people's children.* New York: The New Press.

Dyson, A. H. (1986). Transitions and tensions: Interrelationships between the drawing, talking, and dictating of young children. *Research in the Teaching of English, 20,* 379–409.

Edwards, D., & Mercer, N. (1987). *Common knowledge.* New York: Routledge.

Graves, D. H. (1994). *A fresh look at writing.* Portsmouth, NH: Heinemann.

Graves, D. H., & Hansen, J. (1983). The author's chair. *Language Arts, 60,* 176–183.

Gundlach, R. (1982). Children as writers: The beginnings of learning to write. In M. Nystrand (Ed.), *What writers know: The language, process, and structure of written discourse* (pp. 129–148). New York: Academic Press.

Heibert, E. H. (Ed.). (1991). *Literacy for a diverse society: Perspectives, practices, and policies.* New York: Teachers College Press.

Labbo, L., Hoffman, J., & Roser, N. (1995). Ways to unintentionally make writing difficult. *Language Arts, 72,* 164–170.

Lensmire, T. (1994). *When children write.* New York: Teachers College Press.

McIntyre, E. (1995a). The struggle of developmentally appropriate literacy instruction. *Journal of Research in Childhood Education, 9,* 2.

McIntyre, E. (1995b). Teaching and learning writing skills in a low-SES urban primary classroom. *Journal of Reading Behavior: A Journal of Literacy, 27,* 2.

Moll, L. C., & González, N. (1994). Lessons from research with language minority children. *Journal of Reading Behavior: A Journal of Literacy, 26,* 439–456.

Pappas, C. C. (1997). Making "collaboration" problematic in collaborative school-university research: Studying with urban teacher researchers to transform literacy curriculum genres. In J. Flood, S. B. Heath, & D. Lapp (Eds.), *Handbook of research on teaching literacy through communicative and visual arts* (pp. 215–231). New York: Macmillan.

Pappas, C. C., Kiefer, B. Z., & Levstick, L. S. (1994). *An integrated language perspective in the elementary school.* White Plains, NY: Longman.

Pappas, C. C., & Zecker, L. B. (in press a). *Teacher inquiries in literacy teaching-learning.* Hillsdale, NJ: Erlbaum.

Pappas, C. C., & Zecker, L. B. (in press b). *Working with teacher researchers in urban classrooms.* Hillsdale, NJ: Erlbaum.

Reyes, M. de la Luz (1992). A process approach to literacy instruction for Spanish-speaking students: In search of a best fit. In E. Hiebert (Ed.), *Literacy for a diverse society* (pp. 157–171). New York: Teachers College Press.

Sudol, D., & Sudol, P. (1991). Another story: Putting Graves, Calkins, and Atwell into practice and perspective. *Language Arts, 68,* 292–300.

Sudol, D., & Sudol, P. (1995). Yet another story: Writers workshop revisited. *Language Arts, 72,* pp. 171–178.

Vygotsky, L. (1978). *Mind in society: The development of higher psychological processes.* Cambridge: Cambridge University Press.

Wells, G. (1986). *The meaning makers: Children learning language and using language to learn.* Portsmouth, NH: Heinemann.

Wells, G. (1990). Talk about text: Where literacy is learned and talked. *Curriculum Inquiry, 20,* 369–405.

Wells, G., & Chang-Wells, G. L. (1992). *Constructing knowledge together: Classrooms as centers of inquiry and literacy.* Portsmouth, NH: Heinemann.

Willinsky, J. (1990). *The New Literacy: Redefining reading and writing in the schools.* New York: Routledge.

8 Doing His Own Thing: A Mexican-American Kindergartner Becomes Literate at Home and School

Margaret M. Mulhern

"Did you bring books? How much did this cost? Where did you buy it? Do you have a library card?" This was one of the many strings of questions asked by kindergartner Rubén Gutierrez when I visited his home. Rubén, never at a loss for words, was described by his mother as *"muy preguntón"* (very inquisitive). At school, his teacher noted that Rubén had a knack for "doing his own thing," rather than following her directions. High on Rubén's agenda was learning to read and write, a task he approached with as much gusto as he ate jalapeño peppers, biting into them whole and raw, with great joy.

Looking back, it is not surprising that Rubén caught my attention during my first visit to his classroom in the early fall of his kindergarten year. Eventually, I selected him as one of three Mexican-American children whose Spanish literacy development I would document at home and school (Mulhern, forthcoming). Though most of the children in the classroom were eager learners, Rubén's energy was electrifying and contagious. I wanted to find out more about Rubén, especially his home life and the ways in which his home and school worlds would connect during his kindergarten year. To do so, I spent one day a week in Rubén's classroom in the fall and two or three days a week between January and June, alternately observing the three focal children. I also accompanied Rubén home from school weekly, interacting with him and his family members for three or four hours. His family welcomed me, a Euro-American woman who had learned Spanish as a second language, into their home during that year and I continued to visit them for the two years I remained in Chicago.

Reprinted from *Language Arts*, October 1997.

Why Rubén?

Rubén, like most of his classmates, was the child of Mexican immigrants, many of whom themselves had not had extended opportunities for schooling. Almost all of the children in Rubén's Chicago neighborhood and school were of Mexican origin and, like Rubén, many were placed in Spanish bilingual classrooms. His classroom was crowded with 27 children identified as needing additional instructional support. Rubén was one of four children who had attended preschool and this probably contributed to his teacher's and my identification of him as a child with a high developmental knowledge of literacy as compared to his classmates. For instance, Rubén was able to write his first name and seemed comfortable with literacy activities, while many children struggled to copy one letter of their names.

My interest in studying Rubén and his classmates was driven by the lack of information on how children construct literacy as they move between their home and school worlds (Sulzby & Teale, 1991). I believed that, by attempting to look through the eyes of a child crossing the home-school border, a fuller understanding of the varied ways that children go about becoming literate could be revealed. Those ways are undoubtedly influenced by family perspectives on literacy learning (Goldenberg, 1989; Solsken, 1993) and teachers' approaches to literacy instruction (Dahl & Freppon, 1995). By looking through this broad lens, I hoped to gain insights into the ways in which home-school links and literacy instruction could be strengthened to better meet the needs of children.

My use of the term *literacy* refers to print literacy or written language, rather than the multiple literacies that are part of children's lives. Farr (1994) notes that the Mexicano families she worked with, who also lived in Rubén's neighborhood, viewed literacy (the ability to read and write) as a cultural tool connected to schooling. In clarifying my primary focus on children's acquisition of school literacy, I do not want to discount the importance of "funds of knowledge" (Moll & Greenberg, 1990), oral literacy activities (Vasquez, Pease-Alvarez & Shannon, 1994), and *consejos*, "spontaneous homilies designed to influence behaviors and attitudes," (Valdes, 1996, p. 125) that have been documented in Mexican-origin families.

In recent years, much attention has been placed on the need to involve parents (especially those from low-income backgrounds) in their children's early literacy learning. The burgeoning family literacy movement is one manifestation of the goal to increase parent involvement (Mandel, 1995). While such programs may be valuable for those families who choose to participate in them, I wanted to document the ways in which Mexican-immigrant parents are already involved in their children's education. I believe that parent programs should not lessen the responsibility teachers have for learning more about home literacy practices and reaching out to parents who may be unfamiliar with instructional approaches in U.S. schools. If parent involvement programs are implemented at all (see Valdés [1996] for arguments against them), they need to take into account the sociocultural practices of families (Auerbach, 1995), including the ways in which written language is used in homes.

In this article, then, I share Rubén's experiences as a literacy learner who negotiated meaning as he crossed the home-school border. I have included additional information on Rubén's home background, for readers who may be less familiar with the home lives of Mexican-immigrant children. While what is true in Rubén's case cannot be generalized to apply to other children, it does provide insights into the potential for interconnectedness between a child's home and school learning experiences. His experiences can also inform teachers who wonder about home support for literacy learning and the role of the school in communicating with families like Rubén's. Finally, Rubén's talent at making links between a variety of literacy activities, both within the classroom and between home and school, suggests ways that teachers can foster similar linkages for other students.

Rubén at School

Rubén was a child who commanded attention in the classroom. Physically, he was always shooting up his arm or jumping up with excitement. Verbally, his constant initiations, rapid speech, and deep voice drowned out many of the children. Rubén's enthusiasm for learning to read and write was evident in his choice to continue his engagement with literacy during free play periods and in his persistent questioning about the texts that surrounded him. Even reminders from his teacher that he needed to listen did not sidetrack Rubén from his pursuit of literacy. The result of this interactive stance was that Rubén could easily "steal the show," as he vocally participated in whole group activities far in excess of any other child.

Setting His Own Agenda

Rubén was intently focused on learning, but what he had in mind to learn did not always match his teacher's agenda. This caused some tension for both Rubén and Mrs. Martinez (a ten-year veteran of kindergarten teaching), although, for the most part, Rubén was able to negotiate lessons to fit his interests. For instance, during a phonics lesson on 'B' syllables, Mrs. Martinez said, *"Eso es una ballena"* (That is a whale), and Rubén followed with, *"Si viene un niño, la ballena se come un niño"* (If a child comes, the whale eats a child). Rubén's comment momentarily turned the phonics lessons to one of his favorite topics—animals, what they eat, and how they live. Thus, one way Rubén remained engaged during skill instruction was to personally create a more meaningful context for the syllables presented.

Sometimes Rubén told his teacher he didn't want to complete the assignments as directed. For instance, when instructed to write an ending for a story, Rubén said, *"Maestra, ya no quiero escribir"* (Teacher, I don't want to write anymore). When she didn't answer, he tried again, *"Maestra, ya no quiero hacer nada"* (Teacher, I don't want to do anything anymore), and finally, *"Maestra, ya acabé"* (Teacher, I finished already). This tactic didn't work, however, and Rubén was told to continue writing. While other children appeared to have similar feelings on occasion, few were as vocal as Rubén in expressing their opinions.

Rubén's frequent assertions could, at times, get him into trouble and he had to stand apart from the group for a few minutes. Mrs. Martinez felt that Rubén liked to make jokes so the other kids would laugh. One day, as she explained that only mothers or fathers could come pick up report cards, Rubén suggested that the cat could also come. Another time, when Mrs. Martinez started to read a book saying, *"Vamos a ver quién es el autor"* (Let's see who the author is), Rubén interjected his best friend's name and, once again, he had to take a *time out*.

Rubén's tendency to want to follow his own agenda was apparent to Mrs. Martinez, who often told him that he wasn't listening and told me that Rubén "does his own thing." It appeared to me that Rubén's desire to make his own choices resulted in his tendency to do as he pleased. He thought worksheets were "easy" and wanted to rush through them so he could read a book. If an activity was interrupted because the children had to leave the room, Rubén didn't want to stop working and he would stand at the table writing, even after the lights were out and all the children had left. Finally, he would run out the door and catch up. Rubén did test the teacher's limits at times, but, for the most part, he figured out how to negotiate doing his work as well as doing what he wanted.

Engaging in Literacy Activities

In Rubén's classroom, literacy instruction was conducted almost exclusively in Spanish, thus allowing the children to acquire literacy in the language they knew best before making the transition to English instruction. The traditional approach included direct instruction of Spanish syllables (i.e., *ma, me, mi, mo, mu)* and the completion of worksheets. There were also regular opportunities for the children to explore written language through shared book experiences and independent reading, as well as writing stories, journal entries, and letters. Mrs. Martinez sometimes made connections between the syllables the children had been taught and the whole text activities; however, most of the phonics instruction was isolated from more meaningful contexts. The classroom was print rich; the walls were covered with posters and signs and there were over 300 books available for reading.

Overall, Rubén enjoyed the literacy activities available at school. He caught onto graphophonemic relationships easily and would name the beginning syllables of words he encountered throughout the day. If he had any questions about them, he was not hesitant to ask an adult for assistance, and he elicited information at his level this way. Rubén was very attuned to environmental print. For example, he asked me to read posters and bulletin boards when we walked down the hallways and he always knew whose birthday would be celebrated, by referring to the classroom bulletin board. Rubén eventually learned the letters of the alphabet and the associated pictures posted in the classroom, although these were not a focal point of instruction.

Rubén had a great affection for books. During shared book reading, he sat in the front of the group, often getting up on his knees to see the book better. He had so many comments and questions (15 or 20 per book was not unusual) that Mrs. Martinez had to ask him to hold his questions until the end. Even with this warning, Ruben interrupted frequently, commenting on content *(¿Verdad que el tigre es el amigo del león?*—Isn't the tiger a friend of the lion?) and graphophonemic relationships *(Búho empieza con la 'bu'— Búho* [Owl] begins with *'bu').* Rubén read both alone and with others. He did this during independent reading as well as many other times, but always after requesting permission from the teacher. Claiming that he could read, Rubén reconstructed the meaning of books from memory and picture cues.

Rubén was eager to obtain books to read at home. He often spoke of getting a library card, as Mrs. Martinez had suggested, and one day he asked me to give him a dollar for the card. He asked the school librarian when he would be able to check books out, and he often ran over to peruse the piles of books at the beginning and end of library class. Short texts in basal workbooks did not hold Rubén's interest, however. When he left one of these selections on the table one day, I reminded him that the teacher had asked the children to take them home and read them to their parents. He grimaced at the idea and told me to take it, instead.

Rubén's desire to engage in writing activities wavered, depending on his mood and his confidence in his ability to write. Assignments which involved writing to a known audience (e.g., a card to a classmate's mother who recently had a baby and, on another occasion, a mother's day card) were exciting. Being able to choose his own topic also seemed to foster Rubén's interest in writing. Rubén was the first child in the room who noticeably started to think about encoding his message using his graphophonemic knowledge. In January, while writing about a zoo visit, he isolated and recorded Z for *"zoológico"* (zoo). Then he said, *"Yo miré focas"* (I saw seals), and wrote the letter O for *"foca."* (In Spanish, invented spelling often consists of vowels rather than initial and final consonants.) Rubén often used me as a sounding board, wanting me to verify his letter or syllable choices and read his invented spelling. Yet there were times that spelling seemed to be too much work for Rubén and he wrote children's names and lines across the page "to finish quickly." Mrs. Martinez commented to me that Rubén didn't want to make a "mistake" and therefore became very hesitant in his writing. This hesitancy may also have stemmed from the phonics lessons where the children were expected to write initial syllables correctly.

Rubén often chose to go to the writing table during free time. He sometimes succeeded in calling his friends over to write and draw with him, but they didn't seem to have his staying power. Near Valentine's Day, though, four children joined him after he started writing notes to his friends and putting them in a postal area set up for the holiday. Most often, Rubén drew favorite objects, sometimes connecting the pictured items with an oral "story." He also labeled his drawings, especially those portraying Ninja Turtle characters. As he wrote, Rubén told me that he would show his work to his mother because she would compliment him. Rubén also used the free-play period to listen to books on cassettes, read books, and complete leftover worksheets. At the end of the school year, Mrs. Martinez commented about Rubén, "When we have free play he won't play, he wants to just do writing."

Rubén at Home

Rubén walked home from school with his mother until close to the end of the year when he began to walk alone or with me on the Thursdays I visited. Rubén's street was like many in the neighborhood. It was filled with three- or four-story older houses that were divided into several apartments. While the conditions of the housing varied, the buildings were old and problems with plumbing and roach infestations were common. The steps to the homes came right to the sidewalk and there were few gardens or lawns and very few trees. When Rubén and his classmates got excited about seeing a squirrel at the zoo, it struck me that they didn't see them in their neighborhood very often. The sidewalks had many gaping holes that were slowly being repaired by the city; meanwhile, old tires or pieces of wood covered the holes to prevent accidents.

A few blocks from Rubén's home was the central commercial area of the neighborhood. Local businesses catered to the community—there were photo studios for special occasions, *tortillerías, panaderías* (Mexican bakeries), and stores selling clothing, music, and other merchandise from Mexico. The high concentrations of *Mexicanos* made the neighborhood a comfortable entry point for immigrants who often already had an established social network of family members and neighbors from their home towns in Mexico. However, gang activity was a great concern within the community.

The Gutierrez's apartment made up the entire second floor of one of the houses. The front door opened into a large living/dining room, warmed by a large space heater. Rubén and his sisters, four-year-old Erica and two-year-old Lucia, and I watched TV, read books, or played in this room. Several photographs of the children hung over the couch and their artwork adorned the door. When he could not work at his construction job because of foul weather, Rubén's father played cards with friends and relatives in this room. Three bedrooms, a kitchen, and a bathroom made up the rest of the apartment.

Rubén's parents were 24 years old and had emigrated eight years before from the Mexican state of Durango where they had lived on *ranchos*. Their home was busy with people coming and going, so it took me a while before I sorted out who lived there. Señor Gutierrez's brother, his wife, and Señora Gutierrez's brother also lived in the aparment. Having at least five adults in his home, it became clearer to me why Rubén felt so at ease with adults in the classroom.

On a typical school day, Rubén played outside, watched television, and did literacy-related activities until he went to bed. Rubén watched cartoons or the public television channel his teacher had recommended. He enjoyed the programs about animals, and asked me to interpret the English narration for him. Rubén's chores were to take out the trash and put away his toys. On the weekend the family mostly stayed at home, but Rubén liked to go to the park or play outdoors when the weather was favorable.

On warm days, the streets were full of activity—everyone was relieved to be outdoors after the cold winter. On the sidewalk in front of Rubén's house, the neighbors sold corn on the cob and cucumbers from a small stand. On the hottest and muggiest days of summer, the fire hydrant was opened and cold water flooded the street as the children cooled themselves off. Sometimes Rubén's grandfather came by with his popsicle cart and treated the children. Ball games, hopscotch, and piggyback rides were the children's favorite outdoor activities. Rubén was asked to watch his youngest sister if she went outside with him. He had to be very mindful, since she was as active as he was—Rubén had to track her down once when she climbed in the window of the neighbor's house. Rubén, too, could get into dangerous situations—on the way to the store, one day, he picked up a discarded hypodermic needle he saw under a car. His mother explained to him why it wasn't safe to pick it up.

Rubén's activities within his home and neighborhood provided rich contexts for learning outside of school. He interacted with the many adults in his extended family, as well as with family friends and neighbors. Rubén had responsibilities within the family and integrated play and literacy learning into his daily activities. In the next section, I provide some background information regarding Rubén's family members' perspectives on literacy learning, in order to further contextualize his home literacy experiences.

Situating Rubén's Home Literacy Interactions

Of the family members, Señora Gutierrez and her sister-in-law, Amanda, had the highest levels of formal education and read and wrote most frequently. They were also enrolled in school, Amanda in the eighth grade, and Señora Gutierrez in ESL classes at a community center. Señora Gutierrez took care of many of the literacy needs in the home—reading school notices, communicating with her family in Mexico, and filling out forms related to her husband's employment. The majority of observed and reported literacy events in the home were related to education (e.g., doing homework, playing school, reading children's books, and reading school notices) and daily living routines (e.g., shopping, writing letters, reading mail, paying bills, and taking down phone messages). Rubén's mother was the most involved in his literacy interactions, answering his questions and checking his school papers. She informed the teacher when Rubén had the chicken pox and asked for homework to bring home to him.

Señora Gutierrez, herself, had enjoyed school in Mexico, finishing the six years of primary school. She remembers her brother helping her write the alphabet. She was taught through a syllabic approach using a school textbook, and noted that literacy was being taught to her children in a similar way. One difference she noticed between U.S. and Mexican schools was that the schools in Mexico were harder, with more homework. She gave the example that, if one misspelled a word, it had to be practiced five times. Señora Gutierrez continued to write new words several times when she was studying English.

Asked about literacy and the availability of books in her parents' home in Mexico, Señora Gutierrez recalled her school books. There was no library in the town, and her family did not have money to buy books. When I spoke of my mother reading to me, she explained, *"Es que no había este costumbre allá, pero la gente que tenía dinero iba al pueblo y compraba libros para sus niños y la gente que no tenía ni sabía que habían libros"* "It's that there wasn't this custom there, but the people who had money went to the town and bought books for their children and people who didn't have money didn't even know that there were books). Lack of resources also prevented her from pursuing her education after primary school. At the age of 16 she came to the United States with her older brother so she could help support her family in Mexico.

Rubén's father did not like school, as a child, and after four years, he decided to leave to work with his father. When I asked Señora Gutierrez what her husband read, she told me, *"Él no lea, no le gusta"* (He doesn't read, he doesn't like it). If Rubén asked his father a question about written language, he would refer him to his mother. But, according to Señora Gutierrez, her husband thought highly of Rubén's great interest in learning. *"Pues, dice que está bien porque a él no le gustaba. Dice ¡qué bueno! que a él le gusta porque ahora que está grande dice que hace falta saber. O sea como no salió de sexto dice que a él le gustaría haber salido"* (Well, he says that it's good because he didn't like it [school]. He says it's good that he [Rubén] likes it because now that he's older he realizes that it's important to have knowledge. As he didn't finish sixth grade, he would have liked to have finished).

Señora Gutierrez did not particularly like living in Chicago, but she planned to stay for her children's schooling. She felt that the most important value she could teach her children was *"la educación,"* which included both the importance of behaving well with others and studying. Her hope was that her children would "come out ahead" in life.

Engaging in Home Literacy Activities

No less talkative at home than at school, Rubén used the dinner hour to tell his mother about various school events—things he did there (that he had read five books to me, or that he had played Red Riding Hood in a dramatic reenactment), something interesting he had learned, or other children's behavior. Señora Gutierrez felt that Rubén knew a lot because he asked so many questions, often about literacy. If she was too busy to answer his questions, he found someone else to ask. Rubén used any available print at home to learn about written language—he asked his mother to read him school notices, frequently referred to the calendar, dictated letters to his mother to send to his grandmother in Mexico, and he often played school.

Rubén's interest in literacy was evident during all of my home visits. On the days I visited, Rubén engaged me in literacy interactions, and I learned from his mother the extent to which similar activities took place when I was not present. He initiated most of the activities we did together, pulling me away from the kitchen table, getting my bag of books and saying, *"Quiero hacer algo"* (I want to do something). Besides reading books, Rubén wanted to draw, write, and do "work." For instance, Rubén initiated a letter naming activity in which I was to put an 'X' on any letters he did not name correctly. Letter naming was not a common literacy activity at school, but Rubén made good hypotheses about letter names. For a letter name Rubén didn't know, he generated a hypothesis that, if he said the beginning sound of a word that started with that letter, it would be the correct letter name. This worked for some letters, like *B* (pronounced /be/ in Spanish) for the word *bebe* (/bebe/). Yet, he called the *Q* /ke/ instead of the Spanish /ku/, because he associated the letter with the word *queso* (/keso/, cheese) which was pictured next to the *Q* at school. Similarly, he called the letter *G* /gwa/ instead of /he/ because he thought of the pronunciation and spelling of his classmate's name, Guadalupe. This activity again indicated to me how aware Rubén was of the environmental print in the classroom and that he was applying the knowledge gained at school to his home activities.

When a classmate asked Rubén why I went to his home, he responded, *"para leer libros"* (to read books). Indeed, reading and talking about the books I brought were major activities during my visits. Rubén took advantage of my access to children's books since the books in his home were limited to a Bible, a set of medical encyclopedias, and books related to the family members' schooling. His first question when I walked in the door was, *"¿Trajiste libros?"* (Did you bring books?). He would sometimes run to the kitchen to show his mother a book and tell her that he wanted her to get him some. Despite frequent requests for books, Rubén was, at first, not very successful in obtaining them. His mother was concerned about him being responsible enough to care for books, and she worried he would leave them out where his little sister could get them. Moreover, Senora Gutierrez did not know where she could purchase books. Unfortunately, the two best Spanish language bookstores in Chicago were located at the other end of the city; the local bookstore had a small selection of children's books, most of which were highly priced and poor in quality. Yet, later in the year, she was able to borrow some books from the community center where she studied English, and Rubén brought them to school so Mrs. Martinez could read them to the class. Rubén listened to his mother read the books I lent or gave him and he engaged in pretend reading on his own. His mother was grateful for the bit of quiet time this activity allowed.

While reading seemed to be Rubén's preferred home literacy activity, he also liked to write. Labeling his drawings, writing names of family members, and occasionally writing a letter were most typical. When Rubén wrote at home, he solicited assistance with spelling from me and his mother. He wanted his mother to validate, by reading aloud, the emergent writing he did on his own at home. But she was often unable to read his invented spellings and modeled conventional spellings. According to Señora Gutierrez, one day when Rubén had brought a paper to her saying, *"Aquí dice tortuga"* (Here it says turtle), she told him, *"No, asi no lo dice"* (No, like that it doesn't say it), then she wrote the word correctly for him. Her response reflected her experiences with learning to write in rural Mexico. In addition, although an emergent approach to writing was being used in Rubén's classroom, no explanations of this perspective were provided to parents, who continued to draw upon the literate practices they had been exposed to as children.

Rubén was not always pleased with his mother's view of his writing and responded to her comment that his writing didn't say anything by telling her that she "didn't know." He tried to better understand how written language worked, by asking his mother, *"¿Por qué tu haces muchas letras y dice algo?"* (How come you make a lot of letters it says something?). She explained that she had already learned how to write and he was still learning. Thus, there was some tension around writing at home, as there was at school—Rubén was unsure when his writing was legitimate and he wanted to spell correctly. Still, he held onto his desire to write and continued to take risks as a writer.

Rubén's family contributed to his literacy learning. His parents were pleased with his avid interest in learning and his mother responded to his many inquiries about written language. Señora Gutierrez talked with Rubén about school, made sure he completed his homework, participated in writing activities with him, read to him at his request, and made an effort to provide books for him.

Learning from Rubén: Implications for Fostering Connections in Children's Literacy Experiences

By spending time with Rubén, I learned more about his world and the role of literacy in his life. Rubén's orientation to literacy learning was similar at both home and school, and he managed to "compose a place" for himself (Dyson, 1993) as he moved between these two settings. This process involved the negotiation of some tensions that arose because of differences between how Rubén and others perceived literacy learning. Many of the strategies Rubén used in becoming literate were effective ones. He had a strong sense of himself as a reader/writer and he seemed to instinctively know what would help him to become literate—access to books, time to read and write, choice of books to read and topics for writing, and adult scaffolding. His inquisitiveness and straightforwardness allowed him to pursue literacy by "doing his own thing" and resulted in rapid acquisition of knowledge about written language.

The following points highlight the lessons I learned from Rubén about how teachers might foster literacy learning in and out of school.

Connect Skill Instruction to Meaningful Contexts

Rubén was a highly motivated child who realized that he could learn more about the world through books and that he could communicate with others through his writing. His teacher helped foster these understandings by providing opportunities for reading and writing. Planned activities that were the most authentic (i.e., reading trade books, writing to a known audience) seemed to engage Rubén the most. He showed disinterest in or resistance to writing on assigned topics that did not spark his interest and he disliked reading basal stories, preferring to keep the "word" connected to his "world" (Freire & Macedo, 1987).

Rubén was attuned to meaning and wholeness when he engaged with print. He found ways to add meaning to teacher-directed skill lessons, by associating the syllables to words that were meaningful to him or by commenting on words such as *ballena* (whale). Rubén was also adept at noticing beginning syllables of words in books and other print, picking up on his teacher's modeling during read alouds. His ability to listen for the initial consonant or syllable of any word he wanted to write was exemplary, especially since there was infrequent discussion or teacher modeling of ways to think about using the syllables the children were taught during skill lessons. Rubén's strategies indicate how important it is to connect skill learning to contexts that are meaningful to children. Teachers can observe the strategies children use to make sense of print and they can have children share their strategies with their peers (Mills, O'Keefe, & Stephens, 1992).

Connect Home and School Literacy Experiences

Rubén's case suggests ways in which the connections between home and school literacy experiences can be encouraged. Because these links were a central focus of my research and because I was present in the home and school settings I had a greater role, in making the connections recommended here on an informal basis, than Rubén's teacher did. However, as a result of the study, she came to see the need to improve home-school relationships.

Rubén's love of books and his ongoing crusade to obtain them suggest the need to increase children's access to books. Señora Gutierrez was not familiar with the cultural practice of sharing books with children, but she enjoyed reading to her children those books I made available. It is critical to understand that the infrequency of reading to young children in some Mexican-origin families is neither an indication of neglect nor disinterest in children's educational success (Heath, 1986; Valdés, 1996). Rather, many parents had not been introduced to this practice in Mexico and are not familiar with ways to access books. Given the importance of book reading for young children and, as in Rubén's case, children's enjoyment of books, support for this activity could be provided by allowing children to borrow books from the school or classroom library. Currently, many schools do not allow kindergartners to take books from the library. Modeling of shared book reading could occur by inviting parents to visit the classroom, or by sending home a teacher-made videotape of lap reading.

In suggesting that books be sent home with children, I am not implying that parent-child book reading is the only or most critical use of the books, or that some parents are not already reading with their children. Parents may not read the books with their children for various reasons, including limitations on parents' time and literacy abilities (Purcell-Gates, 1996) or lack of knowledge of English, when only English books are sent home. Yet, children can benefit by engaging in pretend reading, or reading books with a sibling or neighbor, as Rubén did. An explanation of the value of pretend reading is warranted because parents or older siblings who have not seen young children engage with books may expect children to be able to read them if they are sent home by the school. While this was not true in Rubén's case, I have observed this reaction in other families.

Clearly, teachers must make efforts to inform parents about school literacy practices. Tension arose between Rubén and his mother over writing because Señora Gutierrez was not aware of the school practice of allowing children to write using invented spelling. While some tension in literacy learning is inevitable (Solsken, 1993), and may, in fact, be helpful in furthering children's understandings of written language, Rubén's case study points to the need to better inform parents. It was when I interviewed Señora Gutierrez about Rubén's home literacy activities that I learned of her perspective on his writing. Señora Gutierrez's conception of literacy learning, which required correct answers, made sense, given her own literacy background and the worksheets Rubén was bringing home. However, when I provided an explanation of the concept of emergent writing, Señora Gutierrez seemed to better understand how Rubén's spellings were indicative of his competence with written language. Having a particular perspective on literacy learning does not preclude parents from considering alternative perspectives. Changes in literacy approaches have necessitated educating all parents about the ways children are being taught. Non-mainstream parents, who do not directly question teachers about their methods, should not be left out of discussions of literacy instruction.

One caution to educators as they foster home-school connections is to avoid advocating only literacy activities valued by schools, in case culturally specific literacy practices are replaced (Auerbach, 1995; Valdés, 1996). While this critique has been made of family literacy programs, it also applies to teachers' approaches to involving families in their children's schooling. Auerbach (1995) notes that ethical issues are raised whenever we intervene in families' lives, so "we need to proceed with caution and humility" (p. 649). It is critical to learn more about the ways in which families use literacy and how they perceive written language learning, simply because there is variability across families. Moreover, it is necessary to acknowledge home activities as potential learning experiences for children, which can be tapped into when planning school instruction (e.g., see Moll & Greenberg, 1990).

Learn about Students' Out-of-School Lives

Rubén's case study provides not only a description of his literacy learning experiences, but also a portrait of an active, inquisitive child from a loving family. Just as Rubén was able to share his school activities with his mother, his home experiences could be tapped into for literacy learning at school. Mrs. Martinez helped children make home-school connections when she provided space for children to discuss their home lives, when she allowed children to choose their own topics for writing, and when she shared with the class books children brought from home. By doing so, she opened the door to learning more about the children she taught.

Too often in my work, I hear negative stereotypes about Mexican-immigrant families and their role in their children's education. In sharing a small piece of Rubén's world, I hope I have dispelled some of these stereotypes by offering an inside look at the whole child and how literacy fit into his world. Clearly, Rubén's family, like others I know, and those written about elsewhere (Carger, 1996; Delgado-Gaitan, 1990; Delgado-Gaitan & Trueba, 1991; Goldenberg, 1989; Moll & Greenberg, 1990; Valdés, 1996), are interested in their children's educational and social success. Educators working with children like Rubén will be best prepared to teach them if they make the effort to learn more about their lives and to understand their parents' perspectives on education. Such efforts open the door to increase communication between parents and teachers and *smooth* the transition for children as they learn at home and school.

References

Auerbach, E. (1995). Deconstructing the discourse of strengths in family literacy. *Journal of Reading Behavior, 27* (4), 643–661.

Carger, C. L. (1996). *Of borders and dreams: A Mexican-American experience of urban education.* New York: Teachers College Press.

Dahl, K. L., & Freppon, P. A. (1995). A comparison of inner-city children's interpretations of reading and writing instruction in the early grades in skills-based and whole language classrooms. *Reading Research Quarterly, 30,* 50–74.

Delgado-Gaitan, C. (1990). *Literacy for empowerment: The role of parents in children's education.* Philadelphia, PA: Falmer Press.

Delgado-Gaitan, C., & Trueba, H. (1991). *Crossing cultural borders: Education for immigrant families in America.* Philadelphia, PA: Falmer Press.

Dyson, A. H. (1993). *The sociocultural worlds of children learning to write.* New York: Teachers College Press.

Farr, M. (1994). *En los dos idiomas:* Literacy practices among Chicago Mexicanos. In B. J. Moss (Ed.), *Literacy across communities* (pp. 9–47). Cresskill, NJ: Hampton Press.

Freire, P., & Macedo, D. (1987). *Literacy: Reading the word and the world.* South Hadley, MA: Bergin & Garvey Publishers.

Goldenberg, C. (1989). Making success a more common occurrence for children at risk for failure: Lessons from Hispanic first-graders learning to read. In J. B.

Allen & J. M. Mason (Eds.), *Risk makers, risk takers, risk breakers: Reducing the risks for young literacy learners* (pp. 38–78). Portsmouth, NH: Heinemann.

Heath, S. B. (1986). Sociocultural contexts of language development. In *Beyond language: Social & cultural factors in schooling language minority students* (pp. 143–186). Los Angeles, CA: Evaluation, Dissemination and Assessment Center.

Mandel, L. M. (Ed.) (1995). *Family literacy: Connections in schools and communities.* Newark, DE: International Reading Association.

Mills, H., O'Keefe, T., & Stephens, D. (1992). *Looking closely: Exploring the role of phonics in one whole language classroom.* Urbana, IL: National Council of Teachers of English.

Moll, L. C., & Greenberg, J. B. (1990). Creating zones of possibilities: Combining social contexts for instruction. In L. C. Moll (Ed.), *Vygotsky and education* (pp. 319–348). New York: Cambridge.

Mulhern, M. (forthcoming). *Esperanza, Rubén and Yesenia: The emergent literacy of three Mexican immigrant children.* Albany, NY: SUNY Press.

Purcell-Gates, V. (1996). *Other people's words: The cycle of low literacy.* Cambridge, MA: Harvard.

Solsken, J. W. (1993). *Literacy, gender, & work: In families and in school.* Norwood, NJ: Ablex.

Sulzby, E., & Teale, W. (1991). Emergent literacy. In R. Barr, M. L. Kamil, P. Mosenthal, & P. D. Pearson (Eds.) *Handbook of reading research. Volume II* (pp. 727–757). New York: Longman.

Valdés, G. (1996). *Con respeto: Bridging the distances between culturally diverse families and schools.* New York: Teachers College Press.

Vasquez, O. A., Pease-Alvarez, L., & Shannon, S. M. (1994). *Pushing boundaries: Language and culture in a Mexicano community.* New York: Cambridge.

III How Politics Have Shaped Our Thinking and Our Classrooms

Of all issues in our schools that have sparked political interest, two of the most pertinent for teachers of language arts are the phonics–whole language debate and standardized testing. These issues have gained increased attention in the political arena as government representatives argue for a standardized method of reading instruction and improved test scores, and as teachers and teacher educators fight back against this "one-size-fits-all" mentality.

The four pieces in this section foster political awareness and involvement. They inform the reader of these two issues as well as give accounts for how some educators have become actively involved in their communities, as well as their local, state, and provincial governments. Denny Taylor, in a chapter from her book *Beginning to Read and the Spin Doctors of Science,* uncovers the alliance of politicians, journalists, and scientific researchers working in Texas—and elsewhere—to control how reading gets taught. Taylor shows how these groups cooperate in distorting research on whole language instruction in an attempt to promote the big business of basal readers and phonemic awareness instruction.

Constance Weaver supplies us with explicit definitions of whole language and phonics, while Jeff McQuillan analyzes state legislation of reading instruction in California and criticizes the use of standardized test scores in decision making.

Finally, in "Believing in What's Possible, Taking Action to Make a Difference," Ellen Brinkley and others describe the formation of the grassroots group Michigan for Public Education, an organization that promotes education equality and excellence. In addition, she offers suggestions to help educators become more actively involved in strengthening public education.

9 In Which Governor Bush's Business Council Holds a Pre-summit Meeting in Texas

Denny Taylor

In Texas, the discourse of management and control is readily available for us to read in the transcript of the 1996 pre-summit workshop of Governor Bush's Business Council. In the next few pages I will quote from the document, staying as close to the text as I can, but I encourage every educator to read the original transcription to discover firsthand how the ideological tendencies about which Giroux writes "strip literacy from the ethical and political obligations of speculative reason and subjugate it to the political and pedagogical imperatives of social conformity and domination" (p. 149).[1]

"Lack of educator training in how to teach reading is a hurdle that must be cleared," Governor Bush's Business Council states in the foreword to the transcription of the meeting. "Currently, many teacher training programs are not research based. Structured programs that are based on good research offer one solution" (p. 1).

"Most children must be explicitly be [sic] taught to read," the Council continues amorphously. "Teaching and practicing the alphabet, the sounds of letters, decoding and blending are important. Frequent testing of progress is necessary" (p. 1).

Charles Miller, the chairman of Governor Bush's Business Council, opens the meeting. "Good morning. Welcome. . . . I don't want to exaggerate, but I believe the Governor's Reading Initiative could be one of the most important steps towards improving Texas education that we've ever taken. However, it's

---

Reprinted with permission from Chapter 6 of *Beginning to Read and the Spin Doctors of Science* by Denny Taylor. ©1998 by Denny Taylor.

going to take continued and sustained effort by a large part of the
community in Texas to succeed. You could say we're in the beginning
skirmishes of a major battle" (p. 2).

Miller talks for a while, and then he thanks the press. "First I want to offer
special thanks to the people representing the media. The *Houston Chronicle,*
Dallas Morning News, and the *Texas Monthly* are with us today. In our efforts
to reform education, the support from those three publications has been
extremely valuable. They have been positive and constructive. I want to thank
them personally and on behalf of the Governor's Business Council" (p. 3).

The press is part of the spin, and part of the pre-summit workshop,
together with the government representatives and researchers from the
scientific community. Forget neutrality. Forget integrity. Forget accuracy.
Ominous news accounts of illiteracy misrepresent reality, present selective
information, offer worst-case scenarios, and are used to legitimize the claims
of "scientific" studies on phonemic awareness. In 1997 the *Dallas Morning
News* published an article called "Sounding Off" with graphs that look
remarkably like those generated by Foorman and her colleagues. The article
states, "On tests of ability to read words, children with low phonological
awareness (PA) scored below their grade levels and below children with
normal PA. . . . When given specific instruction in phonological awareness,
phonics, and text reading, children who started out with low PA showed
dramatic improvement in their ability to read words." There are no alternate
perspectives presented. In this article all the "experts" agree, including Lyon
of NICHD.

"We're not here for public record in the sense of being newsworthy, but
we are going to publish virtually anything that's said today," Miller says as he
finishes. "I would just encourage you not to hold back during that process
because of that possibility. What we really need is frank, open, clear
discussion of the most hard-hitting and constructive type."

The participants of the pre-summit introduce themselves. Patrick Oxford,
a lawyer in Houston; Marina Ballyntyne,[2] the founding head of the John
Cooper School; Peter O'Donnell, president of the O'Donnell Foundation;
Rosie Zamora, on the Board of Regents of Texas Southern University; Henry
Tatum, associate editor of the *Dallas Morning News* editorial page; David
Langworthy, the opinion page editor for the *Houston Chronicle;* Carolyn
Bacon, from the O'Donnell Foundation; Jim Nelson, chair of the new State
Board of Educator Certification; Jim Ketelson, retired chairman of Tenneco;
Leonel Castillo, assistant to Houston's mayor on educational issues; Beth
Ann Bryan, from the Governor's Business Council; Greg Curtis, the editor of
the *Texas Monthly;* Ed Adams, who among his other credentials is the

president of Texans for Education; Michelle Tobias, special projects counsel for Governor Bush; Margaret La Montagne, senior advisor to Governor Bush; Wanda Watson, principal of Ryan Elementary School; Lenox Reed, director of the Neuhaus Education Center in Houston (which trains teachers in Alphabetic Phonics); Marsha Sonnenberg, consultant in reading and curriculum alignment in the state of Texas; Sandy Kress, president of the Dallas School Board and a consultant to Governor Bush's Business Council; Carmyn Neely, deputy director for statewide initiatives; Mike Moses, Commissioner of Education; Darvin Winick, who we've met before and who is consultant and advisor to Governor Bush's Business Council; Douglas Carnine, professor at the University of Oregon who has long been associated with DISTAR; Jean Osborn, from the Center for the Study of Reading at the University of Illinois, who is associated with the Reading Mastery program, which is the latest version of DISTAR; Barbara Foorman, from the University of Houston and an author of the Scholastic Spelling program; Johnlyn Mitchell, principal of Kramer Elementary School in Dallas; Alda Benevides, principal of E. B. Reyna Elementary School in La Joya; Suzanne Slevinsky, third-grade teacher at Bowie Elementary School at HISD; Felipe Alanis, Associate Commissioner with the Texas Education Agency; Dub Rider, a businessman; and Jodie Jiles, member of the Governor's Higher Education Coordinating Board.

Back to Charles Miller. He tells the participants at the pre-summit that the Governor said, "If the existing programs don't work, get another program." He talks about statistics. "The National Adult Literacy Survey in 1993 found that nearly half of America's adults are poor readers or functionally illiterate." He mentions another study and then continues arbitrarily using statistics. "The overall literacy rate has gradually eroded from 97 percent in 1950 to less than 80 percent today," Miller states. "More than 3 out of 4 that goes on welfare are illiterate, 85 percent of unwed mothers are illiterate, and 68 percent of those arrested were illiterate." He concludes, "Must be some kind of causal effect there." He continues with his statistics.

"No topics are prohibited, no comments should be off the table," Miller ends by reminding the participants, "and we should try to build a record today that can be used to start discussions across the state."

He turns the meeting over to Winick who talks about microphones and tells the participants to speak up. Then he introduces Mike Moses, the Texas Commissioner of Education, who begins with a story.

"My son came home during the last six weeks and his reading grade was not very good. I said, 'Mason, this reading grade is not acceptable. If you don't do better at the end of this six weeks, somebody is going to get a whipping.'" Moses tells the participants what happened next. "He went to school the next day to see his teacher. He went up to her. He said, 'Mrs Dawkins, I don't want to scare you or anything, but my daddy said if my reading grade doesn't come up, somebody is going to get a whipping.' And I had to call her and explain that it was not she that had anything to worry about."

Moses gets serious. "The fact of the matter is we're not doing it very well. We're not doing anywhere near what we need to be doing in Texas in terms of teaching our children to read." Moses talks about scores on the MAT and the TAAS, then about the Governor, NAEP, and TV. "I think the problem is obvious," he says, and he begins his wrap-up with "I don't know that it needs a great deal more elaboration."

Winick introduces Sandy Kress and tells everyone that he will be wearing his Dallas School Board hat. Kress talks about reform in Dallas, and about increasing test scores. He says he wants to talk about what they did before "the experts in reading" speak. He talks about accountability.

"We need to measure student performance," he says. "And there has to be consequences from the performance, particularly the adult performance." Kress elaborates, "We found, for example, all over our district principals who simply were not paying attention to their mission." He praises the Dallas principal who is at the pre-summit. Then he continues. "A principal who is not focused on the Governor's goal to get the youngsters reading by grade 3 is probably going to be a principal of a school that doesn't make a lot of progress with us." He talks some more about principals and then says, "This is at least what we found in Dallas."

Kress is on a roll. "My bad news for those cities across Texas who just offered the TAAS test as a principal means of testing, if you're not testing youngsters K, 1, and 2, and you don't offer a test until the State requires one, at the end of grade 3, I want to suggest to you that you're going to be operating at a school that does not have the diagnostic tools in order to help youngsters grow and know that accountability is taking place and that teachers are performing."

Kress ends by coming back to accountability. "This can be done. This is not as difficult as a lot of things we do, measuring them and holding adults accountable for their growth," he says. "But it's going to take us, as adults and business leaders in every city across Texas, saying, 'This is our mission,' working with a focus, working with our school districts, and making this kind of change take place."

Winick introduces Carmyn Neely, the deputy director of statewide initiatives, who reads from the McGuffey First Eclectic Reader—"Ned is on the box"—before reading from a book she says her granddaughter might read in school this year—"Once in the deepest ocean there was a little fish." She talks about teachers.

"Teaching students to read continues to be tremendously demanding of our educators," she explains. "It involves constantly unpacking our ideas about reading and instruction."

Neely's presentation is conciliatory, deferential, but at one point there is a bite to what she says. "In the early days of America notions about literacy were rather simple and basic," she says. "One source tells us that in the early 1900s, of the 100 children who would start to school at age 7, only 13 would still be there at age 16. The literacy level at that time [that] came close to being universal was fifth-grade level." She ends this thought by stating, "Only very lately has literacy been addressed in classrooms that included young women, learning-disabled students, those students who are physically challenged, where all students read, not just recite, and all students write, in other words, compose, not just copy."

Neely talks about a report that is being written that came out of a meeting that Moses organized. She explains, "So Dr. Moses' group did not aim toward balance by picking and choosing the best from competing theories and practices. This cafeteria approach would sound like the eclecticism advocated during the sixties and seventies. If balance were achieved simply through a pick-and-choose method, there would cease to be either a definable or defensible position to articulate."

Neely states categorically that "balance" means that "[s]tudents engage in decoding and spelling activities through explicit and implicit instruction in developmentally appropriate skills and strategies."

After Neely finishes speaking, Moses talks about "a student who has a second language" who is exempt for two years but in the third year must take the TAAS in English. The question of Hispanic American children taking the TAAS test has been mentioned several times, and he says that the exemption is a real problem and that he is trying "to have a state Board rule that would tighten that up."

Winick introduces the experts. He talks of their "impressive research credentials" and their "illustrious academic records."

"I would like to comment," Winick states, "that we sought out qualified individuals who were serious about the need to pick reading skill development programs and strategies after careful review of experimental findings."

"Our next presenter is Jean Osborn."

The Treacheries of Reading Education

After a short preamble Osborn states, "Let's just focus on beginning reading, which is probably the most controversial topic in education. Lots of people have belief systems about how to help children learn to read. Teachers have belief systems. Researchers—some of them—have belief systems. Some of them have research. Parents have opinions. Professors—they're among the most questionable." Osborn continues for a while and then says, "The problem is lots of children do not learn to read the words very well, and yet the adults go on in this ideological and often very nasty warring with each other about how children should learn to read."

She talks about points of agreement: "oral language knowledge is related to the understanding of printed language"; "learners need lots of good experiences with print"; "and most everyone in the world agrees reading aloud to young children is good." Osborn lists the controversies. She talks about whole language and gets to phonics.[3]

"Teaching the sounds of letters interferes with reading as meaning," she says, stating the controversy. "Now, for those of you unexposed to the treacheries of reading education, this is a big, big item. There are those who say if you say, 'Look, here's an M and it makes the sound "mmm"' you're abstracting meaning from print, you're making it automatic, and you're going to, the more extreme will say, ruin children for reading."

"There are others," Osborn explains, "who say this is a sensible way to teach children to read. Teach them letter names with the sounds the letters make and some procedures for combining them. That's a big argument right there."

Now to the research.

"Systematic phonics instruction is effective. There happens to be a lot of data that supports that, but there happens to also be a lot of people who say it's not necessary or it's damaging to children."

Osborn talks of other reading methods. Of reading by colors or by drawing boxes around words. No kidding. She says, "There's a current view that says different children learn to read in different ways and all you have to do is to find out if a child likes to read in a hot room or a cold room."

She continues with language experience and "Read Along with Uncle Bob," before returning to whole language.

"I don't know specifically how popular whole language is in Texas classrooms, but if it's like most states, I would assume it's swept the state." Osborn gives her hot room/cold room version of whole language, and then she states, "it also discards any organized and grade-level-calibrated basal reading program."

This is, of course, a big problem for researchers who are authors of basal programs. Osborn herself is an author of the Reading Mastery program.

"There are too many casualties," she says. "Let me tell you what these children do. They look earnestly at the teacher, who will give them some advice. They guess. They look at the pictures. They remember. They have all kinds of strategies, some of them excellent, for not dealing with print."

I am neither a whole language educator nor researcher, but I do support those who are, and this is disinformation, propaganda, not even "techo-babble—which would be preferable because at least then we would have to work to deconstruct the spin she's in.

Osborn talks about "research."

"[M]y third caution is that we know something from research and from science about reading," says Osborn, pulling on what Winick called her illustrious academic record. "We have information. We have evidence that has enormous implications toward the teaching of beginning reading." Osborn warms to the hegemonic project. "And I think the time has come in our evolution as reading educators to really take advantage of what science can tell us. So right now I would like to talk about some research-based education for beginning reading. Any questions so far?"

"All right. Let me hold up a couple of things here." Osborn holds up a copy of *Becoming a Nation of Readers*. She encourages everybody to read it. She holds up the summary of Adams's government report, *Beginning to Read*. Osborn calls Adams's book "totally and wonderfully fascinating." Referring to the summary, she says, "We just felt there was such an important message in that book that we wanted to get it out in a form that a lot of people would consider reading." She talks about the reading of isolated words. How adults read, according to Adams. Then she talks about children.

"They have to understand that spoken words can be divided into sounds," she tells the participants in the pre-summit workshop. "Now, a lot of children, young children, do not know that. Study after study can show you that."

Not so.

"There is a high correlation between that kind of knowledge in children coming into kindergarten and ease of learning to read."

That depends on which tests you administer and the synthetic programs you use.

"Because after all, it is the sounds of spoken words that map on to the letter. Right?"

I disagree. Osborn is ignoring linguistic ambiguity. But, even so, in classrooms where children are deeply engaged in developing their own individual and shared literacy configurations, they are continuously engaged in activities that build on their understandings of the relationships between spoken and written language.

"It's not the meaning that's the first level. It is the sounds."

Throw out Piaget, Vygotsky, and Ferreiro.[4] Scrap the work of Dyson. Forget Yetta Goodman. Tear up Ken Goodman's forty years of research. Toss out *Family Literacy, Growing Up Literate, From the Child's Point of View.* Ignore the research on practical intelligence and everyday cognition by Barbara Rogoff and Jean Lave. Get rid of Michael Halliday and, of course, James Wertsch.

"[I]f you're going to say the word Sam by its sounds, 'sss aaa mmm,' you have to have another set of skills, which is to put it back together again," Osborne says. "A lot of children could go 'sss aaa mmm' and the teacher will say, 'What word is it?' and the children will say 'sss aaa mmm' because they don't know how to blend."

Patrick had to write "sssssssssssss" before "un" when he was "blending" sun—I counted the "s's." But he also had to write "eeeeeeeeee" before "gg" when he was blending "egg." Wouldn't this make it ēgg? You might not agree. But I can document ethnographically that while Patrick was having difficulty blending in school, he was writing stories at home with me. Perhaps it has something to do with the activity?

Osborn is stuck on blending. "Teachable," she says. "It's absolutely teachable."

"Now, all this research that Marilyn and others have pooled together, this should make you believe in the alphabetic principle. So often people say, 'Well, there are so many irregular words in English.'" Osborn contends this fact. "Written English is far more regular than not."

Actually, based on the scientific study in the late 1960s of phoneme-grapheme correspondences to improve spelling conducted by, among others, Paul Hanna, John Carroll, Edgar Dale, Harry Levin, and Ruth Strickland, she's got it wrong. In the conclusions to their study, these researchers and their colleagues state that "About half (49+ percent) of all the words in the 17,000+ word corpus" they studied "can be spelled correctly on phonological bases alone." They then state, "To the extent that the corpus is a representative sample of the entire lexicon, this statement can be generalized to hold for the entire lexicon" (p. 122).[5]

These researchers then emphasize that "No member of the research team would advocate that these rules be memorized and used in a *deductive* manner by elementary school children"(p. 123). Later they state, "Complex, abstract understandings require a great deal of previous concrete, multisensory learning" (p. 128). . . . . "[E]xperiences should proceed from the concrete to the abstract" (p. 128). "Furthermore, the lines of evidence that have been presented here suggest that the encoding process of spelling possibly can be learned more readily when children are given the opportunity to discover for themselves that basic structural properties underlie the spellings of many words. Further, children should be given numerous opportunities to apply this knowledge in their writing" (p. 128).

Thus we can state that American English is far more *irregular* than many researchers believe it to be, and we can use this information to ask why they would insist on teaching children to read phonetically.

Back to Osborn.

"So here's a recipe. Learn about teaching sounds and how they relate to symbols. Of course, there's a problem with vowels. Some vowels are, quote, long. Some vowels are short. Some vowels are silent. There are problems with consonant letters that have two sounds. So one of the implications of this is that you don't do it all at once. You have a sequence. You have a plan for teaching this. Blending is essential. Blending is a very important component of beginning reading instruction."

Osborn talks about her experience in a school that was in "big trouble" in Ohio. She says they adopted "a very systematic program of instruction." She tells the pre-summit that in this school they had two language arts sessions in the morning and two in the afternoon.

"They teach reading twice a day. Full reading instruction twice a day," Osborn states. "So two language arts in the morning and two in the afternoon. They gather children with similar needs into groups and classes. They track."

"Book reading is the spare-time activity by design," Osborn states. "I'd walk in last fall, and kids were drawing pictures in their spare time. I said, 'We're not going to have many artists out here. We've got to have readers.'"

If you are like me, reading such statements makes you reach for Maxine Greene. And please excuse the aside if I stop to tell you that one of the teachers with whom I've been talking sent me a short piece by Maxine "to lift my spirits" as I worked on *Spin Doctors*. I cannot call her Greene, because to those she mentors through her writing, she will always be Maxine. In the piece that the teacher sent to me, "What Matters Most," Maxine expresses her concern about the dismissal of the arts by educational reformers. She reminds us that in *Local Cultures* Clifford Geertz writes of "art as a cultural system . . . as wide as social existence and as deep." She also shares a quote from John Dewey. In *The Public and Its Problems,* he writes, "Artists have always been the real purveyors of news, for it is not the outward happening in itself which is new, but the kindling by it of emotion, perception, and appreciation" (p. 35).

"Personal agency, passion, imagination, and a making of meaning: all of these must be part of full engagement with the arts," Maxine tells us, "and it is difficult to accept a call for excellent teaching and 'teaching for America's future' that pays no heed to the awakenings the arts make possible."

The idea that children would be forced to spend most of the morning and most of the afternoon in a direct instruction phonics program and then forced to read is an anathema to me. I think of the five-, six- and seven-year-old children I taught in a "lower working class" community in the East End of London. In our classroom, art was a means of communication, a celebration. We made our own books, wrote stories, and drew pictures. In Spain, where I taught American engineers' children who were too young to be sent away to school, the arts were central to our literate activities. When I was working on my doctorate at Teachers College, a group of kindergarten kids used to come to my house and sit around the kitchen table and paint pictures and write stories. Sometimes their paintings filled the counter tops and spilled onto the floor and stretched out into the front hall, and invariably these paintings were splashed with writing that became integral to the visual composition.

I think of the children in *Family Literacy* and *Growing Up Literate.* I think of Patrick, whose first forays back into the world of print occurred as he tentatively began to draw pictures and then write about what he had drawn. In the Biographic Literacy Profiles Project, we spent years studying what Dyson calls the "symbol weaving" of children. It was impossible for us to interpret their writings without interpreting their drawings. In all of these different settings children learned to read. Irrespective of the social circumstances of their everyday lives, they loved to read stories and they loved to paint pictures. Both were aesthetic and intellectual activities which expanded the boundaries of the children's existence.[6]

Osborn reaches the end of her presentation.

"So I say we get to work on successful research-based and successful practice-based programs," she says. "Thank you."

Just in case the pre-summit participants missed the sales pitch, Margaret La Montagne, senior advisor to Governor Bush asks, "Is that a specific product program, and if so, what is it called?"

"Yes," Osborn replies, unabashedly pushing her own program. "It's Reading Mastery Program, and it goes from first grade."

Other questions follow. "If research is so clearly in favor of things like phonics and clearly not in favor of whole language," an unidentified speaker asks, "why in the world is there such a—"

Osborn interrupts. "It is a mystery to me why we are so reluctant, we as a profession, are so reluctant to take up research."

"Is that a diplomatic answer?" the unidentified speaker queries.

"Well, it's maddening."

"What are you doing about retooling teachers before they become teachers at the university level?" Rosie Zamora asks.

"Good luck."

"Why?"

Osborn hesitates and says she has to be careful. "A lot of professors of education are not really knowledgeable about what goes on in the schools." She talks about professors' romantic notions.

Peter O'Donnell talks about increasing the number of courses in reading at the University of Texas.

Osborn says, "I agree."

The question-and-answer session continues. Winick tries to move the meeting on, but there are more questions. Again it's an unidentified speaker.

"You're not suggesting, are you, it's either-or, either phonics or whole language?" the unidentified speaker asks. "You're not suggesting it's one or the other? Are you?"

"I'm saying at the beginning you'd better be serious about systematic instruction," Osborn responds.

Winick introduces Barbara Foorman, who tells the participants in the pre-summit that her talk follows Osborn's "nicely."

The Design of This Study Is Hopelessly Complex

Foorman talks about NICHD and the Institute's years of research in literacy, research on the alphabetic code, genetics, attention deficit disorders, the etiology of learning disabilities, early intervention, and epidemiological research that shows that girls have as many reading problems as boys. She discusses the epidemiological study and says that the growth of reading achievement was measured on the Woodcock-Johnson. She says, "it is a very excellent test." She talks some more about girls and boys and then gives her definition of reading disabilities.

"Reading disabilities reflect a persistent deficit rather than a developmental lag," she explains. "You need to intervene early because these are deficits in particular areas, not lags. They don't go away without intervention."

She talks about learning disabilities and says they are "conceptually flawed" and "statistically flawed," and she talks about her preference for mathematical growth modeling.

"There's nothing special about reading disabilities," Foorman explains. "It's a continuous distribution. And where you make the cut mark and decide who you're going to serve is largely just your decision on how much money you have and who you can serve. *There is no statistical basis on which you can make that decision*" (emphasis added).

Isn't that exactly what Foorman and her colleagues did? They defined reading disabilities statistically. Go back and take a look at Chapter 4. Their cut-off was at the 25th percentile on the Woodcock-Johnson.

Foorman then gives an Adams definition of reading. She talks about correlations, growth curves, reading achievement, about her handout and the "powerful effect."

"It shows you the critical performance of early successful rapid decoding," she explains, "and the ability to do that kind of decoding is dependent on the ability to segment words and syllables into phonemes."

"Deficits in phonologic awareness reflect the core deficit in dyslexia," she continues, "and the good news, it's treatable."

"Now, in terms of the NICHD Intervention Findings, disabled readers do not readily acquire the alphabetic code due to deficits in phonological processing." Foorman is focused. "Thus, disabled readers must be provided highly structured, intense programs that explicitly teach the application of phonologic rules to print by well-trained teachers."

Foorman talks about "controlling factors," and here's the critical statement.

"Controlling for socioeconomic status, dialect differences mediate the level at which phonology predicts word reading for disabled readers." Foorman makes the statement and moves on, but we need to pause and think about the implications of her statement.

Dialect was not discussed in any of the Foorman studies that I read, and yet it is presented here as a factor that had to be "controlled." In the Foorman studies there were many children speaking many different "dialects" who had to respond to the experimental tasks phonetically. On the pseudoword tasks, the experimenters were given "real" words to guide them with their pronunciation of the pseudowords. Some of the children in the research were in the process of learning American English. How were their interpretations of pseudowords scored? Who determined the correct pronunciation for the African American children? The Asian American children? Or the children from Michigan? New Jersey? Alabama? Indiana?

"And the ethnicity differences turn out to be all in the phonological area and with African American differences in language." Foorman states later in her presentation. She says "ethnicity differences diminished, disappeared over the course of the year by having a good phonological awareness training program."

Whose phonemes? Did Alphabetic Phonics wash the ethnicity differences out? Did the Northern European nursery rhymes get the children to speak like me? Are we talking about first-language loss phonetically?

"When I came to Texas, I was lost," Foorman says. "I had never heard of 'fixin' to go' and 'might ought to should.' It took me five years and I was right in there being a good Texan with my Southeast Texas dialect. And Houston was an interesting place to study. There were a lot of people from Detroit and New Jersey and all over the place and native Texans, and I always have a native Texan on my research project because they need to tell me that *r-e-a-l* on my word list is pronounced *rill, r-i-l-l. I* need that person to help me."

On blending phonemes into "nonwords," who decides whether a child's response is correct or in error? Who decides on the pronunciation of "y-a-s"? The experimenter's pronunciation key says it rhymes with "gas," that "th-u-ng" rhymes with "rung," and "f-ir-t-u-s" with "circus," and "n-i-s-p-a-t with "mistake." I'm presuming that this last one should be "nispate," and that it was a "mistake."

How do you deal with all this dialectically?

"Dialects differ in all aspects to some degree," Ken Goodman wrote in the early 1970s. "Some aspects, vowels for instance, are easily observed while others are more subtle or lost in misconception. Systematic difference often is treated as isolated error."

"Vowel difference is notable in the way speakers of English dialects would pronounce this list," Goodman states, "been, bean, bin, Ben, being. Any two or more of these will be homophones," he writes, emphasizing that some of them will sound alike.

"Dialects of English vary in the number of vowels they use. Furthermore, there is not a consistent correspondence from one dialect to another. The vowel in the following group may be the same or the group may split in two," Goodman adds, "though not consistently for all dialects," and he presents the *list*, "*log, dog, fog, hog,* cog, *bog, frog,* smog, flog, grog, jog." Then, always personable, Goodman writes, "Those italicized rhyme for this writer (the vowel is /ə/) while the others rhyme (the vowel is /a/)."

To emphasize that Foorman's "one native Texan" won't do, let's continue.

"/r/ and to a lesser extent /l/, particularly in the final position, vary considerably in English dialects," Goodman explains. "A speaker from Maine and one from Michigan might hear each other's pronunciation of *media* and *meteor* as exactly opposite."

"Consonants vary less notably than vowels but some variation does exist," he continues. Goodman gives as examples *dis/this* and *nuffin'/nothing*.

My nephews in England say "nuffink."

"Some consonants vary in certain sequences (Etna/Edna) or in clusters (Eas'side/Eastside) or final position (col/cold)."

Goodman then states the problem.

"What complicates dealing with and accepting phonological differences is that there is an artificial phonology, sometimes based on spelling, that confuses many teachers on what is acceptable in any dialect" (pp. 63, 64).

Once again I ask, given this complexity, how do you teach a child to read phonetically? A final quote from Goodman. "No language, and no dialect of any language, is intrinsically superior to any other in coping with any specific area of human knowledge or learning in general" (p. 62). It's important to keep this in mind, especially when we are considering studies that report the elimination of ethnic differences.

Foorman next turns her attention to the Chapter 1 study, the one that has been the center of national attention. She talks about the manipulation of classroom instruction.

"[T]hey either got a direct instruction program which consists of phonological awareness, phonics, and text reading; an embedded phonics program, which practiced phonetic patterns in context. I'll call them spelling patterns from now on. Or, a whole language program, which focused on a print-rich environment."

"The design of this study is hopelessly complex," Foorman says. "If just looking at this gives you a headache, you'll know how I feel every day trying to monitor this."

She gives a definition of whole language.

"Within this whole language philosophy, students are given a wide variety of opportunities to read, write, learn and construct meaning within a meaningful context. In this interactive, student-friendly learning environment, learning is not only active and meaningful, but also fun, with the ultimate goal being to instill the desire for life-long learning."

Then Foorman deftly confounds her own study.

"I don't know what it means," she says. Then she tries to recover what she has just said. "I mean, my project director is a committed whole language person."[7]

By her own admission, Foorman conducted a study comparing training in phonemic awareness and whole language and she doesn't know what whole language means. Problematic? Definitely.

She provides a context for the study.

"When the study started, the superintendent was fired for her whole language belief. The school board took over curriculum decisions and decided in the middle of our study that we should stop the study because in NIH when a drug works, you stop it, and everybody gets the good drug." Foorman then explains, "And they had already decided that phonics worked, so they wanted the whole district to have the phonics program. But we persisted and continued the study, but it's very difficult to do good research in these settings. There are too many stakeholders who know the answers before you start."[8]

Once again the study is confounded and biased. Again, forget neutrality, because the study lacks a key ingredient of experimental research, and that is objectivity. If the superintendent is fired for her whole language philosophy, what chance do the teachers have of dealing with the school board's negativity? How can they participate in a study when the principal researcher doesn't understand the way they teach?

Later in her presentation Foorman talks about the two whole language groups as she shares the results of her study on a graph, and for the sake of making a cohesive presentation let's take a look at what she says.

"There are two groups of whole language. There's the group that we saw and we trained, and then there's a control group from the district that was actually the lowest SES [socioeconomic status] group, which isn't a good control. But the amazing thing is how similar the two bottom lines are."

How can a "control group" be drawn from the lowest SES group? By definition, a "control" group, if you agree with this type of research, must be drawn at random from the entire population, in exactly the same manner as the "treatment group" is drawn. Otherwise you're comparing apples with oranges and any comparative analysis is meaningless.

It's time to turn to Robert Rosenthal and his 1960s research on pygmalion effects. Rosenthal upset experimental researchers by conducting experiments in which he found that students lived up or down to their teachers' expectations. In 1973 Rosenthal presented another series of studies to support his theories. In one he stated, "In spite of the fact that all experimenters read the *same* instructions to their subjects, we found that they still managed to convey their expectations" (p. 56).[9]

Rosenthal writes of one study in which the teachers of Headstart children were told that they could expect poor performance from the "below average children" and exceptional performance from their "bright children." There were in fact no measurable differences between the children. The teachers and children were then observed.

"The teachers worked much harder when they believed they had a bright child," Rosenthal writes. "In a unit on word learning for example, 87 percent of the teachers of the 'bright' children taught eight words or more words." But then making his case he states, "[O]nly 13 percent of the teachers of the 'dull' children tried to teach them that many. Not surprisingly, 77 percent of the 'bright' children learned five or more words, but only 13 percent of the 'dull' children learned that many" (p. 62).

Rosenthal emphasizes, "The expectations may be translated into explicit, overt alterations in teaching style and substance."

"There are very large teacher variability in these studies," Foorman states, "and we are going to average the growth curves for children in each of those methods to answer the question of whether the direct instruction program reduces teacher variability."

"One alternate possibility, *vis-a-vis* teacher knowledge and competence," Lyon writes in his *Education Week* official version of Foorman's study, "that could account for the failure of the whole language approach to enhance reading-skill development in the Houston study is that many College of Education professors may themselves not be fully prepared in their understanding of reading development and reading disorders, and that the information passed on to their students is equally limited and fragmentary in theory, content, and application.

"In short, the conventional wisdom imparted to whole-language teachers during their preparation may not be very wise and is sadly conventional." Lyon is in a tale-spin. "While this may seem to be a harsh interpretation, our studies of teacher-preparation practices indicate that it is accurate."

The tale gets taller and he digs himself in. "It is also important to note that the children in the literature-based groups were taught and assessed according to whole-language philosophy and principles." Apparently Lyon is being disingenuous, because the test reported by Foorman and her colleagues was the Woodcock-Johnson. "Portfolio assessments were carried out frequently during the year, as were continuous observations of oral reading of predictable texts." The children might have been in whole language classrooms and their teachers might have practiced portfolio assessment, but Foorman did not include portfolio assessment in her study. How could she? She is not trained in the disciplined observational techniques used to systematically document children's early literacy learning, and it is highly questionable whether she has the analytic training to interpret the complexities of the children's literacy configurations that are revealed by this approach to instructional assessment.

"Because deficits in phonological skill are prime candidates for what is specific about specific reading disability," Foorman and her colleagues write in the NICHD proposal referring to a 1989 paper by Foorman, "measurement of phonological awareness is central to the prediction of growth in reading and spelling skills as well as achievement outcomes" (p. 57).

In the Chapter 1 study, teachers must have been aware that Foorman and her colleagues were advocates of phonemic awareness and phonics. Other studies had already taken place. Foorman and her colleagues appear to genuinely believe that "reading disabilities," as they define them, are caused by deficits in phonemic awareness skills. Consequently, they used the Woodcock-Johnson word and pseudoword tests—which are essentially tests of phonemic awareness—as their measure of "reading achievement." They trained children with synthetic phonemic awareness drills. Four times during the year they tested the children with their own phonemic awareness pseudowords, and as tests teach, when they tested them again on the Woodcock-Johnson, the children were better at decoding a few more pseudowords.

Teachers aren't daft. They understand the old "raisins in a bottle" routine, even if the researchers don't. Already disparaged in the district, the superintendent was sacked, and the pressure was on to include more synthetic phonics and phonemic awareness training in the kindergarten and first-grade classrooms. It's impossible to imagine that the whole language teachers were not mindful of the researchers' bias. They must have been aware of their unfavorable position, and it's entirely possible that they transmitted their response to the situation to their students. Similarly, there is a strong possibility that the expectations of the teachers of the phonological awareness and phonics treatments affected the way in which they worked with the children.

In addition, some of the poorest children in the district were in the whole language "control" group, and Rosenthal emphasizes that the pygmalion dilemma is doubly significant for children who are poor and for African American children.

"Teachers were much less favorable to the lower-class children than they were to middle-class children," Rosenthal states, quoting another study. "[L]ow income children who had *higher* IQ's [than middle income children] tended to have teachers who viewed them *negatively,* and this was especially true for lower-income children who were black" (p. 63).

Once again Foorman's study is confounded. Who knows what Foorman was actually measuring? Maybe what she did just confirms the ways in which we treat children who are poor and African American children. The researchers didn't expect them to achieve, and this was transmitted through the teachers to the children.

"The two whole language groups' growth rates are bunching around zero," Foorman says. "Zero growths."

Under these circumstances we have to ask: What did the researchers do to these children? Zero growth? That's simply not possible unless there was something seriously wrong with the experimental design, with the ways in which the study was conceptualized and organized, with the tests that were administered—what Rosenthal refers to as "the prejudice of stunted expectations."

Let's backtrack for a moment and pick up Foorman's presentation as she talks about the use of Open Court as one of the treatments.

"Just a word why we use that program," she tells the pre-summit participants. "We reviewed the literature. We were going to use the Reading Mastery program many know here as DISTAR because the literature supported that program with children of low socioeconomic status."

Foorman's presentation is disorganized here but I will present it exactly as it appears in the transcript.

"This is a brand new program" (I presume referring to Open Court). "I didn't know about it. But I called my friend, Marilyn Adams, and I said, 'Help. I'm not allowed to use DISTAR,' which is what happened. In the eleventh hour before the grant proposal was signed off the district said I couldn't use it. However, they said I could use Open Court because they were using Open Court math, but I had to pay for it myself.

"Well to equip 18 classrooms and teacher training would have cost me close to $100,000. NIH doesn't have the money. I certainly don't in my checkbook. So I called my friend Marilyn Adams and I said, 'Help. What am I to do?'

"And she said, 'Well I happen to know of a program you might try.'"

The program was Open Court, and of course Marilyn Jager Adams is one of the program's authors.

So, here's the question. Who paid for Open Court? Not the school district. Not NIH. Not Foorman. So, who paid? The basal company that publishes and profits from the adoption of the program?

On the title page of "Early Interventions for Children with Reading Problems," in which they present a synthesis of all five studies, Foorman and her colleagues thank "Open Court Publisher for providing materials and trainers." In the description of the Chapter 1 study the experimenters state, "Open Court trained the teachers delivering the DI curriculum as well as one of our research staff members so that she could monitor the teachers during the year."

Then in the "Research Update" Foorman, writing apparently on her own, states, "The fact that Open Court helps economically disadvantaged, low achieving children to perform near the national average is very impressive."

The Marlboro Man meets Joe Camel. How did reading research become such a corrupt business?

"The results make a strong positive statement for teachers using the Open Court system," Mary Kay Simpson of SRA/McGraw-Hill writes in a letter to the superintendent of the school district in which Foorman's studies took place. She encloses a copy of a memo from Mike Moses, the Commissioner of Education who is at Governor Bush's pre-summit, which announces that "the second year of funding for *Academics 2000: First Things First,* the Texas Goals 2000 initiative, was approved by the U.S. Department of Education." Mary Kay Simpson, representing the publisher of Open Court, reminds the superintendent that government funds "are available."

Winick next introduces Douglas Carnine. I have never heard or read a presentation quite like Carnine's, and I will present excerpts without commentary. Once again I urge you to read the original transcript which was distributed and is a part of the public record.

We've Got to Get Straight and Help Educators Get Straight That We're Going to Build a New Culture

Carnine focuses on procedures.

"Educators are hooked on procedures. They're not hooked on results. That's the challenge," Carnine states. "What we have to find are programs that work that produce results with kids."

"We've got to get straight and help educators get straight that we're going to build a new culture that is performance dominated, not philosophies, and not procedures."

He talks about a "billion-dollar study in 1990 dollars" that compared reading methods and of the superior performance of direct instruction.[10] He talks about different methods, then focuses on child-centered approaches to reading instruction.

"When we don't use research and we don't know how to provide services that make a difference, we're going to let the child figure it out," Carnine explains. "This will change, but it will only change with leadership from people such as yourselves that help education become a performance-oriented culture, because it will not change from within. The incentives are not there. And the know-how is not there."

He talks about one method that works. The unnamed program must be DISTAR, with which he is closely associated.

"Now, fortunately, there was one approach included in this massive study that was very structured, very intensive, and very academically oriented, and there were very strong and very positive results."

He talks about the results. He talks about children in first, second, and third grade with low IQs and the gains they made. Then he says that the scores for kids with high IQs also went up.

"We actually don't want to close the learning gap," Carnine explains. "Don't get caught on closing the learning gap or you'll create problems for public education."

"What happened as a basis of this research? Well there were reasonably sized projects in Chicago, Houston, Dallas, San Diego, New York City. But you know what happened? Structured teaching fell out of favor. All programs were closed down."

He tells the pre-summit what happened. He says in California a language arts specialist taught a child with Down Syndrome to read. He explained that a curriculum specialist listened to her read.

"And you know what her response was?" Carnine asks. "The curriculum specialist said, 'Yeah, but you taught her how to read.' That's frightening. That's right."

"Now, there are three things that I think are very important to keep in mind. These are all points that you need to help educators do. First, get it straight. What works? What do we know about effective instruction? The inspiring part of this meeting is you didn't bring in educational innovators. That's why I'm happy to be here. You brought in people who can deliver results. That's the new message. That's the new culture."

"Do not underestimate the difficulties of getting things to work on a broad scale. And, finally, keep it straight. You have to set up a safeguard to prevent the educational establishment from wiping out effective programs and replacing them with new fads, such as happened 20 years ago after the release of the data I described."

"Unfortunately, there's no other field where we do such important work and there are absolutely no safeguards or controls."

This is a point on which Carnine and I agree, even if tangentially.

"There needs to be ways in which the profession figures out what it knows and acts on that knowledge. One thing that most people usually don't realize is that, unlike other professions, teachers cannot be sued for malpractice. And the reason for that is that the courts have ruled that educators don't know anything. That's true. There's no tort claim.

"We've got to recognize that in education it's not simply a won't-do problem. A lot of times it's a can't-do problem. These schools really don't know how to fix themselves. They need help. You've got to give them help that will work. We can't send in any more fads."

He talks about state assessment in Texas.

"Now, here's two pieces of advice. If you want to level the playing field on TAAS. They're not easy to do. First you don't test grade-mates, you test age-mates. Then all advantages of retaining kids to inflate scores are gone.

"Second, you multiply the school score by the percent of kids who took the test. Very simple. Very controversial. But what it does, it excludes all advantages for retaining kids and it excludes all advantages for exempting kids."

He talks about report cards.

"The report card I'm recommending for California is quite simple. You get the scores for your kids, and right above it you get the scores for an average of 15 percent of the highest scores in the state."

He talks about high-performing schools.

"Again, if you look at modern management, the idea is not to punish the employees. The idea is to make those employees as productive, as profitable as they can be.

"Now many educators will object to this notion of copying high-performing schools, but let me tell you an example. Let's say I'm running down the concourse to get a plane. I'm almost late, and I drop. The next thing I know, I wake up and I'm in the operating room and the heart surgeon is there and he's going to open up my heart. And he says, 'I'm not a typical surgeon. I do not copy the open-heart surgery processes that have been validated hundreds and hundreds of times. I am creative. I am going to do something new with you.'

"The hallmark of a profession is knowing when and what to copy. That's it," Carnine says, having made his case. "I want things very routine, professional and routine."

He discusses his credentials.

"My training was not as an educator. I was trained as an experimental psychologist."

He talks about England. Russia. Strategies of infiltration and subversion.

"You have to be very careful in terms of the people you appoint and make sure that they are going to share and value this new culture of results-oriented.

"Just be aware that there is an understandable struggle about what shall prevail in education and what the rules shall be, and that was the choice I had to make—either change the rules or get out of the business.

"I appreciate the opportunity to be here today because you have the influence and the intelligence to understand the need to change the rules and do something about it, and I hope that I can be part of that process. Thank you."

Presentations from three educators followed, but they were not included in the transcript of the pre-summit meeting. No explanation is provided of why their presentations were excluded. We can only surmise the reason.

Miller sums up.

"I'd like the group to know that we didn't, let's say, cherry-pick the experts to lean one way or the other. We did look for research or substantial backing for people's opinions or concepts, in other words, that there was scientific, quantitative or research backing for their opinions. That's why we ended up with the folks we had.

"The encouraging part is we know what needs to be done," Miller tells the group. "The discouraging part is that our school system seems to resist proven practices and ignores the lack of achievement. Most energies are not directed toward improvement. So that's a big problem.

"Challenges that we can hear out of this meeting today is that it's important to build awareness and acceptance. The Governor's initiative seems to be going well, but it's very important that we keep momentum.

"Any of us that have worked in the area of changing education, education reform, whatever you want to call it, know that entrenched interests make that difficult. So we need to move to a research-based, accountability-driven system. That's the way to do it.

"We have to reorient. We have to help reorient a large number of educators who are poorly informed about reading skills development."

Teaching Reading Has Become the Task of the United States' Conservative Generals and Their Subaltern Intellectuals

Gramsci writes about a certain type of "intellectuals" whose fortunes are linked to industry. He calls them "subaltern[11] officers in the army" who carry out the plans of the "industrial general staff." He says "some intellectuals become more and more identified with the industrial general staff," and that sometimes the intellectuals reach a point where they think "they *are* the State." Gramsci writes that when this happens there can be "important consequences" and "unpleasant complications" for those who live in the State.

It's as if Gramsci had just visited Texas.

Teaching children to read has always been a part of the struggle for democracy, a human rights issue. But recently teaching reading has become the task of the United States' right-wing generals, such as those in Governor Bush's Business Council, and their subaltern intellectuals, who, together with the publishers of basal reading programs, are exercising power through constituting alliances and winning consent for their hegemonic project.

First, speaking for Governor Bush as a member of his "general staff," Miller establishes his political authority. "The Governor said, 'If the existing programs don't work, get another program,'" he tells the pre-summit. Then he expresses his concern for the erosion of the national literacy rates from 97 percent in 1950 to less than 80 percent today. Untrue, but a good spin.[12] Moses, another member of the governor's general staff, establishes that there is also a local problem. "The fact of the matter is that we are not doing very well." Kress, a member of the lower echelon, but still in a position of considerable authority, elaborates, "We found, for example, all over our district, principals who simply were not paying attention to their mission." He talks of schools without the diagnostic tools to "help youngsters grow," or for "accountability to take place," or for the general staff to know that teachers "are performing."

Kress talks about holding teachers accountable. The teachers in the hegemonic project are, as Giroux puts it, "the clerks." They are low-paid paper-pushers who "know nothing" according to Carnine, and are "variables" to be "reduced" according to Foorman. But they must nonetheless be held accountable, according to Kress, who states, "It's going to take all of us, as adults and business leaders across Texas, saying, 'this is our mission,' working with our school districts, making this kind of change take place." From this perspective, teachers are not even adults, because it's the "adults" who are going to make the changes and hold the teachers accountable. So the teachers will be damned if they do and damned if they don't. If children don't have high reading scores when the generals test them, it will be the teachers' fault. If the children score well, then it will be in spite of the teachers, because the generals and their subalterns have controlled "teacher effects" and reduced them to a "know nothing variable."

The subaltern intellectuals then make sure of the teachers' compliance in this impossible situation by stating categorically and with absolute authority that the artificial programs that they are promoting are supported by the indisputable findings of the "true scientific method." In her presentation, Osborn, as a subaltern intellectual, supports the generals by disparaging and distorting more democratic approaches to reading instruction. Then with a one-two punch she KOs more holistic approaches by comparing them learning to read by colors and with reading in a hot or cold room.

The way is then clear for her to introduce her own "scientific" version of how children should be taught to read. "We know something from research and from the science of reading," she says. "We have information. We have evidence." By using "science," Osborn fulfills her role as subaltern, while at the same time she ensures that the links with the publishers of basal reading programs are maintained as she highlights the four-times-a-day language arts use of Reading Mastery, the reading program of which she is an author. Foorman then adds to the "science" by talking about "deficits," "lags," "controlling factors," and "powerful effects," before she plugs Open Court, the program that Adams, her "good friend," co-authored.

In case there is any dissent, the subaltern intellectual who talks as if he is the state proclaims the new culture. Carnine tells the generals on the Business Council that they have to "get it straight" and "keep it straight." He reminds them that "[w]e actually don't want to close the learning gap." He talks of the "new culture" of "people who can deliver results." He says that's the "new message," and he cautions the generals about educators' "strategies of infiltration," "subversion," and the "understandable struggle about what shall prevail." Carnine cautions the generals as he expounds the virtues of the "new culture of results."

"Just be aware that there is an understandable struggle about what shall prevail in education and what the rules shall be," he says, as he deftly invalidates all other approaches to reading instruction and promotes his own commercial program. Ingratiatingly, he talks about the intelligence of the generals in understanding "the need to change the rules," and presents himself as a willing candidate to assist them in making the necessary changes.

Osborn, Foorman, and Carnine are or have worked as consultants for the state of Texas. However, I've been told that their actual job positions are being "kept anonymous."

Conflicts of Interest and Ethical Problems Involved in Researchers Publishing Findings Which Support Commercial Programs That Provide Financial Incentives

Make no mistake about it, for many researchers, teaching children to read is a way of making money, a lucrative business, a commercial enterprise. This is fine as long as we know of their affiliations with publishers when we evaluate their research findings. It doesn't necessarily mean that their findings are tainted, but this possibility exists, and educators who read and perhaps use their research findings should be able to make that judgement for themselves. Public disclosure is of critical importance so that research can be reviewed for possible bias, because the financial incentives, which can be enormous, create the potential for serious conflicts of interest.

I suspect that there are very few teachers or members of the general public who are aware of just how much money can be at stake. To give you an example, several years ago a well-known literacy researcher and whole language pedagogist was offered $250,000 to work for a basal publisher. The researcher refused, but as you can imagine, with children in college putting the telephone receiver down was not an easy thing to do.

In years past I've also received calls from publishers of basals, but I've always said no, and no money has ever been mentioned. However, last year I received a call from the Early Childhood Division of Scholastic inviting me to be a guest at their annual advisory board meeting in New York, and as I have been impressed with Scholastic's publication of children's books and by their early childhood magazines, I agreed to go. Unfortunately, it wasn't until I visited the exhibits at the International Reading Association's Annual Convention that I realized that Scholastic is now the publisher of a basal reading program, and also that the company is heavily invested in the publication of synthetic materials to systematically train children in phonemic awareness. My first impulse was to cancel my participation in the meeting, but I decided to go and share my concerns at the meeting about the research on phonemic awareness and to explain why the research is extremely problematic. This I did; however, for ethical reasons, I declined the $3,000 honorarium for my attendance at the meeting. Those at Scholastic who had invited me to participate in the advisory board meeting did not question my decision. They expressed their willingness to work with me to choose books to be paid for with this money to send to Letta Mashishi in South Africa for the parenting center she is trying to establish for families living in Soweto, and to Red River Parish in Louisiana, where the conditions of the schools in which children are educated are worse than you will find in any other supposedly "enlightened" industrialized nation.

I want to emphasize that, just as I would defend any researcher's right to work with a basal publisher, I would also defend the right of basal publishers to produce these commercial programs. Similarly, I hope researchers and publishers alike will defend my right to dispute the research findings, to raise objections to the manner in which the research was conducted, to question the role of basal publishers, to point out the possible conflicts of interest and ethical problems involved in researchers making claims and publishing findings which support commercial programs in which they or their colleagues have financial interest, and to caution people about making inaccurate references to the indefensibly flawed research findings of some of the studies on phonemic awareness.

If research on reading is to be fairly evaluated, full public disclosure is essential. In the financial community, public disclosure is a legal requirement, and investment bankers and major brokerage houses have to disclose their vested interests when making recommendations, or their licenses would be revoked. Similarly, news organizations such as *Time* and *Newsweek* routinely disclose their parent companies' vested interests when the company might stand to gain from the publicity resulting from an article in one of their newsmagazines. If medical researchers are funded by pharmaceutical companies, then professional ethics demand that such funding be disclosed when the research findings are published in the *New England Journal of Medicine* or the *Journal of the American Medical Association*. The *Reading Research Quarterly* has no such requirement, and unfortunately the same standards of professional ethics do not apply.[13] In fact, in the past, editors of the journal have also been paid by publishing companies for their work as basal authors.

Now that we are out of the quagmire of the pre-summit meeting of Governor Bush's Business Council in Texas, let's pull together the various threads of the arguments that I've presented. If you recall, Grossen writes that the usual nature of research in education is to present untested hypotheses as proved theories, but that in a true scientific paradigm, theories are tested by doing everything to try to prove the theory incorrect. The same applies to scientific arguments. Perhaps the events taking place in Texas are anomalous, and maybe there is no hegemonic project. After we've visited the state legislature in North Carolina, where I'll develop the arguments further, I'll let you decide. But first let's tie some of the loose ends together.

Notes

1. The unedited transcript of the pre-summit meeting of Governor Bush's Business Council was distributed at the Governor's first Reading Summit which took place in Austin, Texas, on April 26, 1996.

2. In the transcript Marina Ballyntyne's name also appears as Marina Ballyntine.

3. Once again I urge you to read the original transcript—not the edited version—to read the complete presentations of Osborn, Foorman, and Carnine.

4. In an article entitled "The Creation of Context in Joint Problem-Solving," James Wertsch, Norris Minick, and Flavio Arns discuss the work of Piaget and Vygotsky, and they draw attention to the important distinctions between the social theories of these researchers.

It is important to emphasize here that while the theories of both Vygotsky and Piaget are excluded from theoretical consideration by the advocates of systematic, explicit instruction in phonemic awareness and phonics, their social theories of learning are quite different. Wertsch, Minick, and Arns refer to the research of Piaget as "[t]he most important individualistic theory in modern developmental cognitive psychology," and they note that Piaget, "examined social activity solely from the perspective of how it influences the individual's development" (p. 152). Writing of Vygotsky's social perspective theory, on the other hand, these authors state, "he considered social factors to play a central role in explaining ontogenetic change, and he recognized that the nature and evolution of these factors cannot be explained on the basis of a set of principles relating only to the individual" (p. 153).

As a point of interest, Ferreiro was a student of Piaget, and she continues to work within the Piagetian tradition although her research is distinctively her own.

5. In the report of the study on phoneme-grapheme correspondences directed by Paul Hanna, reference is made to the study of the alphabetic nature of American-English orthography by Ernest Horn. Horn analyzed and noted:

1. More than one-third of the words in a standard reference work on the pronunciation of American English showed more than one accepted pronunciation.

2. Most sounds can be spelled in many ways, one spelling not being sufficient to call it the most 'regular' spelling.

3. Over one-half of the words in a conventional dictionary of American English contain silent letters, and about one-sixth contain double letters when only one letter is actually sounded.

4. Most letters spell many sounds, especially vowels.

5. Unstressed syllables are especially difficult to spell.

6. In the Biographic Literacy Profiles Project, we shared the work of Gunter Grass in *Show Your Tongues*. Writing about it in *Teaching without Testing*, I state, "it is one of the most socially significant examples of symbol weaving that I have so far encountered, just as the illustrated poems of William Blake are artistically/ linguistically significant and Benoit Mandelbrot's *The Fractal Nature of Geometry is* scientifically significant." Then, speaking specifically about the project, "Our observations of print in everyday settings support the need we feel to extend the ways in which we think about the symbolic representations constructed by children. The more we focus our attention upon their productions, the more convinced we have become that our classrooms must be multimedia centers that encourage the exploration of complex symbolic systems" (p. 69).

7. The definition of whole language used by Foorman in the Houston study is not the definition of whole language used by the district, and the project director was not from the district.

8. As of March 1998 the district in which Foorman and her colleagues conducted their research has not adopted Open Court and continues to use a wide variety of approaches and methods to teach reading.

9. Robert Rosenthal's "The Pygmalion Effect Lives" was published in *Psychology Today* in 1973.

10. The project to which Carnine refers was Project Follow Through. His interpretation of the project is challenged in Chapter 14 of *Spin Doctors,* which focuses on the events taking place in California.

11. The 1914 Chambers English Dictionary gives the following descriptions for subaltern: sub'al-tern or su-bal'tern: *adj* a subordinate. - *n*: an officer in the army under the rank of captain.

12. At the beginning of Chapter 14, on California, you will find some alternative perspectives on literacy rates in the United States.

13. In the November 1997 issue of *Worth,* there is an article on Intel. At the end of the article there is a statement which begins in bold caps which states: **"FULL DISCLOSURE:** A *few editorial employees at* Worth *own modest positions in Intel stock, the result of purchases made before this special report was conceived. No purchases were made while this project was in preparation. Under the magazine's conflict-of-interest policy, no employee may acquire shares of a security slated for mention in the magazine. Employees are also required to hold any stock noted in* Worth *at least 30 days past the date that subscribers receive the magazine. None of the senior editors with a hand in this project, including the editor-in-chief, owns shares in Intel"* (p. 144).

It's time that academic journals were required to make similar disclosures of their authors' associations with basal publishers.

References

Dewey, John. (1927). *The public and its problems.* New York: Holt.

Giroux, Henry A. (1988). *Teachers as intellectuals: Toward a critical pedagogy of learning.* Granby, MA: Bergin & Garvey.

Goodman, Kenneth. (1974). Urban dialects and reading instruction. In Joseph P. Kender (Ed.), *Teaching reading: Not by decoding alone* (pp. 61–75). Danville, IL: Interstate Printers and Publishing.

Hanna, Paul R., Hanna, Jean S., Hodges, Richard E., & Rudorf, Jr., Edwin H. (1996). *Phoneme-grapheme correspondences as cues to spelling improvement.* Washington: U.S. Government Printing Office.

Rosenthal, Robert. (1973, September). The Pygmalion effect lives. *Psychology Today,* 56–63.

Taylor, Denny. (1990). Teaching without testing: Assessing the complexity of children's literacy learning. *English Education* 22(1), 4–74. Reprinted in 1993 in *From the child's point of view.* Portsmouth, NH: Heinemann.

Wertsch, James V., Minick, Norris, & Arns, Flavio J. (1984). The creation of context in joint problem-solving. In Barbara Rogoff & Jean Lave (Eds.), *Everyday cognition: Its development in social contexts.* Cambridge, MA: Harvard University Press.

10 A Note on Terms: Conceptualizing Phonics and Whole Language

Constance Weaver

Both phonics and whole language are sometimes characterized as approaches to reading, especially by the media. In truth, neither one is. Phonics is less than a complete approach to reading, while whole language is fundamentally much more—a research-based theory of learning and teaching, which gives rise to certain kinds of practices in helping children develop literacy, but is not confined to reading and writing. Two other terms used frequently in this volume also require some definition: phonological awareness and phonemic awareness.

Let us start with the least familiar terms, phonological and phonemic awareness. *Phonological awareness* refers to awareness of the sound system of the language and, more specifically, to units of sound within the language. In order of descending size, these include syllables; the major parts of syllables (onsets and rimes, which are defined elsewhere in the book); and phonemes, the sounds that we adults have learned to hear as separate within words. Sometimes the more inclusive term phonological awareness is used as synonymyous with phonemic awareness, awareness of the "separate" sounds in words. Hearing individual phonemes is not an easy task—nor, even, is hearing the "separate" words in a sentence. Take, for instance, "I'm going to go," which is often pronounced /ahm gunna go/ or even as one giant word, /ahmunnago/ (slant lines are used to enclose attempts at indicating pronunciation). Or take "What do you want?", which is often pronounced in two word-like segments, /wadduhyu want?/. Hearing the "separate" sounds within words can be even more difficult, especially with

---

Reprinted from *Reconsidering a Balanced Approach to Reading,* edited by Constance Weaver.

the shorter vowel sounds. For example, the "a" sounds in *bat* and *bank* are not really identical, even though we adults have typically learned to think of them as a single sound. When researchers and educators talk about developing children's phonemic awareness, they are talking about developing children's ability to hear such sounds, and particularly to analyze words into their "separate" sounds.

Sometimes phonemic awareness is considered to be part of phonics. Basically, phonics is the relationship between the spelling system of the language (the orthographic system) and the sound system (the phonological system) (see K. Goodman, 1993). Thus when we speak of phonics relationships, we are talking about correspondences between sounds and letters, or more often between sound patterns and letter patterns. Since one needs to be able to hear the "separate" sounds of the language in order to make connections between single letters and sounds, phonemic awareness is required; thus, phonemic awareness is sometimes included in the term "phonics." Other educators keep the terms separate because phonemic awareness can be taught through oral activities only, as well as through reading itself and through activities with written language. They keep it separate also because phonemic awareness correlates highly with standardized test scores.

The term "phonics" is used in other ways, too, depending upon the writer's purposes. For example, I talk about "phonics knowledge," by which I usually mean a functional knowledge of letter/sound patterns that is not necessarily conscious, but that readers can and do use in processing both familiar and unfamiliar print words. Derived from actual reading and writing as much or more than from any direct instruction in phonics, a functional knowledge of phonics is much more complex than what can reasonably be taught. A functional knowledge of phonics is typically derived from our knowledge of words that all too often represent alternative pronunciations of the same letters. For example, what about the various pronunciations of "a," as in *cake, above, bat, bar, father, awe* (which is not different from the "a" in *father*, in some dialects)? What about the various pronunciations of "ea," as in *treat, sweat* (the two most common pronunciations), but also *great, heart,* and the ambiguous *lead*? Or *cove, love, move,* and the ambiguous *dove*? Or *slow, grow,* and *know,* versus *cow, plow,* and *now*? Consonants are much more stable in pronunciation, though "c" and "g" at the beginnings of words are usually pronounced one way if certain vowels follow, and another way if other vowels follow. The "th" in *think* is not the same as the "th" in *this*. And what about the "ph" in *telephone* versus *telegraph*? The "s" in *sun* and *suggestion,* versus *sugar* and *sure*? Or the "c" in *medicine* and *medical*? Part of our functional knowledge about phonics is the knowledge, commonly unconscious more than conscious, that there is often more than one relationship between letters and sounds.

It should be clear even from this brief description of phonics that we must use grammar (syntax) and meaning (semantics) as we read, plus everything we know, in trying to make sense of texts. Thus phonics is by no means a complete approach to reading, however phonics may be defined. Phonics refers to only one of the language cueing systems, and readers need to learn to attend to and orchestrate all of them: phonics (the relationships between the orthographic and the phonological systems), syntax, semantics, plus prior knowledge and experience as well. Teaching phonemic awareness and letter/sound relationships is not the same as teaching children how to read.

Whole language, too, is often misunderstood. It is often assumed to be merely a method of teaching children to read, or to read and write. However, whole language has become a full-fledged, though still evolving, theory of learning and teaching that guides instructional decision making. It exemplifies a constructionist view of learning, according to which concepts and complex processes are constructs of the human brain; therefore, research suggests, the greater the intellectual and emotional involvement in learning, the more effectively the brain learns, uses, and retains what is learned. From this basic theory of learning derive other whole language principles: not only that people learn best when actively involved in learning, but the corollary that making many of one's own decisions about what to read, write, and learn will often generate greater involvement and thus deeper learning. Three other principles especially important to whole language are (1) that collaboration and support often enable individual children to do their personal best; (2) that children will not all learn the same things, much less learn them at the same time, no matter how we teach; (3) and that educational assessment of learning should both focus on and promote continued learning. Given these principles, it follows that children will learn to read and write by being supported in actually reading and writing whole texts—not by being required to do limited activities with bits and pieces of language. Given these whole language principles, it also follows that less proficient readers, writers, and learners can still engage in the same kinds of challenging educational experiences as their more proficient classmates; they will simply need more support—for example, in reading and writing whole texts that interest them. In whole language classrooms, children with less developed reading and writing skills are not consigned to do isolated skills work. They still engage in "authentic" reading and writing, though with/of less sophisticated texts and with more support, as needed. They are given help developing needed skills and strategies in the context of reading and writing meaningful, interesting texts. For a deeper understanding of whole language, see such references as Church, 1994; Altwerger, 1991; Gursky, 1991; Monson & Pahl, 1991; K. Goodman, 1989; Y. Goodman, 1989; Watson, 1989; Newman & Church, 1990; and Weaver, 1990.

One popular misconception about whole language is that whole language teachers do not teach phonics. However, phonics—the relationships between letter and sound patterns—has always been at the heart of whole language, acknowledged and taught as one of the three major language cueing systems that must be orchestrated as one reads. (See, for example, Mills, O'Keefe, & Stephens, 1992, and Powell & Hornsby, 1993; Wagstaff, 1994, also relates different ways of teaching phonics to some common whole language experiences.)

In summary, then, neither phonics nor whole language is, properly speaking, an approach to reading. "Phonics," however, is often used, by the media and others, as a synonym for a method of teaching reading in which children are provided with direct, systematic, and extensive instruction in sound/symbol relationships (and now phonemic awareness) before any other reading instruction or reading experiences. I refer to this as "phonics first," or as "phonics first and in isolation." Often it becomes "phonics first and only." Similarly, "whole language" is often considered as synonymous with teaching all cue systems together, including phonics, and teaching the cue systems and reading strategies in conjunction with what children are reading and writing. This can be referred to as teaching "phonics and other cue systems and strategies in context."

These two approaches, phonics first and in isolation versus phonics and other cue systems and strategies in context, are grounded in two very different ideas about how children learn and, in particular, how children learn to read. The first reflects a behavioral model, according to which knowledge is transmitted from (in this case) a teacher to children. From this perspective, children learn only what they are directly shown or told. They do not learn by developing inferences, concepts, and other generalizations through experience. In contrast, the latter approach reflects a constructivist model, according to which knowledge is constructed by the learner, and therefore the more meaningful and natural the context in which something is taught, the more likely it is that what's taught will be learned and used. So the idea of teaching phonics first and in isolation differs sharply from a whole language approach to literacy, according to which phonics is taught gradually and in context. But on the other hand, phonics is not enough to be an approach to teaching reading, while whole language is considerably more than that.

Works Cited

Altwerger, B. (1991). Whole language teachers: Empowered professionals. In J. Hydrick (Ed.), *Whole language: Empowerment at the chalkface*, (pp. 15–29). New York: Scholastic.

Church, S. (1994). Is whole language really warm and fuzzy? *The Reading Teacher, 47,* 362–70.

Goodman, K. S. (1989). Whole-language research: Foundations and development. *The Elementary School Journal, 90,* 207–21.

Goodman, K. S. (1993). *Phonics phacts.* Portsmouth, NH: Heinemann.

Goodman, Y. M. (1989). Roots of the whole-language movement. *The Elementary School Journal, 90,* 113–27.

Gursky, D. (1991). After the reign of Dick and Jane. *Teacher Magazine,* August, 22–29.

Monson, R. J. & Pahl, M. M. (1991). Charting a new course with whole language. *Educational Leadership, 48,* 51–53.

Newman, J. M. & Church, S. M. (1990). Myths of whole language. *The Reading Teacher, 44,* 20–26.

Mills, H., O'Keefe, T., & Stephens, D. (1992). *Looking closely: Exploring the role of phonics in one whole language classroom.* Urbana, IL: National Council of Teachers of English.

Powell, D., & Hornsby, D. (1993). *Learning phonics and spelling in a whole language classroom.* New York: Scholastic.

Wagstaff, J. (1994). *Phonics that work! New strategies for the reading/writing classroom.* New York: Scholastic.

Watson, D. J. (1989). Defining and describing whole language. *The Elementary School Journal, 90,* 129–41.

Weaver, C. (1990). *Understanding whole language: From principles to practice.* Portsmouth, NH: Heinemann.

11 Believing in What's Possible, Taking Action to Make a Difference

Ellen H. Brinkley *with* Connie Weaver,
Pen Campbell, Marianne Houston, Jean Williams,
Virginia Little, Mary Monaghan, Lauren Freedman,
Bob and Jo Bird

What happens when a handful of people come together because of their commitment to and concern about public education? When they decide to do something rather than nothing? When they make time in their professionally hyperactive lives to speak out about unjust proposals and unwise legislation that threaten to weaken or even destroy public education? This article tells the story of the creation of a grassroots organization that grew out of the concerns and determination of a handful of people who care about public education.

Michigan for Public Education (MPE) began in the fall of 1994, when a group of teachers, librarians, and other citizens began meeting to discuss our concerns about attacks on public schools. At first, most of our concerns were curricular. Some of us knew, for example, that effective teaching of phonics, spelling, and grammar in the context of reading and writing was being attacked as a departure from teaching "the basics." Some of us were especially aware of attempts to censor books and curricula dealing with a wide variety of topics, including critical thinking. A Michigan author of children's books, for example, was *un*invited to read and talk about her new novel in a local school because taking drugs was mentioned in the book. We all knew that multicultural education was being threatened, because our local newspapers had reported comments made by an outspoken Michigan

Reprinted from *Language Arts*, November 1997.

legislator about proposed English language arts standards: "The emphasis on multicultural diversity is a bunch of garbage. We're a Western civilization. Lots of times with this multicultural stuff, they try to bring out an isolated society and make it look like the norm" (Hornbeck, 1994, p. 3A). And all of us knew from personal experience or from newspaper accounts that in some school districts, groups of parents and citizens with very conservative agendas had taken control of the school board and/or the curriculum. And soon we all came to realize that the concept of genuine public education itself was being challenged by Michigan politicians, despite substantial evidence for the successes of the public schools.

These concerns shaped the vision and led us to the pnmary mission of Michigan for Public Education: to research and disseminate accurate information about public education and about effective teaching practices and, thereby, to advocate for educational equality and excellence. More specifically, MPE's goals are to:

- support and strengthen public education;
- preserve First Amendment separation of church and state in the public schools, without censoring religion or denying its role in society; and
- provide a challenging, quality education for *all* students.

Those of us who founded MPE believe achieving these goals will promote not only subject-matter knowledge, but communication skills, critical and creative thinking, problem-posing and solving, responsible decision-making, and civic responsibility. We further believe that education for the twenty-first century must demonstrate and promote democratic principles, including respect for cultural pluralism.

How We Got Started

None of us had much background as political activists, but we all had a passionate commitment to our cause. And we were eager to learn fast and speak out about issues that affect all of Michigan's children. But how we got started is more complicated. Recently, when we reflected on our beginnings, we realized in retrospect that previous experiences nudged some of us toward greater advocacy roles. Connie Weaver, for example, remembers that when she was Director of NCTE's Commission on Reading in 1989, someone brought a paper titled "Illiteracy: An incurable disease or education malpractice?" to the annual commission meeting. Signed by Robert Sweet, founder and president of what is now the National Right to Read Foundation, this document concluded that "The overwhelming evidence from research and classroom results indicates that the cure for the 'disease of illiteracy' is the restoration of the instructional practice of intensive, systematic phonics in every primary school in America!" (U.S. Senate Republican Policy Committee, 1989, September, p. 13). Connie says, "What I couldn't understand is why this document was headed 'U.S. Senate Republican Policy Committee.' What did phonics have to do with politics? A lot, as we've discovered to our chagrin."

My own experience as President of the Michigan Council of Teachers of English (MCTE) in 1992–93 had led me into the midst of an equally politicized curricular issue. During long discussions, our MCTE Executive Board had struggled to decide whether we should contract with our state's Department of Education to design the newly mandated High School Proficiency Test in Writing or whether we should collaborate with the Mathematics, Science, and Reading groups to try to fight the tests. Finally, the MCTE Board decided, as did the other professional associations, that Michigan students might be better off if Michigan teachers designed the test ourselves rather than if we later had to accept whatever might be created by an out-of-state national testing company. I wrote the grant and chaired the group that designed the Writing test, so that by the time MPE was formed, I had already spoken several times to the State Board of Education and worked with a broad network of stakeholder groups.

In 1994 the fall elections shifted the political balance of the State Board of Education. Newly elected State Board members promised to promote charter schools and school choice, and some planned to back voluntary school prayer and the teaching of creationism in schools (Foren, 1994). Given the increase in state-level curricular challenges, threatened local school board takeovers, and a pervasive anti-public school mood in the state, we became more worried but even more determined. We felt that somebody had to do something—that WE had to do something.

Figuring out what it was we could do—and should do—wasn't so easy. During the next several months we met informally, inviting several people to join us to discuss how we might focus our action. Eventually, we evolved into a small active, committed group. We also solicited and received advice from a former state legislator, a corporate public relations specialist, an attorney, and other community leaders about how our group might function. Through conversations with these advisers, we realized the focus of our concerns was statewide, rather than just local. So we revised our thinking about forming a local group and became Michigan for Public Education.

By the summer of 1995 we were presenting testimony at State Board of Education meetings, frequently targeting specific issues that appeared on the Board's agenda. On one occasion, for example, we challenged the provision of expanded funds for technology for quasi-public charter schools while the governor was saying he would not support additional funding for technology in the regular public schools. At another meeting, we expressed concerns about who could start a charter school (virtually anybody). We also testified at state legislative hearings, appeared on local talk radio programs, participated in a state teleconference, responded to requests for statements on education issues from the press, and contacted key legislators and State Board of Education members regarding education issues.

Along the way, we took care of practical, nuts-and-bolts tasks, such as designing a letterhead, getting a post office box, and opening a bank account with small contributions of our own. We also established a fax connection and a database identifying volunteers willing to write letters, attend meetings, make statements, write columns, etc. Once we realized there was a real need for an organization whose only agenda was to support and strengthen public education, we wrote bylaws and filed papers to become a nonprofit corporation. Our newsletter, published more or less bimonthly that first year, informed those on our growing mailing list about upcoming events, legislation and State Board decisions.

All the while we were still refining our notion of who we were as a group and what we could do especially well. As we talked to friends and colleagues, and as our public statements began to attract attention to the group, we found ourselves networking with a variety of organizations that some of us hadn't had professional connections with before, such as People for the American Way and Americans for Religious Liberty. Through the Michigan Public Education Task Force, we began working with leaders from the League of Women Voters, the Michigan Education Association, the American Association of University Women, the American Civil Liberties Union, and others. From these groups we gained information, advice and support. We soon realized that what we could give in return, that is, one of the things we could do especially well, was to apply our research and writing skills to current, controversial issues, such as charter schools and vouchers, state-level content standards, and education in moral values. We could offer facts, but also background and perspective on specific issues, suggest resources, and encourage specific action. As a result, we have freely shared the materials we produce through our newsletter, public statements, and website (http://www.ashay.com/mpe), and we have been pleased that so many of the groups we network with have reproduced and distributed our materials to their own constituencies.

Why People Got Involved

Writing this article has given us the chance to reflect on how and why we became active members of MPE. Board member Marianne Houston is a middle school language arts and social studies teacher and facilitator for the national Courage to Teach Teacher Formation Program, which provides retreats where teachers focus on "inner" work rather than on instructional strategies or techniques. If you get to know her well, eventually you'll discover that in 1993 she won the Milken Family Foundation National Educator Award. Marianne explains her involvement with MPE this way:

> I am marked by an overall passion for justice, but in education espe-cially because of the obvious implications of inequality in education. These implications extend not only to our immediate communities but also to our nation and our world. As one of the founders of MPE it encouraged me immeasurably to find a group of like-minded people who shared not only my passion, but also my energy to actu-ally *work* for change.

Another founding member, Virginia Little, is a former alternative high school teacher who is now breaking new ground as she teaches creative writing in an online program that links students in nine different Michigan school districts. Ginny explains that:

> I became active because of what I saw as a process of dismantling public education in Michigan through laws being enacted by the leg-islature and under the rule of a governor who shows little compas-sion or knowledge about the educational issues.

Ginny shares Marianne's passionate concern for children: "I am a child advocate, and I believe in fighting for social justice. Many of these students do not have any other safe place to be, any other place to gain needed skills or find mentors to guide them in their lives. Without schools, they have no chances. I believe hope is necessary to life." Such beliefs also motivated activist MPE members Jo and Bob Bird to work tirelessly to inform teachers and the public about the need to defend public eduation: "MPE provides a forum for progressive public education. . . . It produces positive press. It legitimizes the agenda of promoting public education."

Pen Campbell, a school volunteer and part-time school employee while her children were young, now teaches high school English. She's a gifted writer who explains reasons for becoming an active MPE member that express what many of us have felt:

> I became involved with MPE because I realized that I had been think-
> ing about the challenges in our schools, had been taking specific,
> local, everyday actions, but I was still seeing the puzzle as if I were
> only as tall as the edge of the table. Each conversation, each action
> seemed like a puzzle piece lifted and slid around on a surface I
> couldn't see until maybe it fell into place—in a puzzle I couldn't see.
> I wanted to be taller. I wanted to be able to see the whole picture,
> all the pieces, and the pattern on the box as well.
>
> The first time I was invited to an MPE meeting my initial thought
> was "I don't know enough to do something like that." "Well, duh,"
> as the kids would say. That was the very reason to go. And it has been
> the very reason to stay involved. It forces me to learn more, to take
> the time to read what I want to read anyway but would otherwise
> put off because I don't really NEED that for tomorrow's lesson plan,
> and there are only so many hours in the day I'll put it on my sum-
> mer reading list. Being involved gives me people to discuss the big-
> ger issues with and to trade ideas with to see how our local
> challenges match up with ones in other areas of the state. It ener-
> gizes and informs what I do in the classroom because it broadens
> my perspective. And sometimes we laugh a lot. It makes me taller.

What We Have Learned

To be sure we've been fortunate to attract talented and strongly committed members, though not all seek the spotlight. Founding member Jean Williams, for example, is a public school librarian with a long history as a community, political, and public school activist. She explains:

> My role in MPE is not showy, but it is important and I feel good about
> that. I'm helping to make a small difference. As a citizen, I believe
> that it's my responsibility to be involved in something that benefits
> the society in which we all live. Because I receive all the member-
> ship applications and donations, I have learned that there are many
> people in our statewide community who support public education
> and understand its importance to the health of our country. This
> gives me encouragement when I learn about another attack on pub-
> lic education.

Our newest Board Member, Lauren Freedman, is a teacher educator and fommer middle school teacher who recently moved to Michigan. She explains:

> I believe that the transformation of education in this country is most definitely a political enterprise. . . . Through MPE I have learned a great deal about the school systems and their political relationships with the governmental bodies in Michigan. As a new resident, it became clear to me very quickly that the governor was not pro-education and is literally 'out to get' teachers and the public school system.

We think that many MPE members would agree with the following items that come from Ginny's realistic list of positives and negatives:

> I have learned a great deal about charter schools, about ways politicians circumvent or refuse to listen to the constituency they are there to serve, about how to organize a political organization, about how futile it often seems to try to change the tide of power. I have learned that networking with like-minded organizations and informing the public about the actions of politicians and governments is much needed. I have learned how difficult it is to enact change. I have learned the bias of the media and how it silences voices which grate against preferred truths.

Others among us have also learned disheartening lessons. For example, I (Ellen) have a stronger sense now of how fragile public education is, how dependent upon the public's good favor. And I've learned that legislators often have no idea of the classroom implications and impact of the laws they enact. Pen described another sadder-but-wiser perspective that many of us feel:

> In my naivete, I suppose I just assumed that 'of course' everyone would want public education to work. Why wouldn't they? What could be gained by failure? I assumed that our elected and appointed officials would naturally want what the teachers, administrators, and parents I'd come in contact with wanted: success both for their students and for the public schools themselves. The only real problem was to figure out the best way to achieve that, then we'd all work together. Now that I'm aware of the threats to public education posed by well-funded, state-level campaigns (see Guyette, 1996), I no longer think that is the case.

On the other hand, our involvement in MPE projects has reinforced and refined our sense of who we are as teachers and as citizens. Marianne reminded us that:

it is *who we are,* our identity and our integrity, which informs our teaching and all our work. As we in MPE have pursued, together, our goals of quality and equality in education, the 'clear eye' of one or the other of us has helped our group to maintain our vision, and given us courage and energy. This is the way community evolves and works whether within families, classrooms, schools . . . yes, even functional states!

Suggestions for Others to Try

In Michigan we have learned from the successes of others. It was a group in Pennsylvania, the Freedom to Learn Network, that provided us with both a model and the spark for a statewide organization in Michigan. Members and leaders of the Freedom to Learn Network (FLN), which was formed just a few years before MPE, include a wide range of people who are not professional educators. How exciting to see not only their commitment to public education, but also the deep understanding they possess about educational issues, the result no doubt of constant study and networking. The FLN already sponsors outstanding annual conferences and clearly makes a positive difference in Pennsylvania. Based on what we've learned from the Pennsylvania group, and our own experience, we offer the following suggestions to help *Language Arts* readers who wish to become active, speak out to support, and to strengthen public education in all the states and provinces:

1. Talk to others in existing groups about issues you feel passionate about. Decide whether there's a need for a separate group. When you can, work as a task force or ad hoc committee within an already established organization to focus on needs.

2. If you decide there's a need for a new organization, don't think you need a cast of thousands to begin. Start with a handful of people and coffee and rolls in someone's living room. We're pleased to know that groups similar to MPE have started out this same way in Texas, Arizona, and Ohio.

3. Think through the issues carefully. Try not to spin your wheels need-lessly as a group, but don't get frustrated too quickly and give up in defeat when you're in a just-talking phase. It took us several months of discussion, reading, investigating, and discussing some more before we could articulate a very clear sense of direction and purpose.

4. Don't be afraid to speak out about controversial topics. Speaking on behalf of a group builds confidence. Take someone with you so you're not alone.

5. Write out "talking points" ahead of time before speaking, prioritizing the most important points you want to make as you talk formally or informally about the issues. Writing out your own views and searching for analogies, etc., can help you distill your thinking about what stand you want to take. Take care to write clearly and carefully to best communicate your message. Learn to articulate your message to people who aren't in education. We're so used to educational jargon. If we use expressions like "accessing prior knowledge," "student-centered learning," "critical pedagogy," etc.—which roll off our tongues so easily— our general audience will quickly tune us out.

6. Take multiple copies of any formal written statement you plan to read in a public forum, and distribute them to members of the board or group you're speaking to and to the press if they're in attendance.

7. Encourage others to express their views by providing them with brief, easy-to-read information that highlights a particular problem or need. Provide addresses of key decision-makers who hold the power to effect change. Include e-mail, phone, and fax numbers for quicker impact.

8. Take a stand on targeted issues that are most important in your area. Develop the positions you take with care, speaking with passion but offering rational, well-reasoned recommendations. Exaggerated, inflammatory, or sarcastic rhetoric may get you quoted in the newspapers but will usually work against your purposes in the long run. By polarizing viewpoints, you may help audiences see contrasts and alternative possibilities, but by publicly characterizing other positions as extremist, you may lose as many or more supporters than you gain.

9. Seek out coalitions and network groups that share similar or related concerns about public education. Although it may seem way beyond your reach initially, if there seems to be no existing network, consider inviting representatives from potentially allied groups to meet to discuss common concerns. Perhaps your group could function as a coalition or network through which information can be shared and joint action can be taken.

10. "Just do it." We all know why we just can't get involved. We don't have time or energy to do one more thing. Our students' and school districts' needs take every minute. Our families deserve our attention. We need

some time for ourselves. Active MPE member Mary Monaghan spent many years as a school librarian and understands the demands on our time. Nevertheless, she insists, "If you feel you don't have time to become more active in supporting and expressing your views, MAKE THE TIME. Others before you have found time to establish politically active groups and associations that have brought you the benefits you have today. . . . Get political! Get more involved if you possibly can. Every voice is needed to defend public school education and the democratic process that sustains it." Pen, who drives an hour each way for MPE Board meetings after she's taught all day, says that when she thinks about the time she's taking, "those old responsibility refrains Mom was always coming up with have a way of popping up to bite you right in the agenda: 'If you don't vote, you can't complain.' 'Put your money (or your time—which we all know is more precious than money any day) where your mouth is.' 'If you want something done, . . .'"

MPE's Effects on Our Advocacy

When we consider how MPE has affected the stands we take as advocates of critical literacy and of public education, there are two common features that are striking. First, the fact that we're part of an organization that we feel a responsibility for has compelled us to stay better informed. Lauren, for example, explained that MPE has been:

> very helpful with providing information I could readily use to think through and make decisions about where I stand on the issues fac- ing public education in the state of Michigan. Because of MPE I have been a much more critical reader of the news media's account of education events in the state and can make sounder judgments about the issues.

Even more significant, however, is that the act of organizing and of becoming a part of a new, grassroots organization has made us more bold in taking a personal, professional, and public stand on issues that matter to us. We realized the difference early in the process on those first occasions when we introduced public statements by saying, "I'm speaking on behalf of Michigan for Public Education, a citizens' group advocating educational equality and excellence." For me (Ellen), it makes a difference that I'm no longer speaking just for myself on such occasions—important as that is. I speak with greater confidence and commitment, knowing that others are counting on me.

Others in our group report similar experiences. Pen explains that, "MPE has taught me to do scary things—like stand up to speak in front of people who weren't my students and talk about something that mattered to me and to speak my mind in casual political conversations." Even Bob and Jo, who were already experienced advocates, explain that "MPE helps provide us a support group at hearings. . . . There's strength in numbers, MPE provides encouragement. It increases our credibility, we're part of a recognized group. It has synergistic effects from combining talents of membership." And even Connie, a prolific author who has given speeches around the world, describes MPE's effect on her own advocacy: "It's had a profound effect. Working with others dedicated to public education and effective language arts/literacy education has encouraged me to learn more and given me the courage to speak up in public forums."

Marianne's words echo those of others: "Perhaps the most significant thing I've done . . . is to better educate myself with regard to the issues, and then grow in courage to address these issues when it may be easier to keep quiet and simply complain later in the teachers' lounge!" These aren't idle words. In a televised public forum she pressed the issue of the reputed success of charter schools. She reminded the audience that research had shown her that results are mixed and generally not supportive of the enthusiasm with which the Governor and some Board members greeted them. She was able to use facts to move the discussion to a more balanced perspective.

Mary, a retired media specialist and educator, also reports that, "MPE has given me more confidence to speak out." In Mary's case, she too has done considerably more than just talk. She and an active group of MPE members in Lansing, Michigan's capital city, have formed the MPE Capital Focus Group with two purposes—(a) being an advocate for public schools and showing concern for their problems, current reforms, and their future, and (b) being an advocate for MPE. The work done by members of this group is especially valuable, since they're able to attend and participate in the many groups and events that take place in their city. Recently, Mary has found a new way to inform community groups about current educational issues. She watches—or programs her VCR to record—State Board of Education meetings and other programs offered on MGTV (Michigan Government TV). Then she uses videotaped excerpts to stimulate discussions at senior citizens' residences. Now she's planning to extend this service to other civic groups. As she points out, "Many people don't even know who the Board members are, but are becoming more interested since the recent proposal . . . to eliminate the Board by a referendum of the people." Mary's goal is to "save our State Board of Education—as a representative voice of the people!"

Doing What We Can

This article presents the voices and thoughts of just a few of the many MPE members who have found unique forms of advocacy and action. Lest we sound too self-congratulatory, though, we should end on a humble note. The truth is that most people in Michigan have never heard of Michigan for Public Education. We have just a few hundred members. In spite of all that's described above, probably none of the state's movers and shakers consider us a serious threat to their agendas. We've learned that networking among citizen groups isn't usually enough to sway public opinion in general or to produce dramatic changes in legislation. Those in Michigan who seek to discredit public education as a step toward using the public's money for private education have incredibly deep pockets. We don't.

Still, we do what we can do. We can help each other be stronger advocates. And we can research the issues and disseminate information about what's unjust. We can articulate a vision of what's needed to help solve the real problems of public education. We can be—we ARE—one voice among several promoting equality and excellence in public education. And, we're convinced that the combined advocacy from our group and others has influenced Michigan lawmakers and voters. When the Governor sought $1.5 million for start-up funds for charter schools, some of which are for-profit corporations, the combined protests of many voices surely played a role in substantially reducing that amount. Data gathering and reporting by our group and several others in many parts of the state have resulted in new requirements for greater supervision of and accountability from the charter schools. Our signature motto is, "Together we make a difference!"

What follows is one of the statements that we've created to focus on recommendations that can make a positive difference in public school classrooms. It's written with Michigan in mind, but we're pretty sure that most *Language Arts* readers will find many common concerns expressed.

How Can the Citizens of Michigan Promote Equality and Excellence in Public Education?

   1. **Make a new commitment to genuine public education for all students.**
      Recognize that many problems currently being blamed on schools and

on teachers exist within a huge tangle of societal pressures and problems. If it's true that "it takes a whole village to raise a child," then we must expect community, state, and national bodies to provide public education support that matters—money, time, respect for educators, and support for teacher professionalism.

2. **Hold politicians and private sector stakeholders accountable for supporting children and for providing positive rather than negative incentives.** Many people hold teachers accountable for children's learning, or at least for raising children's test scores. Such demands assume that children are always able and eager to take advantage of what is taught, that what is taught is always learned, and that learning always results in higher test scores. Politicians and private sector stakeholders must address issues of poverty, homelessness, hunger, and fears for physical safety so that children can take advantage of good teaching. They can create positive incentives by rewarding schools that establish strong links with the community, that teach and empower parents to be their children's best teachers and role models. They can support initiatives that create jobs with a livable wage so that parents can support their children. They can promote genuine pro-family programs that make reasonably-priced health care, child care, and transportation accessible for working parents.

3. **Use taxpayers' money to provide equal education in public schools for the personal and collective benefit of all citizens of the democracy.** Like all parents, Michigan's Governor Engler has the right to decide to send his daughters to private school. High-income parents already have schools of "choice" available to them. They do not, however, have the right to expect taxpayers to pay for that choice. Even parents who select private education for their own children have an obligation for democracy's sake to educate all children. Charter schools and school vouchers work to the disadvantage of students whose parents can't afford to transport their children across town. We believe that charter schools set Michigan on a course that leads ultimately to the devastation of public education.

4. **Spend the money that's currently being used to establish charter schools to strengthen Michigan's public schools instead,** i.e., to provide such things as expanded school library resources, computer access for students, and professional development for teachers.

5. **Address real problems that affect teaching and learning, such as providing teaching schedules that allow teachers to perform professionally.** Too often we expect teachers to stay informed about new technology and teaching methods, to plan class sessions carefully, and to meet students' individual needs—all without needed time and support. Secondary teachers, for example, often pay a heavy price and students get shortchanged when teachers try daily to meet the individual learning needs of as many as 125–150 students. With this many students, one written assignment that needs a teacher's response easily requires 10 minutes per paper, eventually demanding 25 hours of the teacher's time after school or on weekends—just to respond to one assignment.

6. **Reject misguided pressures from nationally organized groups and defend democracy for the sake of all Michigan students.** Most Michigan citizens do not agree with spokespersons from nationally organized groups who have expressed publicly their desire to eliminate public schools and replace them with schools that are operated by churches. Democracy in an increasingly diverse society depends on individual abilities used cooperatively for the common good. All of our students deserve an education that allows them to preserve their individual family culture and values and to understand the culture and values of others. Students best prepared for the future will be those who attend schools where the curriculum promotes genuine literacy rather than just reading and writing skills, generates critical and creative thinking, teaches intellectual freedom, and promotes multicultural understanding and democracy.

References

Foren, J. (1994, Dec. 4). GOP control changes face of education. *The Grand Rapids Press,* pp. A1–A2.

Guyette, C. (1996, June 26–July 2). Onward Christian scholars. [Detroit] *Metrotimes,* pp. 10–15.

Hornbeck, M. (1994, Nov. 20). Multicultural curriculum in hands of GOP. *Detroit News,* pp. 1A–3A.

U.S. Senate Republican Policy Committee. (1989, September). *Illiteracy: An incurable disease or education malpractice?* Washington, D.C.

12 The California Reading Situation: Rhetoric and Reality

Jeff McQuillan

This chapter begins by explaining why the California reading situation is relevant to the rest of the nation. Turning to the alleged decline in reading in California, McQuillan explains that there is no evidence for the popular claim that reading scores have declined since 1987, when the state officially adopted a literature-based language arts framework. The widely cited NAEP scores for 1992 and 1994 do not demonstrate substantial change, and the CLAS scores (California Learning Assessment System scores) are incapable of doing so, due to changes made in the test from year one to year two. There are no standardized measures, however, that compare pre-1987 scores with scores in the early to mid-1990s. Thus McQuillan argues that while the NAEP test scores are indeed low, there is no actual evidence to support the claim that reading scores among California's students have declined significantly between 1987 and now.

And what might be some of the causes for such low performance on the NAEP? Citing correlations between children's free reading and their reading achievement, and between school library resources and reading achievement, McQuillan argues that a major cause for a poor showing on the NAEP is the deplorable lack of books in California's libraries and the relative unavailability of books, libraries, and librarians to children. Another factor is the relative poverty of California's children, in part because poverty inhibits the availability of books and other reading materials in the home, since the presence of such materials correlates significantly with reading scores, including scores on the NAEP. McQuillan also notes that the NAEP assessments in 1992 and 1994 provide evidence that whole language and

Reprinted from Chapter 16 of *Reconsidering a Balanced Approach to Reading,* edited by Constance Weaver.

literature-based teaching produces *higher* reading scores than skills teaching, not lower. Thus there is good reason to be concerned about the reading of California's children, but their reading ability has not necessarily declined in recent years, and the alleged causes for California children's low performance appear *not to* be the real causes. McQuillan points out that it would be a mistake to abandon true whole language teaching, as "the most likely cause of California's low national ranking in reading achievement is not a literature-based curriculum but a lack of reading materials for California's students." This conclusion correlates with an increasingly substantial body of research and is an important lesson for all of us.

Portions of this chapter appeared in the *Claremont Reading Conference Yearbook, 1996.* Reprinted with permission of the Claremont Reading Conference.

While predictions of the historical importance of present events are always risky, it does not appear unwarranted to mark 1995 as something of a watershed year for the teaching of reading in the United States. That was the year when the nation's most populous state, California, took dramatic and highly publicized steps toward a renewed emphasis on phonics and skills in early literacy instruction. The significance of California's policy decisions for the rest of the country cannot be underestimated, as the case of whole language's supposed failure in California has been cited as justification for changes in other states and, indeed, for a new national policy on literacy instruction (e.g., Chen & Colvin, 1996). Understanding what really happened in California is necessary, then, if we are to get an accurate picture of the genesis of the current (and perhaps future) phonics-based reforms in reading instruction.

The reasons for California's dramatic shift in educational policy were agreed upon almost unanimously by government leaders and commissions, the media, and many members of the research community (see, e.g., California Department of Education, 1995a; California Reading Task Force Report [CRTFR], 1995; Fry, 1996; Stewart, 1996). First, California's reading test scores were said to have "plummeted" (Stewart, 1996, p. 23) to record lows over the previous ten-year period; second, this sharp decline was said to be directly attributable to the adoption of a literature-based reading curriculum in the state in 1987 (CRTFR, 1995), which de-emphasized phonics and skills instruction. As I will show, however, there is no empirical data to sustain either of these assertions. The shift in reading policy was based upon false information and faulty assumptions.

California Rhetoric: Declining Test Scores

The move to reform reading instruction in California began with the appointment of a special Reading Task Force in May 1995 by Superintendent of Public Instruction Delaine Eastin. The impetus for the task force was the release of two sets of test scores which have been widely cited as demonstrating that California's reading performance has dropped significantly since 1987. The first set is from the National Assessment of Educational Progress (NAEP), a federally funded, standardized reading assessment administered every two years by the U.S. Department of Education to a representative sample of fourth-grade students in forty-one states. In both 1992 and 1994, California's fourth graders ranked among the worst of the participating states. The median score for California in 1992 was 202, the fourth lowest of the states and territories for which data was available, while the overall national average was 215 (on a scale of 0–500). In 1994, California dropped slightly to 197, tying for next to last, while the national average was 212 (Campbell, Donahue, Reese, & Phillips, 1996, p. 25). Rank scores are, of course, slightly misleading, since a difference of a few points can cause a state to rise or drop in rank if the states are clustered closely together. But even when this clustering is taken into account, California still did not fare well: in 1992, the state was in the bottom third, and in 1994, in the bottom quarter (Campbell et al., pp. 59–60). Clearly, California was performing relatively poorly compared with the rest of the nation.

But performing poorly is not the same as declining. To show a decline, one must look at scores from both the beginning and the end of the time period in question. Herein lies the problem: state-level NAEP scores are unavailable before 1992, and the tests are not equivalent to any other standardized reading measure. As such, the NAEP data cannot tell us anything about whether scores went up or down after the implementation of the literature-based curriculum.

The second set of data cited to show California's supposed drop, the California Learning Assessment System (CLAS), suffers from the same lack of comparability. The CLAS tests were administered only twice, in the 1992–93 and 1993–94 school years. Like the NAEP scores, they are not comparable to previous test scores and tell us nothing about how California students performed before and after the 1987 Language Arts Framework adoption which called for a literature-based curriculum. (In fact, due to changes made in the test after the first year of its administration, the two years are not even comparable to each other.) Ironically, the 1993–94 results indicated that more than three-fourths of California's students could read at a "basic" level, a rather strong showing in light of the dismal financial conditions of the state's schools discussed below (California Department of Education, 1995a).

When analyzing the NAEP and CLAS scores, it is important to keep in mind what categories such as "basic" and "proficient" mean in terms of reading proficiency. Both examinations are "criterion-referenced" and have established cutoff points for each level of proficiency. These cutoff points were not made in reference to how schoolchildren performed in the past, but rather were determined on the basis of criteria created by a committee of teachers and researchers. These criteria are different for each test and are necessarily arbitrary (Glass, 1978). On the NAEP test, for example, children who score above the basic level in the fourth grade (a score of 208 on a scale of 0–500) can "demonstrate an understanding of the overall meaning of what they read," can "make obvious connections between the text and their own experiences," and can "extend ideas in the text by making simple inferences" (Campbell et al., 1996, p. 42). For the CLAS examination, "basic" was defined as "literal understanding of a reading selection, both as a whole and in its parts" (California Department of Education, 1995b). Not surprisingly, the two definitions produce two different results. On the NAEP test, only 44 percent of California's children read at or above the basic level; on the CLAS test, more than 75 percent do. It should also be clear from these definitions that scoring at the "basic" level does not mean that children cannot recognize words or will stare blankly when confronted with a text.

A third set of data, commercial test score results, has also been cited by some journalists as evidence of a test score decline (Levine, 1996). The scores are taken from a report by the Policy Analysis for California Education (PACE) group (Guthrie et al., 1988) which equated California's performance on the California Achievement Program (CAP) to national percentile ranks during the early and mid-1980s. At first look, these scores seem to make the case for critics of whole language: as shown in Table 1, California scored near the middle throughout most of the previous decade in the PACE analysis, not near the bottom, as it had done in the 1992 and 1994 NAEP assessments. Upon closer inspection, however, it becomes clear that this data does not show that California ranked around the middle of the states before 1987, nor that scores were rising relative to other states over that same period of time, nor even that more than half of our students were above the national average in the mid-1980s. Let us take each of these claims in turn. First, commercial tests are not comparable in any way to the NAEP tests from which California's low national ranking is determined.

Table 1

Comparison of California Achievement Program Scores to National Percentile Rankings

	81	82	83	84	85	86	87
CTBS[a] 1973 norms	59	60	62	64	69	71	—
CTBS 1981 norms	—	41	45	46	54	55	55

(source: Guthrie et al., 1988, Table 7.5)
[a]Denotes California Test of Basic Skills.

NAEP scores can be compared only with NAEP scores because they are derived from a set of criteria and representative samples particular to that test and are scored according to a statistical procedure very different from that used by most commercial test givers.

Second, national percentile ranks are *not* the same as ranks among the states (such as those that have been used in the NAEP comparisons). A national percentile rank of 50, for example, does not mean that California ranked in the middle of the states. *National* percentile ranks are derived from comparing the median student scores in a state with the scores of all *students* collectively in the country, while *state* ranks are determined by comparing a state's median score with the median scores of other *states.* An example might clarify this difference. Consider the hypothetical distribution shown in Table 2. Although state B is separated from state A by 19 raw score points and 25 percentile points, the state rank—determined only in relation to where the state's score falls relative to the others—is two. This illustrates that

Table 2

Hypothetical Distribution of State Test Scores, National Percentile Ranks, and State Ranks

State	Mean Raw Score Rank	National Percentile	State Rank
A	230	75	1
B	211	60	2
C	207	55	3
D	205	53	4
E	200	50	5
F	180	42	6

there is no necessary relationship between national percentile ranks and state ranks.

With large, normally distributed national samples such as those used in NAEP, students in most states will tend to fall around the 50th percentile—that is the nature of normal distributions. Yet only one state will rank in first place, and one in last, despite the fact that the students in those first- and last-ranking states may score about average. We can now see why distinguishing between national percentile ranks and state ranks is so important: California's low 1992 NAEP ranking was a *state* rank, not a national percentile rank. California's national percentile rank of 55 from the 1986–87 CTBS reading test means that the average California student scored better than 55 percent of all students in the country, *not* that California ranked twenty-seventh out of fifty states in the country in reading.

Another example will help illustrate this difference: In the 1994 NAEP fourth-grade reading test, only fourteen of the forty-two states (33 percent) had average public school scores above the 50th percentile. This is because students are not evenly distributed among the states, *not* because only a third of American schoolchildren scored above average (a statistical impossibility in norm-referenced comparisons). Minnesota, for example, had a state rank of thirteenth in the nation, but scored below the 50th percentile (Campbell et al., 1996).

Third, even the claim about California's mid-1980s above-average national percentile rank is inaccurate. The percentile ranks shown in Table 1 were derived by comparing California's performance to 1981 and 1973 norm groups. But commercial test norms have been rising substantially over the past fifty years (see *The Manufactured Crisis* [1995] by David Berliner and Bruce Biddle for details). This means that comparing test scores from a group of students to a previous norm group will likely overestimate the true percentile rank. It is easy to see that one can inflate percentile rank estimates simply by using an earlier (and lower-scoring) norming population. Notice in Table 1, for example, that students in California had a percentile rank of 55 when calculated with the 1981 norms, but 71 when computed using the 1973 norms—a 15 point difference! If we assume a similar upward trend in CTBS norms for third-grade reading, resulting in a 15 point difference in percentile ranks over the 1981–1987 period, then California's true 1987 percentile is not 55 or 71, but around 40.

Although the 1980s CAP assessments and 1992 NAEP tests are not comparable, it is interesting to note that when uninflated measures of the

CAP scores are used, the national percentile ranks are in fact quite similar. The most reliable percentile rank from the 1980s CAP program is from 1981–82, the year closest to the 1981 renorming of the test. The percentile rank for that year was 41 (Table 1). The state NAEP scores are not reported with a national percentile ranking, but from the information provided in the 1992 NAEP reports (Campbell et al., 1996, Table 2.1, p. 23; National Center for Education Statistics [NCES], 1994), it appears to be in the high 30s, just a few points below the CAP rank. Given the measurement error in both tests, this small difference is unlikely to be statistically significant. In other words, when compared with students nationwide, the average California fourth grader in 1992 probably ranked about the same as fourth graders in the early 1980s, scoring at around the 40th percentile mark.

The CAP scores do not show that California was on average any better in the 1980s than it was in 1992, nor do they show any serious declines after the implementation of the 1987 Framework. Table 3 shows the raw scores from the CAP until its discontinuation in 1990. There were slight increases and decreases across different grade levels, but overall the scores were very stable. California's third graders, for example, were performing at the same level in 1990 as they were in 1985, which would be unlikely if the 1987 Framework had caused a dramatic decline in test scores.

Despite repeated claims to the contrary, then, there is no evidence that California reading scores have declined markedly over the past ten years; rather, there is sufficient data to suggest that little change in achievement has occurred since the 1987 Framework adoption. This stability of test scores is remarkable in light of the declining financial status of California's schools (discussed below), a decline that has been largely ignored in the debates over reading achievement in the state.

Table 3

California Achievement Program Raw Scores for 3rd, 6th, 8th, and 12th Grades, 1984–1990

	1984	1985	1986	1987	1988	1989	1990
3rd	268	274	280	282	282	277	275
6th	249	253	260	260	265	262	261
8th	250	240	243	247	252	256	257
12th	236	241	240	246	250	248	251

(source: Guthrie et al., 1993, p. 34)

California Reality: Disappearing Books

The second part of the argument used to promote a renewed emphasis on skills instruction is that whole language was the cause of California's (nonexistent) decline and (very real) low national ranking. As noted earlier, it is true that California ranked relatively low among the states. Is a literature-based curriculum or whole language to blame? Another look at the 1992 NAEP data reveals that the answer appears to be no. As part of the assessment, fourth-grade teachers were asked to indicate their methodological approach to reading as "whole language," "literature-based," and/or "phonics." The average scores for each type of approach were then compared, and those children in classrooms with heavy emphasis on phonics clearly fared the worst. Children in classrooms emphasizing whole language (reported by 40 percent of the teachers) had an average score of 220, those in literature-based classrooms (reported by 49 percent of the teachers) had a score of 221, and students in phonics classrooms (reported by 11 percent of the teachers) came in last with an average score of 208 (NCES, 1994, p. 284). Similar patterns were observed in the 1994 NAEP results (Campbell et al., 1996).[1]

If these teacher self-reports are accurate, then there is no evidence in the NAEP data that the use of whole language leads to lower reading scores. The cause of California's problems would seem to lie elsewhere. As it turns out, there are several likely sources for the state's low ranking, almost all of which were completely ignored by the state's political and educational leaders and by the media. Consider the following factors.

California Has Some of the Worst School Libraries in the Country

Massive evidence now exists to suggest that greater access to pleasure-reading materials leads children to read more, and that more reading leads to better reading achievement (e.g., Krashen, 1993, 1996; Stanovich & Cunningham, 1992). Specifically, evidence points up the critical role of school libraries in reading performance. Children get anywhere from 30 to 90 percent of their free reading materials from the school and public library (Krashen, 1993), and the impact of library quality on reading scores has been documented in a variety of studies. Lance and his colleagues (Lance, Wellborn, & Hamilton-Pennell, 1993) found in a study of Colorado schools that the quality of the school library had a direct and powerful effect on reading achievement scores, when controlling for the effects of teacher-pupil ratio, overall school spending, and socioeconomic status of the students. On

the national level, Krashen (1995) showed that school library quality was the
only significant predictor of a state's 1992 NAEP fourth-grade reading score,
even when considering median income, per-pupil spending, and the
availability of computer software in a school. My study (McQuillan, 1996a)
also found that public and school library quality were important indicators of
a state's average SAT score. Internationally, Warwick Wiley (1992), in a study
of over 200,000 students in thirty-two countries, found that school library
quality had a significant impact on a country's reading performance,
particularly on students who lived in lesser economically developed
countries.

How does California rank in school library quality? According to the most
recent data available (White, 1990), California places last or nearly last in
almost every category, including per-pupil spending, books per pupil, and
librarians per pupil. Table 4 shows just how far California is behind the
national averages in library quality, and the state's rankings are abysmal:
forty-fifth in per-pupil expenditures, forty-ninth in books per pupil, and
fiftieth in librarians per pupil.

*California Has One of the Worst Public Library Systems in the
United States*

Public libraries also have an important impact on children's reading
achievement. My study (McQuillan, 1996b) found that there is a very strong
correlation (r = 0.70) between a state's 1992 NAEP reading score and public

Table 4

School Library Quality in California and the United States			
Books per Pupil:	Elementary	Middle	High School
U.S.	18:1	16:1	15:1
California	13:1	11:1	8:1
Per Pupil Spending			
U.S.	15.44	15.50	19.22
California	8.48	7.48	8.21
Librarians per Pupil	Overall		
U.S.	895:1		
California	5,496:1		

(source: White, 1990; Snyder & Hoffman, 1996)

library quality in a state. This finding means that nearly *half* of the variance in state NAEP scores can be accounted for merely by knowing the quality of a state's public library system. Mirroring its poor standing on school libraries, California also ranks near the bottom on several measures of public library quality. Chute (1992) reports that, in 1990–91, California ranked thirty-ninth in books and serials held per capita (1.95 versus 2.53 nationally), forty-third in capital outlay per thousand residents ($666 versus $1,912), and fiftieth in hours open to the public per thousand residents (72.09 hours per week).

Not only does California rank relatively poorly now, but the situation has become far *worse* since the late 1980s. As of 1993, Gibson noted that book budgets in the state had been cut 25 percent since 1989, the number of open hours had decreased 30 percent since 1987, and per capita spending had been reduced 36 percent from 1989. Children's services had been hit hardest, Gibson found, with 25 percent of public libraries reporting cutbacks in this area (Gibson, 1993).

California's Children are Poor and Getting Poorer

The only place children can find books outside of the school and public library is at home. But if one is poor, then he or she is much less likely to be able to afford many books. This relationship between poverty, access to books at home, and reading achievement is again seen clearly in the NAEP data: in 1992, the correlation between a measure of poverty and a state's NAEP reading score was –0.73; the correlation between books in the home and a state's average reading score, 0.87 (McQuillan, 1996b). Similar results were found in the 1994 assessment (Campbell et al., 1996). A reasonable interpretation of this data is that children in relatively poor states have less access to books in the home, leading to lower reading test scores.

California ranked ninth in the country in the number of children aged five to seventeen who live in poverty (Bureau of the Census, 1995), with the poverty rate rising an incredible 25 percent between 1989 and 1993 (Schmittroth, 1994). According to the most recent figures, one out of every four California students is living in a family with income below the poverty line.[2] Data gathered in the 1992 NAEP assessment confirms these figures: California ranked tenth-highest among participating states in the number of children who participate in free lunch and nutrition programs. Not surprisingly, the NAEP report also found that the state ranks near the bottom in the percentage of homes with more than twenty-five books in the home (NCES, 1994).

The Verdict on Whole Language

Whole language did not fail in California. There is no evidence that state reading test scores declined after the state implemented its literature-based curriculum framework in the late 1980s. Furthermore, there is very little reliable information on just how widely literature-based reading instruction was actually implemented in the state. The 1992 NAEP reading assessment reported that 69 percent of fourth-grade teachers in California said that they placed "heavy emphasis" on whole language practices in their classrooms, the highest percentage in the country. At the same time, 40 percent also said they gave "moderate emphasis" to phonics and 68 percent said they devoted at least some of their class time to decoding skills (NCES, 1994). Fisher and Hiebert (1990), in an analysis of teacher's self-reported labels concerning reading instruction and their observed reading practices, often found little correspondence between what teachers called their instruction (e.g., "whole language" or "phonics") and what went on in their classrooms. We should be cautious, then, in making any strong claims about just how seriously whole language took root in California based on teacher self-reports.

States looking to learn the "lessons of California" in reading instruction should avoid drawing the same faulty conclusions that the state's media and educational establishment have drawn in regards to whole language. The evidence indicates that the most likely cause of California's low national ranking in reading achievement is not a literature-based curriculum but a lack of reading materials for California's students. Before abandoning whole language, policymakers and teachers would be better advised to look at the state of their school and public libraries, making sure that children have books to read.

Acknowledgments

Portions of this chapter appeared in the *Claremont Reading Conference Yearbook, 1996.* Reprinted with permission of the Claremont Reading Conference.

Notes

1. Chall (1996) claims this interpretation of the NAEP scores is incorrect because "phonics is usually taught in grades 1 and 2, and possibly 3, [and] when

it is taught in grade 4, it usually means that the students were already function-
ing below expectancy" (p. 305). In other words, low-scoring students in phonics
classrooms are there because they are poor students to begin with. Chall argues
that if we looked at the relationship between phonics and test scores in first and
second grade, we would see higher scores for the phonics classrooms.

This interpretation is plausible if we looked only at the results nationally by
individual classroom, as they are reported in Campbell et al. (1996). It is less persuasive, however, when we calculate the correlation between a *state's* NAEP score
and a state's use of phonics in grade four, which (r = .59). If Chall were correct,
it would mean that there is no meaningful correlation between what teachers of
a given state do in reading instruction in fourth grade and what they do in the
first three grades. In this case, it would mean that school districts with a strong
emphasis on phonics in grade 4 do not necessarily use phonics in similar proportions in lower grades.

That is possible, of course, but not very likely. It seems much more probable
that, on the whole, states, districts, and schools that use a lot of phonics in grade
4 also use a lot of phonics in grades 1, 2, and 3. (Imagine if whole language
backers used a similar argument in California—that the real problem was that the
state's first-, second turns out to also be very negative-, and third-grade teachers
were using phonics, and that the emphasis suddenly changed to whole language
in grade 4.)

2. Some have argued (Fry, 1996) that socioeconomic factors cannot account
for California's low ranking in reading, since the median income for the state's
residents in 1992 was above the national average, and both the percentage of
people living below the poverty line and the number of persons twenty-five or
older with a college education were about the same as the rest of the country.
These figures, however, are for the average Californian, not the average California *parent*, who, as the figures above indicate, are indeed poorer than their counterparts in other states.

References

Berliner, D., & Biddle, B. (1995). *The manufactured crisis: Myths, fraud, and the
attack on America's public schools.* Reading, MA: Addison-Wesley Publishing.

Bureau of the Census. (1995). *Statistical abstract of the United States.* Washington, D.C.: U.S. Department of Commerce.

California Department of Education. (1995a). *Educators commit to improving
reading and math; Latest and last CLAS scores released, Press release RL95-
19.* [Online]. Available: Gopher/North America/USA/California/California
Department of Education/CLAS/Press Release.

California Department of Education. (1995b). *Minutes of the Reading Task Force,
May 8, 1995* [Online]. Available: Gopher/North America/USA/California/Cal-
ifornia Department of Education/California Department of Education/State
Superintendent Reading Task Force/RTF Minutes 5/14/95.

California Reading Task Force Report (CRTFR). (1995). *Every child a reader.* Sacramento, CA: California Department of Education.

Campbell, J., Donahue, P., Reese, C., & Phillips, G. (1996). *NAEP 1994 reading report card for the nation and the states.* Washington, D.C.: U.S. Department of Education.

Chall, J. (1996). American reading achievement: Should we worry? *Research in the Teaching of English, 30,* 303–310.

Chen, E., & Colvin, R. L. (1996, July 18). Dole sees problems in schools and blames liberals. *Los Angeles Times,* pp. A3, A19.

Chute, A. (1992). *Public libraries in the United States, 1990.* Washington, D.C.: U.S. Department of Education.

Elley, W. (1992). *How in the world do students read? The IEA study of reading literacy.* The Hague, Netherlands: International Associations for the Evaluation of Educational Achievement.

Fisher, C., & Hiebert, E. (1990). Characteristics of tasks in two approaches to literacy instruction. *Elementary School Journal, 91,* 3–18.

Fry, E. (1996). California students do poorly on reading tests. *California Reader, 29* (2), 9–11.

Gibson, L. (1993). *Status of California public libraries: Final report, abbreviated version.* Sacramento, CA: California State Library.

Glass, G. (1978). Standards and criteria. *Journal of Educational Measurement, 15,* 237–261.

Guthrie, J., Kirst, M., Hayward, G., Odden, A., Adams, J., Cagampang, H., Emmett, T., Evans, J., Geranios, J., Koppich, J., & Merchant, B. (1988). *Conditions of education in California, 1987–88.* Berkeley, CA: Policy Analysis for California Education.

Guthrie, J., Kirst, M., Koppich, J., Hayward, G., Odden, A., Rahn, M., & Wiley, L. (1993). *Conditions of education in California, 1992–93.* Berkeley, CA: Policy Analysis for California Education.

Krashen, S. (1993). *The power of reading.* Englewood, CO: Libraries Unlimited.

Krashen, S. (1995). School libraries, public libraries, and NAEP reading scores. *School Library Media Quarterly, 23,* 235–237.

Krashen, S. (1996). *Every person a reader: An alternative to the California's Reading Task Force Report.* Culver City, CA: Language Education Associates.

Lance, K., Wellborn, L., & Hamilton-Pennell, C. (1993). *The impact of school library media centers on academic achievement.* Castle Rock, CO: Hi Willow Publishing.

Levine, A. (1996, October). America's reading crisis: Why the whole language approach to teaching has failed millions of children. *Parents, 16,* 63–65, 68.

McQuillan, J. (1996a). SAT verbal scores and the library: Predicting high school reading achievement in the United States. *Indiana Media Journal, 18* (3), 65–70.

McQuillan, J. (1996b, August). *The effects of print access on reading acquisition.* Poster session presented at the 1996 Whole Language Umbrella, St. Paul, Minnesota.

National Center for Education Statistics (NCES). (1994). *Data compendium for the NAEP 1992 Reading Assessment of the nation and the states.* Washington, D.C.: U.S. Department of Education.

Schmittroth, L. (1994). *Statistical record of children.* Detroit: Gale Research, Inc.

Snyder, T., & Hoffman, C. (1996). *Digest of education statistics, 1995.* Washington, D.C.: U.S. Department of Education.

Stanovich, K., & Cunningham, A. (1992). Studying the consequences of literacy within a literate society; The cognitive correlates of print exposure. *Memory and Cognition, 20,* 51–68.

Stewart, J. (1996). The blackboard bungle: California's failed reading experiment. *LA Weekly, 18* (14), 22–29.

White, H. (1990). School library collections and *services:* Ranking the states. *School Library Media Quarterly, 19,* 13–26.

This book was set in Optima and Trajan by
City Desktop Productions.
The typeface used on the cover was Trajan.
The book was printed by Versa Press.